WRITERS' FORUM

Vol. 17　　　　　　Fall 1991
Index, Vols. 1-16

Edited by
Alexander Blackburn

Victoria McCabe
Regis College

Craig Lesley
Clackamas Community College

Bret Lott
College of Charleston

The University of Colorado at Colorado Springs
1991

WRITERS' FORUM (Colorado Springs, 1974--)17. 1. Fiction, American 2. Poetry, American 3. Criticism, American West. Editor: Alexander L. Blackburn for the Regents of the University of Colorado. All rights reserved.

Library of Congress Cat. No. 78-649046
ISSN 0163-9072
ISBN 1-878359-01-0

Publication is made possible by a grant from the College of Letters, Arts and Sciences, University of Colorado at Colorado Springs, Dr. James Null, Dean. Special thanks to Myron Wood of Colorado Springs for permission to publish his portrait of Georgia O'Keeffe, taken in 1980 at the artist's New Mexico home, when she was in her nineties. As usual we are grateful to Ruth Wild for manuscript preparation.

Opinions expressed by authors whose work is represented in the magazine are their own and do not necessarily reflect the views of *Writers' Forum* or of the University of Colorado.

WRITERS' FORUM is an independent, noncommercial magazine featuring contemporary American literature with an emphasis on Western American literature. Subscription: $8.95. Back issue sample: $5.95. Add $1.05 for postage and handling. Vols. 1-6 are available on microfiche of archival quality. Vols. 7-17 are in print. Writers' guidelines available on request; please include s a.s.e. Inquiries: Editor, *Writers' Forum*, P. 0. Box 7150, University of Colorado, Colorado Springs, CO 80933-7150; tel. 719-593-3155 or 719-599-4023.

Writers' Forum is distributed by the University Press of Colorado, P. 0. Box 849, Niwot, CO 80544; tel. 303-530-5337.

Printed in the United States of America

FIRST EDITION

WRITERS' FORUM No. 17 Fall 1991

Editorial
Lanniko Louella Lee *Invitation to Lakota Territory* 1

WESTERN WRITERS SERIES
Ann Ronald
Stegner and Stewardship 3

FICTION
Robert Olen Butler
  Love 18
Clay Reynolds
  Etta's Pond 35
Julian Silva
  The Minimalist 61
Peter LaSalle
  A Foil Girl 85
Leigh Cross
  The Pub 107

Diana Abu-Jaber
  At the Continental Divide 131
Max Westbrook
  How Was Your Day 157
Clark Brown
  Elections 167
Greg Luthi
  God's Country 185
Richard Widerkehr
  Soup and Pennies 201

POETRY
Louise Crago 209
James Cushing 183
James Drake 59
Alice Friman 183
Graciela Guzmán 128
Joseph Hutchison 105
P. H. Liotta 106
Joyce K. Luzzi 199
R. Nickolas Macioci 182
Miriam McCluney 198
B. Z. Niditch 165
Ron Offen 165
Paul Ramsey 209
David Ray 57

Gary Short 83
Kelly Sievers 200
Floyd Skloot 80
Larry E. Smith 155
Matthew J. Spireng 166
David Sumner 104
Daniel James Sundahl 154
Sandra Gail Teichmann 129
Terry Thomas 17
Rawdon Tomlinson 32
Ken Waldman 60
David Winwood 156
Harold Witt 82
Lisa Yount 208

NOTES ON STAFF AND CONTRIBUTORS 210

INDEX to *Writers' Forum*, Vols. 1-16 214

Editorial

Invitation To Lakota Territory

Lanniko L. Lee

I see you driving by on Highway 212 and sometimes wave at you when out riding. A few times I've stood by the gravel pile near the intersection of 212 and 63 when the breeze is from the west and watched you whiz by, your eyes staring straight ahead, frozen to the white lines on the road. What is so important that you can't slow down so I can see your face?

I can see that you're from faraway places like Florida, New York and California and I wonder if you remember AIM and the second massacre of Wounded Knee in 1973 and therefore fear to stop. Are you curious as to why the Lakota love this place so much? Our Lakota country is the last remaining part of an ancient, spirit-filled land, but it is still alive with the struggle to remain our home.

With my Grandpa's old diamond willow cane, I like to walk along the gumbo ridge in the early morning dawn and listen to the fresh, new breeze as it tells me again the story of these native grass covered hills. I listen to the muffled thunder of my Grandpa's herd of horses long before barbed-wire fences, and a meadowlark's song in the distance becomes a young lover's bone whistle.

I lie on the mat of the buffalo grass and watch a shag moth hover over a bright yellow cactus flower, looking for a cool place to hide from the dry summer heat. When it flutters away, I reach out and swirl my finger in the center of the flower and watch it slowly close up. And I know how the cactus captures heavy dew in summer. It's a quiet place out here on the open prairie, a quiet absence of man's voice, that is. Otherwise, everywhere, everyone is singing. Cottonwood leaves rustle about down on the Moreau River, like women putting on their jingle dresses for the grass dance.

I have read all about how tired you are these days and I wonder why you've changed so much from those early Frenchmen. I suppose they may have traveled right on through if they weren't riding horseback. There was talk years back by a few who wished those French trappers had ridden straight on through without stopping, but some talk isn't worth listening to, and anyway, who can change the leaves of the cottonwood tree after its roots are set in the mud along the Moreau?

[Ms. Lee's article was written in response to the "Year of Reconciliation" proclaimed by South Dakota Governor George Mickelson. Born and raised on the Cheyenne River Sioux reservation, she is a Minniconjou educator currently working on a M.A. degree from the Bread Loaf School of English, and on a collection of nonfiction about growing up contemporary Lakotan. Ed. note]

Stegner and Stewardship

Ann Ronald

Even though Wallace Stegner has never been specifically labeled as a nature writer or an author of natural history, his prose has always revealed his respect for and his affinity toward the environment. Readers find in his books and essays not only verbal photographs of the West but special feelings for the landscapes of his youth. Nowhere does this fusion of the pictorial and the romantic come together more successfully than in the "Overture" to *The Sound of Mountain Water*. "I gave my heart to the mountains," Stegner wrote many years ago, "the minute I stood beside this river with its spray in my face and watched it thunder into foam, smooth to green glass over sunken rocks, shatter to foam again."[1] Such a line is typical of his heartfelt response to a natural scene undefiled by man.

Susan J. Tyburski published an article about the "Overture" in a 1983 issue of *Western American Literature*. There she generalized about Stegner's vision of the land and argued that "wilderness was a source of religious inspiration and renewal for Stegner."[2] Drawing upon such diverse resources as Max Westbrook and Mircea Eliade,[3] Tyburski determined a geography of "holy places" for Stegner, a geography developed almost entirely from descriptions in *The Sound of Mountain Water* essays and an earlier Stegner chapter of *This Is Dinosaur*. With reference primarily to the most subjective of pictorial passages, she was able to conclude that, "for Stegner, the invasion of commercial elements into a wilderness area constitutes the profanation of sacred ground."

While Tyburski may have been correct in her interpretation of Stegner's "essential source of emotional, aesthetic, psychological, and spiritual regeneration,"[4] her discussion was necessarily selective. She unfortunately focused only on those sentences and paragraphs which supported her thesis, and ignored those words which might confound it. I say this, however, not to point my finger at a particular critic. Rather, I want to point at what is problematic in any generalization about Stegner's environmental point of view.

On the surface, Wallace Stegner's attitude reflects that of any contemporary author who has an emotional attachment and philosophical commitment to the land. Somewhat deeper, though, is a point of view that appears inconsistent at best and downright contradictory at worst. Somewhere deeper still, lies another stratum both organic and rational, both flexible and systematic. Here is the place that I believe constitutes the core of Stegner's sense of the land. Here also is a level no critic has yet explored. So "Stegner and Stewardship"—my name for the heart of his environmental point of view—proposes to sink a shaft through the layers and mine some new terrain.

On the surface, Stegner behaves and writes predictably. His role in the twentieth-century American conservation movement is both wide-ranging and exemplary. It includes not only the production of a number of essays written for *The Reporter*, *The New Republic*, *The Atlantic*, *Harper's*, *The Saturday Review of Literature*, *Blair & Ketchum's Country Journal*, *Esquire*, *American Heritage*, the Sierra Club *Bulletin*, and *The Living Wilderness*, but the editing of a book that helped thwart a proposed Echo Canyon dam.[5] It also embraces such divergent activities as a stint working for Interior Secretary Stewart Udall, two years on the Board of Directors of the Sierra Club, a role as founder and Honorary President of The Committee for Green Foothills in California, and a willingness to give speeches about what Americans are doing to the land.[6] "I can toss my pebbles," he remarked of his quiet activism in 1983, "onto what I wish were an avalanche of protest."[7]

Stegner's most definitive—and best-known—comment on the subject of the environment is his 1960 "Wilderness Letter," the "Coda" of *The Sound of Mountain Water*. Originally written to David Pesonen of the Wildland Research Center at the University of California, Berkeley, the "Wilderness Letter" has been anthologized and reprinted dozens of times. It argues forcefully for the abstract notion of wilderness—"The idea alone can sustain me"[8]—as well as for the tangible desirability of unscarred land. Of the Robbers' Roost country in Utah, he extrapolates: "Save a piece of country like that intact, and it does not matter in the slightest that only a few people every year will go into it. That is precisely its value.... We simply need that wild country available to us, even if we never do more than drive to its edge and look in."[9] Such a statement presages/echoes Edward Abbey and a host of other wilderness advocates, and such a statement is often quoted by those who see Wallace Stegner as a spokesman.

T. H. Watkins, in fact, calls Stegner "one of the central figures in the modern conservation movement." Even though Watkins acknowledges Stegner's discomfort at such a label, he insists upon its appropriateness.

"For forty years [Stegner] has borne witness for the land that has enriched his life and art, and the measured cadence of his splendid prose has played a significant role in the shaping of the sensibility we now call environmentalism."[10] Certainly Stegner's ostensible wilderness position was—and still is—highly regarded for its articulation of a consistent pattern of ecological awareness. And "conservationist" assuredly is the best word to characterize the most obvious pattern of Stegner's ideas.

His conservationism seems to grow from two deep roots, one physical and tangible, the other intellectual and more abstract. The former had its beginnings in boyhood, especially in the early years spent on the Saskatchewan/Montana border; the latter, in the author's study of John Wesley Powell.

Between 1914 and 1920, Stegner's parents homesteaded in the Cypress Hills country of southern Saskatchewan. So the young boy's days and nights were spent in close intimacy with a pristine and relatively inhospitable land. From this experience—the homesteading venture was a failure—Stegner learned exactly what could and could not be done with arid land. *Wolf Willow*, his memoir of the time spent as an erstwhile Canadian, recounts both beauty and despair. He recalls "the mystery of nights when the stars were scoured clean and the prairie was full of breathings from a long way off, and the strange, friendly barking of night-hunting owls,"[11] but he also ponders the futility of such toil.

> How does one know in his bones what this continent has meant to Western man unless he has, though briefly and in the midst of failure, belatedly and in the wrong place, made trails and paths on an untouched country and built human living places, however transitory, at the edge of a field that he helped break from prairie sod? How does one know what wilderness has meant to Americans unless he has shared the guilt of wastefully and ignorantly tampering with it in the name of Progress?

He answers for himself. "One who has lived the dream, the temporary fulfillment, and the disappointment has had the full course."[12]

The boy who lived both the dream and the disappointment never forgot the lessons of his youth. So when he went on to become the man who studied John Wesley Powell, Stegner was ready to espouse the truths spoken by a historical figure whose ideas coincided with his own. In 1954, Wallace Stegner published *Beyond the Hundredth Meridian*,[13] a narration of Powell's exploration of the Grand Canyon and the second opening of the West. Yet *Beyond the Hundredth Meridian* covers far more philosophical territory than its title or subtitle would have the reader believe.

The visionary nature of Powell's conclusions appealed to Stegner, particularly as examined from the perspectives of time and space and history. For Powell said to nineteenth-century deaf ears what a twentieth-century Stegner knew to be true—"the West is defined . . . by inadequate rainfall."[14] Powell suggested a radical but rational solution, "proposing to close, apparently forever, a great part of the remaining public domain, and to bring to a close, except within the irrigable lands, the agricultural expansion which had been part of the national expectation for almost a century." When powerful congressional forces combined to suppress Powell's point of view, the suggestion was defeated and his career was destroyed. Stegner compares his fate with that of "all leaders who go too far ahead, and of all thinkers who think straighter than their contemporaries."[15]

John Wesley Powell's straight thinking about the finite nature of water in the West has come to haunt more recent generations. The West is indeed a dry place. "Aridity, and aridity alone, makes the various Wests one," repeats Stegner in a recent chapter appropriately called "Living Dry." No plan for settlement, for agriculture, for mineral extraction, for industrialization, he argues, can prudently ignore this fact. "And what do you do about aridity, if you are a nation inured to plenty and impatient of restrictions. . . ? You may deny it for a while. Then you must either adapt to it or try to engineer it out of existence."[16]

One would expect any good conservationist, I think, to embrace adaptation while disdaining engineering. Certainly that is the intuitive message of an Aldo Leopold or the battle cry of an Edward Abbey. Certainly that is the gist of Stegner's words much of the time. A fairly predictable sentiment of his can be found, for example, in a chapter called "The Gift of Wilderness" in *One Way to Spell Man*. There Stegner wrote, "We need to learn to listen to the land, hear what it says, understand what it can and can't do over the long haul; what, especially in the West, it should not be asked to do."[17] This passage directly follows a page that implicitly harks back to Leopold and explicitly calls for "a land ethic that unites science, religion, and human feeling."[18]

While such phrases underscore Stegner's prevailing commitment to the ethics of conservation, the latter quotation includes a curious anomaly. The word "science" sounds strangely out of place—naming something closely akin to technology, something many conservationists would blame rather than embrace. Here is the first indication of that layer of environmental viscosity which critics to date have ignored.

Its most blatant manifestation is a full-length book called *Discovery!*, a nonfiction product from 1971 whose focus is engineering. Stegner's *Discovery!* describes the Arabian American Oil Company's corporate implementation of a plan that ultimately sent Arabian oil out to the western world and brought the western world to Saudi Arabia.[19] It is a book apparently commissioned by Aramco itself—at least its title page pronounces it "As Abridged for *Aramco World Magazine*." It does not appear to be a book about which Stegner brags, and few of his readers are aware of its existence.

Whether a curious aberration, however, or an integral part of Stegner's thought pattern, *Discovery!* does exist, and needs to be assessed in the context of his conservationist point of view. At least he took measures to distance himself from the task. Of all Stegner's prose, *Discovery!* is the one text that keeps the point of view at arm's length, so the author must have consciously removed himself from the material in question. The omniscient narrator remains as impartial as possible, making no real value judgments, neither cheerleading nor castigating. Even so, the subject matter itself leads him into paradox.

The Introduction, for example, guides the reader into unfamiliar territory while setting a tone for the book as a whole. "Whatever the uncertainties of the future," Stegner wrote before the days of OPEC, "Aramco can congratulate itself on a record that is a long way from being grossly exploitative or 'imperialist.' Its record probably contains both mistakes and inconsistencies, and it has indeed earned impressive profits, but in general its role and its intention have been to provide an alternative between willful foreign exploitation of the 19th-century kind, and willful nationalization such as has happened more recently." Such a description of the company that changed the course of a nation and of an entire segment of the world sounds very odd indeed. But it does reveal the author's apparent intent—to glamorize Aramco's accomplishments. The whole point of the book is to boast of the changes one powerful corporation brought to the land.

Stegner goes on, then, to recount the course of negotiations, explorations, and discoveries that accompanied Aramco's first decade in Saudi Arabia. Essentially his narration focuses on those who brought Aramco into being, and their energy and zeal. "Predominantly from the western United States," he wrote of their commitment, "the Hundred Men [those who stayed on in Saudi Arabia during the second world war] responded to a reclamation dream as kindling responds to fire." While such a simile makes no directly evaluative statement, it does imply tacit approval of the Hundred Men's task. So do the incidents selected to tell the tale.

The back cover of the book itemizes the contents: "an oil-well fire out of control, a tragic mid-gulf explosion, bombs falling out of a moonlit sky. Above all, it is the story of men—the men who came to Saudi Arabia in 1933, bringing the skills and strengths of another world, and the proud men of the desert awaiting with grave concern the impact that this vital discovery would have on their time-honored ways." Little evidence exists, however, that Stegner has any concomitant grave concern. His narrative voice neither probes the impact nor ponders the results. He simply describes the processes of dealing with the bedouins, of sinking dry wells, of protecting the company's property, of striking it very rich in a foreign desert. Even the wildlife, uniquely precious in that part of the world, is treated from a distance.

Shooting three rare oryx for dinner, or lassoing them for sport, ought to be cause for complaint, I think. Yet the reader learns only that "for the next day or two they ate the best meat that Arabia provided, and they kept the calf, Butch, force-fed with a medicine dropper." Butch's demise is equally unfortunate—both for the oryx and for the conservationist mindset.

He was everybody's baby. But he was symbolic of the losses that accompanied the gains of the industrial invasion. Butch's parents had been unable to escape hunters chasing them in a car, the kind of hunting that was to virtually wipe out both oryx and gazelle before conservation laws were put into effect. And Butch himself, treated more kindly by the newcomers, died of their kindness; born to subsist on an occasional wisp of grass, he fell so greedily upon the alfalfa they brought him in the supply truck from Hofuf that he bloated up and perished in convulsions.[20]

The next paragraph immediately deploys the men against five more of the rare species. While not exactly applauding such behavior, Stegner nonetheless treats the incidents lightheartedly and withholds the judgment a reader might expect. That the baby oryx "was symbolic of the losses that accompanied the gains of the industrial invasion" is the only directly evaluative statement in the book, but even it minimizes the impact of killing endangered species and ignores the more general environmental disruption that must have swept across the Saudi Arabian desert after the Americans arrived.

Stegner's seeming indifference to mineral exploitation counters sharply with his pronouncements of a decade earlier. "For mining I cannot say much good except that its operations are generally short-lived,"[21] he wrote in *The Sound of Mountain Water*. This statement is difficult to correlate with the one hundred ninety pages of engineering enthusiasm that mark *Discovery!*, and even harder to conjoin with the apparent longterm effects of oil production in the Middle East, pipelines in Alaska, open pits or off-shore drills.

But perhaps we can guess how he justified *Discovery!* to himself. In one conversation with Richard Etulain, Stegner defines a theme that is relevant here. "Discovery, raid, settlement," he says, referring to a major American triumvirate, "those make an obvious solid topic; the Westward Movement essentially. I suppose most historians like that because it's romantic, because it's encompassable, and because it makes a nice unified sort of theme."[22] "Discovery" makes a nice romantic title, too, and I find it an appropriate choice for this particular book. First, it distances itself from its companions, "raid" and "settlement." Then it glamorizes a process while dismissing its effects, and allows Stegner the same latitude. At the same time, however, *Discovery!* implies the presence of an author whose themes are not as simple as our conservationists would insist.

Let's go back to that critical essay by Susan Tyburski. At the beginning of this piece I accused her of selecting only a Stegner whose paragraphs led naturally to her conclusions and of ignoring a Stegner whose words might suggest an alternative attitude toward nature. Specifically, I was thinking about page fifteen in *This Is Dinosaur*, the page immediately following one from which Tyburski quoted and the page that is at the heart of another puzzling Stegner conundrum. There, in the book that was to put the first chink in the armor of the Army Corps of Engineers, Stegner positioned an extraordinarily anthropocentric paragraph. "A place is nothing in itself," he declared back in 1955. "It has no meaning, it can hardly be said to exist, except in terms of human perception, use, and response. The wealth and resources and usefulness of any region are only inert potential until man's hands and brain have gone to work; and natural beauty is nothing until it comes to the eye of the beholder."

Observations like "a place is nothing in itself," or "it has no meaning . . . except in terms of human perception, use, and response" sound contradictory when judged against the "Wilderness Letter" or the many other Stegner allusions to the "idea" of wilderness as an abstract necessity. Yet in *Dinosaur* he is insistent about this man-centeredness. "We cannot even describe a place except in terms of its human uses," he contends. "It would be idiotic to preach conservation of such a wilderness in perpetuity, just to keep it safe from all human use. It is only for human use that it has any meaning, or is worth preserving."[23] A lot of environmentalists would disagree.

Sometimes Stegner himself sounds like he disagrees. Just recently, in a lecture series given at the University of Michigan, he quoted the Mormon hierarch, John Widstoe, who said: "The destiny of man is to possess the whole earth; the destiny of the earth is to be subject to man. There can be no full conquest of the earth, and no real satisfaction to humanity, if large portions of the earth remain beyond his highest control." Stegner's immediate response could not be more forthright— "That doctrine offends me."[24] On the other hand, this is the same Stegner who said of the Grand Canyon, "Incorrigibly anthropocentric as we are, we can only respond humanly."[25] And the same Stegner who said of Capitol Reef, "The land is not complete without its human history and associations. Scenery by itself is pretty sterile."[26]

To fabricate a Stegner of utter contradictions might be possible now, but that would be as critically irresponsible as to contrive one stamped from a single mold. The responsible task is to pull the apparent contradictions together in a way that spells out the deep-seated consistency in his environmental point of view without violating his artistic license. For despite the problematic *Discovery!* and despite the anthropocentricity that would alienate many an ardent preservationist, Wallace Stegner does hold a fairly uniform vision of the environment and of man's relationship to it. What he believes—which resembles the thinking of a man like Aldo Leopold but is absolutely contrary to the notions of an Edward Abbey[27]—he calls "stewardship."

The dictionary, tracing "steward" back to two Old English words for hall and keeper, defines the modern term in a number of complementary ways. "A person put in charge of the affairs of a large household or estate." Or, "one who acts as a supervisor or administrator... for another or others." Or, "a person variously responsible." Or, "a person ... in charge of arrangements, ... an attendant, ... an officer."[28] Those dictionary definitions impact significantly upon Stegner's environmental sense of the word. To him, a "steward" is someone in charge of the land around him, someone who consciously takes responsibility for its well-being, someone who acts upon it in ecologically sound ways.[29]

One becomes especially aware of Stegner's use of the word when reading the chapters he wrote for *American Places*. Co-authored with his son and published in 1983, this book focuses on observed interactions between the American people and their surroundings. Stegner's contributions meander across the countryside from New England's Long Pond to a series of small towns along the Mississippi and from the Great Salt Lake to Montana's Crow Country. The word "stewardship" appears with surprising regularity.

The first occurrence echoes a solemnity that pervades Stegner's recent prose. "These are soberer times," he observes of the present-day United States. "What a young American just coming of age confronts now is not a limitless potential, but developed power attended by destruction and depletion. Though we should have recognized the land as a living organism demanding care and stewardship, we have treated it as a warehouse." Here he distantly alludes to stewardship as something we have completely missed in our ongoing transactions with the land.

Then his tone changes to a more matter-of-fact one—"land is a heritage as well as a resource, and ownership suggests stewardship, not exploitation." At this point he implies that, if Americans can learn to recognize the integrity of the land, perhaps stewardship is a concept well within our grasp. Finally, when looking at some Montana property where the owners have cared well for their land, Stegner voices genuine optimism. "Work to be done, the chores of an unremitting but satisfying stewardship." These ranchers apparently understand how to function effectively in their natural surroundings, and their children, especially, suggest to Stegner a kind of interactive continuity. "Ten or fifteen years from now, ... one or more of them will perhaps be running this ranch, exercising the same stewardship"[30] which their parents have been able to display.

That Stegner uses the same word so many times in succession cannot be accidental. He repeats it because it so appropriately defines his sense of man's relationship to the land. Here lies what I earlier projected as the core of Stegner's environmental point of view. Stewardship is the keystone—the concept both organic and rational, both flexible and systematic. It is the tenet that can embrace such diverse things as Stegner's abstract "idea" of wilderness, a book like *Discovery!*, his studied anthropocentrism, some crotchetyness, and an abiding concern that has stayed with him for nearly four score years.

In a literary context Stegner once pinpointed "the human response to a set of environmental and temporal circumstances."[31] That phrase appropriately fits an environmental context, too. I believe he has embraced stewardship today because our twentieth-century environmental and temporal circumstances have dictated such an alliance. As a nation of entrepreneurs, we have changed the face of the land. Now we have a responsibility to see that those changes do not damage the world irrevocably; we are in charge.

Stegner likes to refer to George Perkins Marsh, the author of *Man and Nature* who, in 1864, first warned Americans about the consequences of tampering with the environment. Marsh's book outlined the extent of changes already wrought by human actions to plants, animals, water, and topography, pointed out the dangers of imprudence, and suggested the importance of restored harmony between man and his natural surroundings. Like Powell, his ideas were dismissed in his own time but have been adopted and advocated by subsequent generations. His ideas are particularly relevant to Stegner, for they lead inherently to stewardship. Once man has altered the environment, he cannot stop doing so. Each diversion of a waterway, each destruction of plant or animal life, each transaction with nature inevitably leads to further transactions. Unless these are the result of stewardship, man will unleash destruction in his world.

Aldo Leopold understood Marsh's concept, too, most ironically when he defined a conservationist as "one who is humbly aware that with each stroke [of an axe] he is writing his signature on the face of his land."[32] Leopold, in fact, made this apparent incongruity the basis for his proposals regarding deer hunting in Wisconsin. When potential predators have been eliminated from an environment hospitable to deer, the deer naturally increase out of proportion to the land's ability to sustain them. After this happens, man must take over the role formerly played by natural forces, must accept responsibility for culling the herd and managing the deer population. As Leopold explained in the 1940s, "man-made changes are of a different order than evolutionary changes, and have effects more comprehensive than is intended or foreseen." Therefore, it is man's place to do what is "right . . . to preserve the integrity, stability, and beauty of the biotic community."[33] Consequently it becomes man's place to use hunting as a means of regulating an animal population, or logging as a means of patterning the forests.

Stegner would describe the permutation less indirectly and perhaps more emphatically. In *One Way to Spell Man* he zeroes in on the unhappy consequences of the American Dream. "We have been fruitful, and multiplied . . . but in doing so we have plundered our living space. If we have loved the land fate gave us—and most of us did—we went on destroying it even while we loved it, until now we can point to many places we once pointed to in pride, and say with an appalled sense of complicity and guilt, 'Look what we've done!'"[34]

If he complains about plundering our living space in *One Way to Spell Man*, however, he turns the term around in *The American West as Living Space*. This, his most recent commentary on the subject, proposes new ways in which Americans might further their relationship with the land. The answer does not involve the bulldozer. In the past, "we have tried to make the country and climate over to fit our existing habits and desires," he observes. "Instead of listening to the silence, we have shouted into the void."[35] Without shouting, Leopold made the same point. His best-known book ended quietly, "We shall hardly relinquish the shovel, which after all has many good points, but we are in need of gentler and more objective criteria for its successful use."[36] A generation later, Wallace Stegner more explicitly suggests a solution that lies in adaptation and stewardship.

Part of the burden rests with the individual. From the heritage of his boyhood, Stegner still holds the dream of the yeoman farmer, and from the heritage of his study, he still sings the praises of Thomas Jefferson and St. Jean de Crevecoeur. He even titles the last chapter of *The American West as Living Space* "Variations on a Theme by Crevecoeur," referring the reader to Crevecoeur's *Letters* of two hundred years ago and speculating why the Frenchman's idealized yeoman American farmer has either disappeared or been transformed. So in good faith Stegner can romantically applaud Montana ranching, even though he knows how difficult such a life of yeomanry and stewardship can be.

"They do not kid themselves. Theirs is a holding action, perhaps a rearguard action, and it could easily lose. Many forces, economic and social, work against the subsistence ranch."[37] Yet the stewardship there is satisfying, Stegner thinks, because the men and women themselves cherish the land. And this notion meshes with that puzzling Stegner anthropocentrism from the past. When he wrote, "the wealth and resources and usefulness of any region are only inert potential until man's hands and brain have gone to work . . . the natural world, actually, is the test by which each man proves himself: I see, I feel, I love, I use, I alter, I appropriate, therefore I am,"[38] he could have been talking about the Bench Ranch in the West Rosebud. There, day after day, Jack and Susan Heyneman prove themselves in relationship with, and thus provide stewardship to, the land. I think Oliver Ward, the protagonist of Stegner's novel, *Angle of Repose*, was trying to do the same.[39]

Not all of us can live in a Bench Ranch world, however, so our stewardship must be exercised in a somewhat different way. Stegner suggests a partial reliance on the federal government. In this respect he differs quite radically from a number of his fellow conservationists, since he genuinely believes that proper governmental intervention is a viable course of action. History may have proved otherwise, but Stegner retains a measure of confidence that sounds almost uncharacteristically optimistic. He rejects what he regards as the bad agencies—the Bureau of Reclamation, for example—and embraces the good. The good, in this context, are those land-managing bureaus that "have as at least part of their purpose the preservation of the West in a relatively natural, healthy, and sustainable condition." Indeed, Stegner thinks Westerners especially should rethink their relationship to the government in Washington, D.C.

"The federal presence should be recognized as what it is," he explains, "a reaction against our former profligacy and wastefulness, an effort at adaptation and *stewardship* [emphasis mine] in the interest of the environment and the future."[40] While this faith in federal control sets Stegner apart from many other environmentalists, it does fit the context of Stegner's career. After all, he has for years admired the John Wesley Powell who advocated governmental oversight of Western lands, as long as the parameters were scientifically sound. And he worked for Stewart Udall once, supported the Secretary of the Interior's efforts, and applauded the results. "As a *steward* [emphasis mine] of the land," Stegner once said, "I would rate [Udall] very high indeed."[41]

Perhaps this is the place to fit *Discovery!* into Stegner's career, too. Despite my own reservations, the book does boast a sympathy with the bureaucratic potential to weld a corporate entity with a native population, to marry happily a power with the less powerful. "Not inconceivably," Stegner admits, "the thing they all thought of as 'progress' and 'development' would blow them all up, and their world with it. But that is another story. This one is purely and simply the story of a frontier."[42] I read that final disclaimer not only as the author's attempt to place his book in the context of the pioneering spirit that permeates his fiction and nonfiction alike, but also as an effort to set this particular story apart. *Discovery!* deals with potential, nothing more.

And potential lies at the heart of stewardship's promise. Perhaps that is the beauty of Stegner's organic concept for future generations. Occasionally a curmudgeon and often a grouch, he nonetheless keeps his eyes on the heritage we might leave our children. With the proper restraint, he can envision that heritage as better than what we ourselves received. "America is the world's greatest undeveloped nation," he says ironically, "and by its very premises, nobody can develop it except its citizens." But we have a chance, he conjoins, "to assert the long-range public interest against short-term economic interests—in effect, to promote civilized responsibility, both public and private, over frontier carelessness and greed."[43]

This is a rational view of stewardship, of—to return to those dictionary definitions—persons "variously responsible . . . in charge of arrangements." From the beginning of his career, Stegner has hoped not only that man can accept the appropriate responsibility for his relationship with the earth, but can make adequate provisions for its future. He has persuasively repeated:

> We need an environmental ethic that will reach all the way from the preservation of untouched wilderness to the beautification of industrial cities, that will concern itself with saving the still-savable and healing the half-ruined and cleansing the polluted, that will touch not only land but air and water, that will have as its purpose the creation of a better environment for men, as well as the creation or preservation of viable habitats for the species that our expansion threatens.[44]

Unlike the ardent preservationists, or even the most studied conservationists, Stegner assumes an ongoing need for man's participation in things environmental because, as he well knows, whole ecological systems no longer remain intact. For what the anthropocentric has already manipulated, the anthropocentric must accept responsibility for managing further. In so doing, Stegner insists, we must "apply to ourselves and our habitat the intelligence that has endangered both. That means drastically and voluntarily reducing our numbers, decontaminating our earth, and thereafter husbanding, building, and nourishing, instead of squandering and poisoning."[45] And while our actions must be judicious and respectful, they must also be strong enough to keep the unacceptable alternative at bay.

Stegner looks forward to the challenge. Gone are the negative overtones when he talks about stewardship. "Angry as one may be at what careless people have done and still do to a noble habitat," he summarizes, "it is hard to be pessimistic about the West. This is the native home of hope. When it fully learns that cooperation, not rugged individualism, is the pattern that most characterizes and preserves it, then it will have achieved itself and outlived its origins. Then it has a chance to create a society to match its scenery."[46] In stewardship, he firmly believes, we and the land together have a chance.

NOTES
[1.] Wallace Stegner, *The Sound of Mountain Water* 1980 (Lincoln: University of Nebraska Press, 1985), 42.
[2.] Susan J. Tyburski, "Wallace Stegner's Vision of Wilderness," *Western American Literature*, 18 (August 1983): 135.
[3.] See Max Westbrook, "Conservative, Liberal, and Western: Three Modes of American Realism," in *The Literature of the American West*, ed. J. Golden Taylor, Boston: Houghton Mifflin, 1971; and Mircea Eliade, *The Sacred and the Profane*, New York: Harcourt, Brace & World, Inc., 1957.
[4.] Ibid., 141.
[5.] See Wallace Stegner, ed., *This Is Dinosaur: Echo Park And Its Magic Rivers*, New York: Alfred A. Knopf, 1955.
[6.] I am indebted to T. H. Watkins, "Bearing Witness for the Land: The Conservation Career of Wallace Stegner," *South Dakota Review*, 23 (Winter 1985): 42-57, for specific details of Stegner's contributions.
[7.] Wallace Stegner and Richard W. Etulain, *Conversations with Wallace Stegner on Western History and Literature* (Salt Lake City: University of Utah Press, 1983), 183.
[8.] Wallace Stegner, "Coda: Wilderness Letter," in *The Sound of Mountain Water*, 150.
[9.] Ibid., 153.
[10.] Watkins, "Bearing Witness for the Land," 42, 43.
[11.] Wallace Stegner, *Wolf Willow* 1955 (Lincoln: University of Nebraska 1980), 281.
[12.] Ibid., 281-82.
[13.] See Wallace Stegner, *Beyond the Hundredth Meridian*, Boston: Houghton Mifflin, 1954.
[14.] Wallace Stegner, *The American West as Living Space* (Ann Arbor: University of Michigan Press, 1987), 6.
[15.] *Beyond the Hundredth Meridian*, 307, 366-67.
[16.] *The American West as Living Space*, 8, 27.
[17.] Wallace Stegner, *One Way to Spell Man* (Garden City, New York: Doubleday and Company, 1982), 177.
[18.] Ibid., 176.
[19.] Wallace Stegner, *Discovery!* (Beirut: Middle East Export Press, Inc., 1971), 13.
[20.] Ibid., vi, 170, 139, 140.
[21.] *The Sound of Mountain Water*, 151.
[22.] *Conversations*, 145.
[23.] *This Is Dinosaur*, 15.
[24.] *The American West as Living Space*, 45. Stegner himself quotes from Widstoe's *Success on Irrigation Projects* (1928), 138.
[25.] Wallace Stegner, "Foreword" to *The Grand Colorado*, by T. H. Watkins and Contributors (USA: American West Publishing Company, 1969), 10.
[26.] Wallace Stegner and Page Stegner, *American Places* (Moscow,

Idaho: University of Idaho Press, 1983), 143. Citations from *American Places* will be taken only from chapters written by Wallace Stegner.
27. Shortly after drafting this Stegner essay, I read Edward Abbey's last novel. In its pages, I found Abbey's definition of "what the Forest Service calls stewardship," a counterpoint to Stegner's point of view. "Managing the land for the best interests of industrial society and fuck anything else like deer or elk or black bear or red squirrels or people who like to get out in the woods. . . . To make the forests neat and orderly and easy to cut. Like a cornfield, that's what they want. They want the whole West to look like an Illinois cornfield. Like a farm. We are stewards of the earth, they say, appointed by God to manage the earth (every bit of it) in whatever way seems best (to us stewards). That's our holy mission, to be good little stewards and keep that old raw cranky smelly smelly unpredictable Mother Nature where she belongs." Edward Abbey, *Hayduke Lives!* (Boston: Little, Brown and Company, 1990), 127.
28. *Webster's New World Dictionary*, 2nd ed. (New York: World Publishing Company, 1970), 1397-98.
29. To Edward Abbey, the word's etymology can be interpreted in a slightly different way. "A steward is a sty-warden," he clarifies. "Look it up. It's from the Anglo-Saxon *stigeweard*, meaning guardian of the pigpen. That's what our noble stewards are—people who guard pigs" [*Hayduke Lives!*, 127].
30. *American Places*, 27, 49, 123.
31. *Conversations*, 196.
32. Aldo Leopold, *A Sand County Almanac and Sketches Here and There* 1949 (New York: Oxford University Press, 1981), 68.
33. Ibid., 218, 224-25.
34. *One Way to Spell Man*, 163.
35. *Living Space*, 33.
36. Leopold, *A Sand County Almanac*, 226.
37. *American Places*, 113.
38. *This Is Dinosaur*, 15; see endnote 23.
39. "They were the makers and doers," wrote Stegner of his fictional protagonists, "they wanted to take a piece of the wilderness and turn it into a home for a civilization." *Angle of Repose*, New York: Fawcett Crest Books, 1971, 344.
40. *Living Space*, 38.
41. Quoted in Watkins, "Bearing Witness for the Land," 53.
42. *Discovery!*, 190.
43. *American Places*, 259, 255.
44. Wallace Stegner, "What Ever Happened to the Great Outdoors?," *Saturday Review* 48 (22 May 1965): 36. On the same page Stegner uses the word "stewardship."
45. Wallace Stegner, "Conservation Equals Survival," in *Crossroads*, ed. by Tom E. Kakonis and James C. Wilcox (Lexington, Mass.: D. C. Heath and Co., 1972), 128; rpt. from an article in *American Heritage Magazine*, December 1969.
46. *The Sound of Mountain Water*, 38.

King Kong
and the Big Building

Terry Thomas

You just knew he was a goner when he
put his first hairy paw on
New York's tallest. It wasn't because
he stepped on black superstition or rejected
white affluence (sometimes edited). It wasn't even
because of the mosquito planes

stinging him to death. Oh, no.
His last fall was because of
love and beauty. His primal dream was
to turn the woman into a hairless mate,
but as fate would have it, she became
a final trouble doll. Maybe his macho
instinct turned him to the ultimate

phallic symbol—a steel erection
to the pride of pygmies—finally
rejecting his tiny totem and life.
He dared to love and coveted beauty
(not a building); silly primate.
King Kong died for our sins.

Love

Robert Olen Butler

I was once able to bring fire from heaven. My wife knew that and her would-be lovers soon learned that, though sometimes the lesson was a hard one for them. But that was in Vietnam, and when the need arose once more, here in America, I had to find a new way. You see, it has never been easy for a man like me. I know I appear to be what they call here a "wimp." I am not a handsome man, and I am small even for a Vietnamese. I assume the manners of a wimp, too, and I am conscious of doing that. I have done it all my life. I cross my legs at the knee and I step too lightly and I talk too much on subjects that others find boring. But there are two things about me that are exceptional. First, I was for many years a spy. You think that all spies look like the men in the movies. But real spies have a cover identity, even if that cover was in place many years before they began their secret life. The second thing about me is that I have a very beautiful wife. I married her when she was fifteen and I was twenty-five. Her parents were friends of my parents and they liked me very much and they gave me this great blessing and this great curse.

Her name is Buom, which means in English "butterfly." She is certainly that. She would fly here and there, landing on this flower or that, never moving in a straight line. And how do you summon a butterfly? Only show it a pretty thing. It is not her fault, really. It is her nature. But it is a terrible thing to be married to a beautiful woman. We lived in the town of Bien Hoa, very near an air base and two big American camps, Long Binh and one they called Plantation, and when my wife walked down the street of Bien Hoa she was dressed in black pantaloons and a white blouse like all the other women but it was so clear how different she was. Her sleeves were rolled far up and her top two buttons were undone for the heat and her hair was combed out long and sleek, and the GI jeeps would slam on their brakes and honk and the Vietnamese men would straighten up slowly and flare their nostrils and the Vietnamese boys on their motorbikes would crane their necks going by, even though more than once I saw them run into some automobile or fruit cart or a pile of garbage and fly through the air for trying to look twice at my wife.

Of all these men and boys it was the Vietnamese I worried about. No American ever tried seriously to go out with my wife. They had their Vietnamese whores at the camps, and it should be said for my wife that she never much liked the looks of the Americans anyway. This is true even today, after we have lived in Gretna, Louisiana, for more than a dozen years. It was the Vietnamese who I feared. They loved my wife, all these men, and it was only to be expected that some of them would try to have her. They would believe that she could be had. Why else, they reasoned, would she be so beautiful and swing her hips in that way and unbutton those two extra buttons on her blouse? How much cooler did she really think that would make her?

But these men were warned. And some of them never showed up again after they ignored the warnings. I could bring the fire from heaven to keep them away from my wife. I was a spy, after all. I worked with many Americans at Plantation. They came and they went each year and I would always bring them what they needed. They called me an agent handler, because I had two dozen people working for me. My eyes and ears. The schoolgirls and the woodcutters and the old women and the regional forces soldiers and boys from the neighborhoods on their bikes and others like these—they brought me information and I took the information to the Americans, signing onto the post as a day laborer. Most of what I brought them was tactical intelligence. A VC squad with a political cadre coming down from Lai Khe and working the widows' settlement near Bien Hoa. A rocket attack planned on the air base at dawn from a certain place in the woods. Things like that. And when I gave them this information, I was right often enough that the Americans didn't really question me after awhile, especially about rocket attacks. If I said there were going to be rockets at dawn from such and such coordinates, then first thing the next morning the United States Air Force would come in and blow those coordinates away.

You can see how this might be a great help to a seemingly wimpy man with a beautiful wife. When my people brought me information about my wife and another man, or I used the evidence of my own eyes, I would send a warning to the man. The fire would come from heaven, I told him in a note delivered by one of my agents. I told him that my wife carries this ancient curse with her. The curse of the little man. I would sometimes go into historical detail. Napoleon Bonaparte, for instance, was very small and conquered 720,000 square miles of Europe. Attila, King of the Huns and ruler of an empire of 1,450,000 square miles, was still smaller, thought even to be a dwarf. History teaches, by the way, that not only is the curse I bring upon the would-be lovers ancient, but the problem of the husband is ancient, too. Napoleon had great troubles with his butterfly of a wife and Attila died in the middle of making love, no doubt due to his being foolish enough to have many wives. But, of course, these are observations that I left out of my warning messages, which were clear and forceful. And if they were not heeded, I would find the coordinates of the place where the man cut wood every morning or where he went to eat his lunch or to fish or some other place where the United States Air Force could find him. We are all creatures of habit.

And how did my wife react when she found some man who was pursuing her suddenly disappear? Perhaps the first time or two she felt that it was something she herself had said or done, or perhaps she thought they did not find her attractive anymore. (This makes me a little sad, to think I made my wife doubt herself. But surely she has always known how beautiful she is and nothing could truly shake that.) Later on she must have known that I was responsible in some dramatic way. But however it was that she felt, I can never say for sure. She would always maintain a face and attitude that revealed nothing. I would speak to her, as I often did, of history or politics or matters of daily life, and she would listen, her face bowed over her sewing, until it was time for us to sleep. Only once did she let on that she knew what had happened to her latest suitor. I believe that this man—a woodcutter with a shack by a stream—never understood what I could do. He was a big man, an arrogant man. One evening soon after this particular reported rocket attack was prevented by the United States Air Force, my wife looked up from her sewing. I had just paused for a few moments in speaking to her due to an itchiness in my throat, so at first I thought she wished me to quickly continue the observations that I had been making on the futility of using our Regional Forces irregulars to guard local government buildings. But instead, she said, "It's sad, the mistakes made in a war."

I knew at once what she was talking about. She had made a terrible mistake in letting this man get too close to her.

"Very sad," I said.

"Do you think someone is actually in control of all these things that happen?" she asked.

"I am sure of it," I said, and a clearer reminder than that was unnecessary. My wife is beautiful, but she is also subtle.

So finally history caught up with my country. I could see it coming for a long time. I stopped enough rockets from hitting the air base at Bien Hoa that in repayment my wife and I, along with our two children, flew from there a week before the place was overrun by the communists. I was not so very sorry to go, for I was coming to a country full of men that my wife would not look at twice. And it's true that in

America, things have been much calmer, though this Gretna, Louisiana, is an area with many Vietnamese. But it seems as if somehow the men of Vietnam have lost their nerve in America, even with a beautiful Vietnamese woman. I sometimes receive a respectful compliment about my wife, but these men are beaten down; they are taller than me and even younger than me but wimpier by far.

We live near the Mississippi River and just over the bridge is New Orleans. My wife has seemed happy simply to live in an apartment where she can sit in the living room whenever she wishes and she and her women friends can go out together and shop and get their hair fixed. I work for the telephone company and we have a television set which makes me more interesting to my wife because she does not have to listen in the evenings to the thoughts I have on politics and history and such. I understand her limitations, and a wise man does not try to change the things that can't be changed. It's just that I'd begun to hope that things had changed on their own. For a long time she seemed utterly uninterested in allowing me to be tormented in the ways I was in Vietnam. There was no town street to walk down with the eyes of everyone on the open throat of her blouse or the movement of her hips. The hairdos she liked here seemed intended to impress the other women rather than any man. Things have been very good, very calm. That is, until two months ago.

It was, of course, a Vietnamese. He is a former airborne ranger, a tall man, nearly as tall as an American. And he owns a restaurant in a shopping plaza. The restaurant is called Bun Bo Xao, a name obviously chosen to attract the American diners out for some exotic treat that they can't even distinguish from Chinese. I know this because Bun Bo Xao means Sauteed Beef with Noodles. What if an American restaurant was named Grilled Hamburger with French Fries or Baked Chicken and Mashed Potatoes? Do you see my point? To call a restaurant a name that a whole people will understand as Sauteed Beef with Noodles is an insult to that people. And the bun bo they make there is second rate anyway, and the nuoc mam, the fish sauce, is even worse. This sauce is very special to the tongue of the Vietnamese. I do not expect to taste true Vietnamese nuoc mam in America. The nuoc mam from Phu Quoc Island was the best of all, clear and with an astonishingly subtle taste for a substance that a fish will give up only after a prolonged process lasting several days. But the sauce in this restaurant is from the Philippines, very bad, not from Thailand which at least is a pale second-best.

I do not criticize this man's taste and sincerity idly. These were my first clues. My wife and this man forgot that I am a spy. They may have known that I can no longer command the United States Air Force, but they forgot that I know how to read clues. You see, in spite of the bad bun bo and the worse nuoc mam, this suddenly became my wife's favorite restaurant. We did not know where to go one Friday night, which is the night we usually go to a restaurant, and she said, oh so lightly, so offhandedly, that she heard that this Vietnamese place was quite good. She quoted one of her hairdo companions, a woman who would be plucking chickens and getting high on betel nuts in some Saigon alley if we had won the war. I have tried to avoid Vietnamese restaurants in the United States, but Buom seemed so set on this, yet in such a casual way, that I indulged her. She is, after all, still a very beautiful woman.

We pulled into the little shopping center and found the place just a few doors down from Ngon Qua Po-Boys and the Good Luck Bowling Alley. I noticed how my wife's hand casually slipped off my arm as we stepped into the Bun Bo Xao Restaurant and I only had time to make a quick note of the Chinatown lanterns on the ceiling and the lacquer paintings on the wall mass produced in Hong Kong, when this tall Vietnamese man in a tuxedo was suddenly bowing before us and shooting little knowing glances at my wife. The owner. Tran Van Ha. He was so glad to see us and I felt a chill going up and down me from my scalp to my toes.

So we ate this second-rate food and the owner visited our table twice to make sure everything was all right. I explained carefully to him how it was not, how the food was falling short of this or that standard of excellence. He listened to me with his temples throbbing and I could hear my wife peeping in repressed contradiction to me. It was all so clear that I almost laughed at them then and there and said, Do you take me for a fool? Have you forgotten how severely I deal with matters such as this?

But the fact was that I no longer had access to the fire. I did not even have my eyes and ears who could go out and gather more information for me and deliver the necessary warnings. So I held my tongue about all but the food. Nor did I speak of these things on the way home nor that evening nor even, a week later, when my little butterfly said she had a craving for Vietnamese food and suggested the Bun Bo Restaurant. I simply said no to the restaurant and with my spy experience kept a cool exterior, a calm and placid exterior. Inside, however, I was a whirlwind of feelings and plans. At no time in the past dozen years had I such a strong sense that I was in a foreign country, behind enemy lines, as it were, without any resources but my own. But soon my head cleared enough to understand that no matter where you are in the world, the forces of history and culture have been at work, and these forces create solutions to problems for the man who knows how to find them.

Take New Orleans, Louisiana, for instance. Napoleon snatched the city from the Spanish, who he defeated in Europe, and then two years later he sold it to the United States. This city was the casual possession of a small man who commanded fire of his own. But the city had a long history even before Napoleon held it. For a hundred years it had been a city with French and Spanish people but with many from the

Robert Olen Butler 23

Caribbean, too, the West Indies and elsewhere, black people with fire of a different kind. You can't live around New Orleans without hearing about voodoo. And one night soon after I learned about Tran van Ha, I saw a program on our television where a very thin little black man taught hard lessons to his enemies with voodoo. My wife was sitting there with me and I kept my face very calm, never letting her know that I was listening to the voice of history right there in her presence, and even when the thin little black man made some mistakes that let the lumbering Americans catch him, I knew that I had to grow and learn and command the fire once more.

So on the very next day I called in sick to the phone company and I went across the bridge and past the great mandarin hat of the Superdome and down into the French Quarter where the television and the movies all suggested voodoo was practiced. I walked the main streets of this area and there were boutiques and tee-shirt shops and pizza parlors and jazz places and places where women danced whose husbands, if they had the power I once had, would have long ago bombed New Orleans into rubble. But the shop I found among all of this was run by white people, large Americans with neat shelves full of books and jars and dolls that I clearly sensed had nothing to do with the real voodoo.

So I went out of that shop and looked up and down Bourbon Street and I realized that this was all like Tran van Ha's Vietnamese restaurant, a phony thing. I went up to the next corner and turned down a side street, then took another turn and another until I was in a cobbled street of narrow little houses with spindlework porches and I walked along and I smiled at the black people on their stoops and I stopped at several of the stoops and asked if there was a voodoo man in the neighborhood. I have learned the lessons of history and I felt a kinship with these people and I was comfortable asking them for help, even though most of them looked at me very strangely. Finally an old man with a gray film in his eyes and a walking stick leaning on the post next to him said to me, "What you want him for?"

I said, "I have a beautiful wife who has a wandering eye."

The old man nodded and said, "I know that trouble," and he told me how to find the house of a voodoo man, a Doctor Joseph. He said, "You ax Doctor Joseph what you want. He be a powerful low-down papa." (I learned later that a papa is what many people call a male voodoo witch. And a "low-down" papa is willing to perform black magic and do evil deeds.)

I thanked the old man and made my way to another street much like the one I'd just left. I found the house, but I was expecting something different. This was like all the other houses, no strange symbols hung over the door or animal bones dangling on string or anything at all, except I did see a tiny sign by the doorbell. I went up onto the porch and the sign was a three-by-five card, laminated and nailed there, and it said,

"Doctor Joseph. Hard problems solved." If he had a great power like the old man said, then I liked Doctor Joseph already. This was my own style, of course. Low key. I rang the bell and waited and then Doctor Joseph himself answered the door. I know this because he said so. As if he already knew me and knew what I wanted, he opened the door and instantly said, "I am Doctor Joseph. Come in."

I stepped into a dark foyer that smelled of mildew and incense and my eyes were slow, straining to open to the darkness, and I couldn't see a thing but I followed in Doctor Joseph's wake and we entered a front sitting room. He waved his hand and I sat in an enormous soft old chair and I could feel the springs of the cushion beneath me. Doctor Joseph sat opposite me in a cane-backed chair and he had seemed from the moment he opened the door like a very large man, bigger even than any American, but now that he was sitting before me I could see that I was mistaken. It may have been a little spell he'd cast over me. I hoped so. But now he let me see that he was not big. He was as thin as any Vietnamese and he was a younger man than I'd expected, though this too may have been a spell. His eyes were very clear, very large, and the tight black curls of his hair had not the slightest touch of gray. His lower lip pushed up into an inverted smile and he was obviously ready for business, so I began.

I told Doctor Joseph everything about my wife, about the burden I've had to bear. I did not tell him that I once used the U. S. Air Force to correct my problems. I am still, at heart, a spy, even in the presence of a low-down papa, though being the papa that he was, he probably knew all of this anyway. After hearing me out, he tented his fingers before him and looked past me to the window where the filmy curtains let in the morning light that illuminated the room. He kept his eyes outside for a long while and I finally looked away from him, too. The room was very small, and except for the two chairs and a wooden pedestal table beside Doctor Joseph, there were no objects at all in the room. The empty walls were very dark in spite of the light from the window, and when I looked closer, they seemed to be actually painted black. There was a heavy curtain at a doorway which must have led to the rest of the house and perhaps back there were all the potions and mysterious objects of the voodoo doctor. I don't know. All that was in this room was the smell of incense and the low-down papa's gaze, which was traveling beyond me.

Finally Doctor Joseph's eyes came back to my face and when they did, I felt a burning in my sinuses and a weakness in my arms and legs. Then he said, "How much is this woman worth to you?"

I figured he was talking about his fee. I shrugged and he knew what I was thinking because he kind of snorted and said, "You and I will deal with that later. I'm speaking of a different realm. Three times you will have an opportunity to deny her. If you are going to call on the High Heavens, then you best know exactly what you want and exactly how bad you want it."

I was losing track of his words, but I could sense he wanted some kind of declaration from me before he would proceed. So I gave him the only answer I could possibly give. I did not even think about it. I said, "She is worth bringing fire from heaven."

Doctor Joseph nodded his head at this and his eyes bored deeper into me. I felt like I was about to sneeze. He said, "I could give you some good gris gris for the doorstep of this man, but I think something stronger is called for."

I nodded and I found that I could not raise either of my hands and I twitched my nose at the threatened sneeze, hoping Doctor Joseph would not take this as disrespect. Then he rose from his chair and he did not need to tell me to stay seated because I knew for certain that I had no command of my body at that moment. He disappeared through the curtain and I waited and it struck me that I was not even breathing, but then Doctor Joseph reappeared in the room, a sea wave of incense smells following him. He passed his chair and was looming before me and I sank down, the springs sproinging beneath me, and Doctor Joseph bent over me and I closed my eyes tight. "Here," he said and something dropped lightly into my lap.

I opened my eyes and he had pulled back. In my lap was a small brown paper parcel and Doctor Joseph said, "Inside is a hog bladder. You will also find a vial of blood. You must fill the bladder with the shit of a he-goat and then pour in the blood, tie up the bladder with a lock of your wife's hair, and then at the stroke of noon throw the bladder over your rival's house."

I nodded dumbly.

Then Doctor Joseph's inverted smile poked up again from his chin and he waved his hand and I don't remember getting up and crossing the room and going out the door, though I must have. But I just found myself standing in the street before his house and under my arm in a brown paper parcel was a hog bladder and a vial of the blood of who-knows-what and I was faced with a quest for goat shit. And I thought to myself, What am I doing? I thought of Buom's face and I could see in my mind that it was very beautiful, but history taught that a beautiful woman would always bring torture to her husband. Simply ask the American actor Mickey Rooney. I should drop this paper parcel in the nearest trash can and leave that woman, I thought. It might strike you as strange, but this was not a common thought for me, to just remove myself from the field and let my butterfly fly away. It was a very uncommon thought. In fact, this may well have been the first time I had it. I later realized that this was also my first opportunity to deny my wife. But the thought vanished as quickly as it came. I pulled the parcel from under my arm and looked at it and I wondered where in New Orleans I would find goat shit.

I am a small man but very clever, and soon I found myself

approaching the gate to the petting zoo in Audubon Park. I was in luck, I thought, because it was a weekday morning and there was no one in sight. Just me and a pen full of sheep and goats who were as fidgety as unwilling whores, waiting for the petting that would come at them every day. Before going in, I sat down on a bench to figure out how to handle this. My hands began to work at the string on the parcel, but then I realized that the goat shit didn't have to go straight into the bladder. I could gather the droppings in something more easily handled and then put them in the bladder later. I was very pleased with myself at this thought. I knew how to plan effectively.

So I got up and went back to a concession stand and ordered a box of popcorn, thinking to dump the corn and use the box. I glanced away for a moment, hearing the crunch of popcorn being scooped into the box, but thank Buddha I glanced over to the girl just as she stuck my box under a silver metal spout and reached up to the pump. "No butter!" I cried, and the girl recoiled as if she'd been hit. This could not be helped. I was concerned about inadvertently altering Doctor Joseph's formula. Who knows what butter might have done?

With the box in hand, however, I grew calm. So much so that I returned to the bench near the petting zoo and sat and ate the popcorn and enjoyed it very much. And this turned out to be a big mistake. I did think to wipe the salt out of the box with my handkerchief, but taking the time on the bench to eat the popcorn set up the arrival of a class of schoolchildren just as I stepped into the pen. I heard them laughing and talking and then saw them approaching along a path and I had to decide whether to back out of the pen and sit on the bench and wait for everyone to clear out or head quickly for the goats. The sun was getting high and I figured that it could be one class after another for the rest of the day, so I looked around the pen. There was a scattering of pellets here and there, but I didn't know exactly what a sheep's shit might look like and I didn't want to make a mistake. I spotted a white goat rubbing itself against a wooden post and I went over to it and lingered at its tail.

The goat continued to rub and the children were at the gate and I started to pat the animal on the hindquarters, both to look less conspicuous and perhaps to coax something out. But the goat looked up and twitched its ears at the gabble of the children and the voice of the teacher riding over the others and saying to calm down and be nice to the animals. The goat pulled away from the post and I could feel it tense up and I knew that there were little hands heading this way.

"Come on," I said, low, and I watched the goat's tail flick once, twice, and then there was a cascade of black pellets. I have particularly good reflexes and not more than half a dozen of them fell before my popcorn box was in place and clattering full of what I needed.

Then a child's voice rose from behind me, right at my elbow, howling in amazement, "Miss Gibbs, this man is putting goat doodies in his popcorn!"

It was now that I once again thought about my wife's face. I considered it in my mind and asked if it was worth what I was going through. I knew that many eyes were turning to watch what I was doing and part of me was saying, Let her fly away. And this was the second chance I had to deny my wife. But something was happening quite apart from my free will at that moment. I have heard the one or two rare, brave soldiers that I knew in my home country speak of a time under fire when your mind knows you are in serious danger, but your body will not budge; it holds its position in spite of the terrible force moving toward you. It was this that I felt as the child ranted on about this strange thing that I was doing. I kept my face down, my eyes focused on the flow of goat shit into the box in my hand, and I did not move. I held my ground until the tail twitched again and the flow stopped and the goat wisely galloped away from the little demon behind me.

I, too, moved away, never looking back at my tormentor or Miss Gibbs or any of the others. I followed the white goat; we escaped together along the perimeter of the pen, and it struck me that I must appear to the children and their teacher to be pursuing the goat for still more seasoning in my popcorn. But I veered away at last and waded through the children, heading for the gate and escape. To keep me from seeing the wondering glances of these little faces, I went over in my mind all that I'd just accomplished. I was very conscious of the weight of the popcorn box and the press of the paper parcel tucked tightly under my arm. I could get a lock of my wife's hair tonight. The tough part was done. I had the shit of a he-goat. And this stopped me cold as I touched the gate latch.

A he-goat. I had not checked the sex of the goat. I spun around and there were children all around me, drawn close, no doubt, to see this strange man and his strange snack depart. But when I turned, they drew back squealing. The white goat had stopped by the far fence. I knew it was *my* white goat because it was standing where I had last seen it and because it was looking at me almost in sympathy, as if it understood what I was going through with the attentions of these other little creatures.

It was a very hard thing for me to do, but I moved back into the pen, amidst the children. I would not look at them, but in my peripheral vision I could tell they were all turning to watch me, some of them even following me. I approached the goat and it looked very nervous. I spoke to it. "It's all right," I said. And then the toughest thing of all. I went to the goat's tail and I crouched down, and I heard two dozen little voices gasp. Thanks to Buddha I saw what I needed to see underneath the white goat, and I rushed out of the pen and the park as if the darkest voodoo demon was pursuing me for my very soul.

That night, as my wife slept, I bent near her with her own best sewing scissors and she was very beautiful in the dim light, her face as smooth and unlined as the face of the fifteen-year-old girl that I married. How was it that fate brought such a woman as this to a man like me? Even if my surface hides quite a different sort of man. She sighed softly in her sleep and though it was a lovely sound, it only made me restless. I could not bear to look very long at my wife's beauty until this whole thing was resolved, so I went to the back of her head and gently raised some of her hair so the lock I took would not be missed, and the silkiness of her hair made my hand tremble. Badly. I feared even that I might slip and cut her ear or her throat. But I took a deep breath and my blade made a crisp little snip and I was ready to work my voodoo magic.

The next morning Buom said she was going shopping at the malls with her friends. I said, "You know those women would be plucking chickens and getting high on betel nuts in the alleys of Saigon if we had won the war."

Buom huffed faintly at this and she even whispered to the toaster, "Try saying something new."

It's true I'd made this observation before and I said, sincerely, "I'm sorry, my pretty butterfly. You have a nice time with your friends."

Buom turned to me and there was something in her face that I could not place. Part of me wanted to believe that it was a wistful look, tender even, appreciative that I am the kind of Vietnamese husband who might even apologize to his wife. But another part of me thought that the look was simply repressed exasperation, a Vietnamese wife's delicate loathing. Either way, we said no more and when I left the house I did not head for the telephone company.

I drove to a local library and read the newspapers and the news magazines for a few hours. The world was full of struggle and you had to be clever to survive, that much was clear, and in the back seat of my car in a gym bag was a hog bladder full of blood and the shit of a he-goat and it was tied up (this was not an easy thing to do, as it turned out) with a lock of my wife's hair. I had Tran van Ha's address and I knew the neighborhood he lived in. At a quarter to twelve, I carefully folded the newspaper I was reading and replaced it on the shelf and I walked past the librarians with the softest tread, the calmest face (I was still a splendid spy, after all) and I drove up Manhattan Boulevard and under the West Bank Expressway and a few more turns brought me to Ha's street and I found his house on the corner.

I still had five minutes, so I parked across the street and slumped lower behind the wheel and observed the place. His was a shotgun house in a neighborhood of shotgun houses. They get their name from the fact that you could stand on the front porch and shoot a shotgun straight through to the back porch and the buckshot would pass through every room in the house. It occurred to me that this was the perfect design for a man in my situation. These houses were probably invented by an architect with a butterfly wife. He wanted to make it easy to draw a bead on his rivals. Just as I was about to answer this with the observation that a shotgun was not my style, something struck me about a shotgun house.

Doctor Joseph said I was to throw the bladder over the house. I had a ranch house or cape cod or such in my mind, a place where I would stand near the front porch and throw the bladder over the peak of the roof and it would roll down the other side and the task would be done. But the shotgun house is very long, stretched out deep into the lot. I could not throw the bladder that far. I was not a good thrower to start with, and this was just too far. Would the magic work if I threw the bladder over the house from one side to the other? Ha's place sat very near to the house next door and there was a fence in between.

It was a high, solid fence, I noticed, so that the neighbors could not see into his bedroom window where he met his lovers. This thought made me very angry and I looked at my watch and I had only two minutes to figure this out. I grabbed the gym bag from the back seat and stepped out of the car. Over the house, I thought. Over the house. If it goes over from side to side, it is still over the house. Surely that's all right, I thought. And I was lucky that Ha's house was on a corner lot. I could not deal with the narrow passage and high fence, but the other side of the house was open to the street and I walked briskly around the corner.

On this side there were three large trees, side by side. They seemed to block the house, but looking closer, I could see that there was a space of a few feet between each one. I looked at my watch and I had no time to waste now, only a matter of a few seconds. I set the gym bag down at my feet and drew out the bladder, long and dark gray and with a bandanna of Buom's silky hair. I placed myself between two of the trees and the alarm began to beep on my watch and I did not know how to hold the bladder, how to move my arm. Overhand or underhand? The alarm beeped on and I felt panic like a frightened goat running around in my chest and I chose to use an underhand throw. My arm went down, I kept my eye on the peak of the roof, and I flung the hog bladder as hard as I could, just as the alarm stopped beeping.

The bladder flew almost straight up, hooking just enough to crash through the leaves of the tree to my left and drape itself on a branch. I won't tell you exactly what it looked like to me, this bulbous skin doubled now and dangling from the limb of the tree. Yes I will tell you. It looked like a monstrous set of testicles, and it made me crazy with anger at Tran van Ha and I knew it could not remain there. Hanging there like that, it would probably work magic that was the exact opposite of what I'd intended. I decided that the bladder had been flung at noon and in a real sense it was still in the process of going over the house. The trip had no time limit on its completion, I reasoned, so I went to the tree, which was an oak with some large lower branches, and I began to climb.

As with many small men, I am very agile. I have not had much experience climbing trees, but the sight of the bladder above me and the thought of Ha and his desire for my wife drove me up the tree in a trance of rage. The bark scraped, the leaves grabbed at me, the gulf beneath me grew larger and larger, but I went up and up without a look down or a single thought of my own safety until I was nearly as high as the top of the roof and I'd drawn opposite the bladder. At this point I reached for a limb to steady me but it was dead and cracked off and clattered down onto the roof and my head snapped back with a little shock of understanding. I was in a tree and high off the ground.

But the bladder was hanging just beyond arm's length now and the peak of the roof was only an easy toss away from me and by the High Heavens I was going to complete this curse on Tran van Ha. I wrapped my arms and legs around the limb before me and began to inch my way out to the bladder. The little twigs along the limb clutched at me and I made the mistake of letting my eyes wander from my goal and I saw the distant earth and felt my breath fly away, leaving my lungs empty and my heart pounding. But I closed my eyes for a moment and when I opened them again, they were fixed on the hog bladder filled with the hard-earned goat pellets and I inched farther along, just a little more, a little more, and finally I reached out my hand and grasped the bladder.

And just as I did, I heard a voice from below. "What the hell is this?" the voice said. I looked down and it was Tran van Ha with his shirt unbuttoned and in his bare feet, like he had thrown his clothes on hastily. His face was turned upward to me and when I looked down, he must have recognized me, because his mouth gaped open and he staggered back a step. "You," he said.

"Yes, me," I said and the bladder was firmly in hand. I wondered what would happen if I threw it over the roof now. Would the earth crack open and swallow him up? Would he disappear in a puff of smoke? For a moment, I actually felt personally powerful up in that tree, like I was a B-52 opening its bomb bay doors. I was ready to make one more defense of my wife, my honor, my manhood. But then I heard a woman's voice, and Tran van Ha lowered his face and looked toward the sound.

"Don't," he said to the voice. But already there was a figure gliding across the lawn, a woman, her hair long and black and silky, and the face lifted to me and it was Buom. It was my beautiful butterfly of a wife and she, too, gaped, not expecting to see me. And I didn't feel powerful anymore. I was a small man up a tree holding a hog bladder full of goat pellets while my unfaithful wife stood beside her lover and watched me. This is what I'd come to. The man who once could bring fire from heaven now could only bring shit from the trees. I glanced at the peak of the roof and then I looked down at the two upturned faces and I knew I had to work my own magic here. But just as Doctor Joseph had prophesied, I was visited by my third opportunity to deny my wife. As beautiful as my wife's face was, it had only brought me pain, I thought. The hand with the bladder moved out away from the limb, hovered over this face, and I thought of how this woman had tormented me. But am I truly the right man for a woman this beautiful? Could I truly blame her? I looked at Tran van Ha and there was nothing redeeming at all in his face and I raised my arm not just to drop the bladder but to propel it. This I did, squarely at the amazed forehead of this man who had tempted my wife. I am glad to say that the bomb found its target. Unfortunately, this accuracy was obtained at some cost, for I followed the bladder out of the tree and I now lie in a hospital bed with both legs in traction and my left arm encased in plaster and folded over my chest.

But I am still more than I may seem to be on the surface. Every day I have been in this hospital, my wife has come and sat with me and held my right hand with her face bowed. Then this evening she brought her sewing and pulled her chair close to me, and before she began to sew, she asked what thoughts I had about the ways the Vietnamese in America were becoming part of American society. What did history have to say about all of that? she asked. I have many thoughts on that subject and I spoke to her for a long time. I spoke to her, in fact, until I dozed off, and I woke only briefly to feel her adjust the pillow behind my head and gently cover my good arm with the sheet.

Breakdown

Rawdon Tomlinson

It weaves the plot out near the edge
Like a hurricane at sea
While moving inland gradually;
The people look and talk

With no one inside; they pull apart
Like dolls with little arms,
Whispering how they'll harm
You once they find a way inside;

You grip the steering wheel with hands
That look like yours; you speak
And dress and brush your teeth,
But you know—its hydraulics

Are locked on full capacity
When it strikes, lashing out
With gale-force rage and blackout—
Miraculously you wake in the eye,

And then it snaps—power like that
Doesn't let go—and what you thought
Made it work, is lost.
The place you never own is restored:

See how the patient hands work
The pieces with the mind;
Though you can hear at times
Like these some shape snarling trapped

In undergrowth deep in the forest.
See how a life renews
Itself quietly, continues
Unremarkably each day,

The heart beginning to listen, the hands
Obedient to reprieve;
Every moment you breathe,
Everything you do is prayer.

Lost

Rawdon Tomlinson

The same houses stand
The people die and
Others move in, tell
Their stories and dis-
Appear; the meadow
Fills with trees, bleached bones;
The town on the plain
Succumbs to grass and
Wind; wind and ice
Erase the mountains;
Everywhere I
Look there is no place
To begin from, our
Faces change into
Our mothers' and our
Fathers', into those
We have never known;
On walks leaves shadow
Puzzles across walls
Then all is darkness,
Silence when we wake
Exhausted from some
Place we can't recall,
While time devours

Like ants dismantling
A prize butterfly,
And in age our mates
Turn strangers and die
Saying they never
Knew us, our bodies
Worked into juice by
Bacteria and
Grubs, the bones at last
Carbon reclaimed by
Dirt, with our names snowed
From the fallen stones--
Where we begin each
Day, shoved out the door
By the pikes of fear,
Blesséd pain which moves
Us desperadoes
To faith through the wilds
Of air, our paths
Closing behind us
Traceless as the wakes
Of little sailboats
In a giant race.

Etta's Pond

Clay Reynolds

Walker P. Sloan and Mickey stopped chewing at the same time. It was the first really warm night in a while, and the windows were open. They were having supper when the terror of screaming rubber came through the rusty, thin screens on the house's south side. They immediately looked at each other. Walker P.'s fork, laden with mashed potatoes and red-eye gravy stopped half way to his open mouth. Mickey's cornbread froze in his fingers. Their eyes locked. They both knew what was the matter without saying it, and a hollow feeling replaced the half-eaten meal in Walker P.'s stomach.

"Maybe it was a skunk, or a armadillo," Mickey said.

"Them folks don't stop for that." Walker P. put his fork down, picked up his napkin, and wiped his chin. "Rabbit or possum neither. It's Butch."

Out on the porch twilight was passing. The silver sky in the west outlined the bare trees. It was early spring. Buds hadn't yet appeared on the live oaks and cottonwoods, and the Johnson grass was still yellow and crackly. Walker P. walked to the edge of the warped, gray boards and peered out toward the highway. A pair of taillights blinked away into the night.

"One of them Surburbans," he said. "From over to Punkin Center. Goddamn town people got no sense. Drive too goddamn fast. Don't they know folks live here?" The man and boy stared off into the darkness. "Get my rifle," he said, "And a lantern." Mickey turned and went back into the house.

"You ain't goin' to shoot him, are you?" he asked when he returned and handed the 30.06 to the old man.

"May have to. If he's hurt bad an' ain't dead, I got no choice. Animals can't live with pain. Couldn't keep that damn fool dog out of that road. Should of shot him when they put it in."

"You couldn't of done that, Walker P. He was my dog."

"He was Etta's dog."

Walker P. hefted the rifle in arthritic fingers and limped down off the porch. Mickey lit the kerosene lantern and followed. It was a scant fifty yards out to the barbed-wire alongside the paved state highway. Mickey put a worn sneaker on a lower strand to push it down, and pulled the top wire up. Walker P. leaned the rifle against a cedar post and stooped through the opening, then he held the fence and the lantern for Mickey.

"Butch," Walker P. whistled. "Butch? Yo, Butch Boy?"

"C'mon Butch," Mickey pleaded. "Yo, Butch!" His voice was high and plaintive. It rang off the mesquite scrub along the fence line. The two waded through the dead Johnson grass in the ditch. The rifle wasn't necessary. Butch was dead: back broken, teeth bared back in a fierce grimace against the lantern's glare. Whether it was pain or fear, Walker P. couldn't say. There wasn't much blood. He had died clean.

"Stupid sons-of-bitches," Walker P. said. "Damn fool dog."

"This is where the pond was, an' this is where he liked to be," Mickey said.

"Pond's gone. Damn fool dog should of seen that."

As the last of daylight slipped behind the horizon, Mickey picked up the dog and carried him back through the wire. They buried him on a knoll a hundred yards behind the house, next to Etta's grave.

"There was a time," Walker P. said while he tamped down the newly turned earth over his—Etta's—dog's grave, "when she'd of done anything she could for that animal. Worthless as he was. Who'd of thought he'd outlive her? Hadn't of been for that road, he'd of outlived me, bet you."

"Don't say that, Walker P.," Mickey's voice cracked. He was crying, or fighting it, Walker P. realized. "Somethin' happens to you, what'll become of me?"

"You'll get on, Boy," Walker P. said. He gave the grave a final pat. The lantern's yellow light spilled across it and illuminated them only from the knees down. The night was moonless, dark. "You got on before. You'll get on after." The wind picked up slightly, and Walker P. thought he heard a hymn being hummed from far off. He cocked his head suddenly, but it was gone.

"He was a good dog," Mickey said. Walker P. knew the boy felt the need to say something, wanted Walker P. to say something. He had wanted him to say something when Etta was buried, too. But he hadn't. He'd be damned if he was going to now.

"Yeah, well, what the hell," he said. He picked up the pick and lantern. "Get the shovel. We got a early day tomorrow."

"We got a early day every day."

"Yeah, well, what the hell." They went back to the house to wash up the supper dishes.

***

Walker P. had been getting up at five o'clock for so long that he had no need of an alarm clock. Occasionally a thunderstorm would awaken him earlier, maybe Etta would turn in her sleep and bring him to consciousness. But usually, he just opened his eyes, cleared his throat, and shifted his legs over the side of the bed. By the time he did the milking, gathered the eggs, fussed with whatever piece of equipment he would need that day, the sun was up. Etta would have ham frying along with eggs, biscuits, gravy, potatoes, hot coffee, cool, sweet milk.

Since her death five years before, he sometimes forgot she was gone. When he returned to the kitchen, stopping to remove his dirty shirt and boots before entering the house, he was shocked to discover the stove cold, coffee unmade, the room still dark and still. It was then her death hit him the hardest, then and one other time, when he looked out over the highway and remembered where the pond had been.

The pond was a unique phenomenon in the county. Lots of farmers had tanks, most filled by windmills pulling gyp water deep from the earth and pouring it into man-made sandy ditches for stock to drink. But Etta's Pond was fed by a natural spring. Maybe it was the only one in the whole county, or at least the only one left since irrigation dropped the water table. Walker P.'s father, Sean, found it one Sunday when he took off from the back-breaking toil of laying down the Forth Worth and Denver City Railroad route and went on an aimless walk through the fields nearby the line camp. He had been the son of a farmer in Ireland, and he knew enough of the trade to know that rich soil and sweet surface water meant success was possible. He marked the spring, hiked to town and sat on the sidewalk outside the county courthouse until they opened on Monday. He filed his papers, went back and built a dug-out, and two years later had made enough farming cotton to marry Elizabeth Walker, a sixteen-year-old beauty who gave him Walker Patrick and three other children before she died of pneumonia thirty years later. Sean had a stroke ten years after that. He spent his last year sitting in a rocker on the porch, looking out over the encroaching mesquite around his spring and the small creek that ran out of it, and watching Walker P. take over the farm. The other children—girls all— married and moved away. Walker P. got a Christmas card from each of them and their children, whom he'd never met, every year. Two were dead now. The third was senile.

The spring wasn't a pond then, only a creek, a run really. When Walker P. arose the morning after he and Mickey buried Butch, he peered out into the pre-dawn gloom and imagined that he could still see cotton bolls waving just outside his window. Cotton was his life when he was young. It was hard to grow, hard to keep healthy, hard to pick, cheap to sell. Every square foot of the farm was planted, even the dooryard to the house which Sean had completed after Walker P.'s second sister was born. There were no strippers then, not even tractors. Black laborers and white trash from town hoed the weeds, pulled the bolls, sacked and loaded the cotton onto mule-drawn wagons which Walker P. and his father drove to town. Walker P. was only ten when he drove his first team to the gin. He was past forty when he gave up cotton for wheat.

He started the coffee boiling and went out to the barn and milked his single cow. She was heavy with a calf, and that pleased him. He'd fatten it all summer, butcher it next year: keep half, sell half, eat well for a year. He heard Mickey fussing around in the henhouse, talking to the chickens, gathering eggs. Walker P. poured out a quart of warm white foam into a plastic container, then took the milk pail and set it next to the barn door for Mickey to find. There was no market for fresh milk anymore. Or for eggs. Mickey would slop the hogs with most of both before he came in for breakfast.

The sun was up when Walker P. finished hard-frying six eggs and crisping ten strips of bacon so brittle that they broke from a mere glance. He used store-bought biscuits—never had the knack for bread-making—commercial jelly, too, no gravy. They ate the last of Etta's preserves two years ago. The coffee was bitter and hot, but yesterday's milk was sweet and cold. The two men ate in silence and listened to traffic swishing past on the highway. As was their custom, they didn't speak during a meal.

***

There was a series of mornings—several months' worth—when Walker P. was aroused for his morning chores by something other than his internal clock. The noise of earth-moving equipment started the din. It was followed by bull dozers, heavy trucks, then rollers and asphalt machines. The slamming of doors and curses of working men brought the sun up, put the cow off her milking schedule, stopped the hens from laying. The sows ate their litters that spring. Everything was wrong, but there wasn't a thing Walker P. could do about it.

"We're putting the highway right through here," a khaki-clad engineer told him.

Walker didn't like the man the minute he saw him. He drove up in a new Chevrolet pickup with State Highway Department markings on it, sent Mickey looking for Walker P., and sat there smoking a cigarette while the farmer shut down his ancient International Harvester tractor and trudged up to the house. The man wore a shiny straw hat, short-sleeved white shirt, and a clip-on tie. He introduced himself as Clyde Dayton and told Walker P. what was about to happen: he was going to lose his farm.

***

"Imminent domain," the young lawyer in town told Walker P. "There's nothing you can do about it, I'm afraid." The young man's name was James David Leftwich.

Walker P. scowled at the youth across the mahogany desk in front of him. He never had trusted any man who went by two whole first names. He had been Walker P. since grade school where there was also a Walker K. and a Walker T.

"Never knew that name was so popular," the teacher said. It was the way she had of telling them apart when she called on them, and it stuck.

"Where's Buddy Henson?" Walker P. asked the attorney. "I always do my law business with Buddy. He won't let 'em take my farm."

"You know Buddy's retired," James David smiled sadly. "I'm his nephew, and I'm handling his practice. Have been for two years." He adjusted his cuffs underneath his suit-coat. "And they're *not* taking your farm. They're just building a highway through it."

Buddy never wore a suit-coat inside of doors in his life, Walker P. thought. His only fault was that he sometimes drank too much. It was a vice Walker P. respected. James David Leftwich didn't look like he had ever had a sip of decent whiskey in his life. No backbone, Walker P. scowled to himself. Half-decent shit pain'd cripple him.

"Now," Leftwich went on as he scanned the papers Dayton had given to Walker P. "They're offering you a fair price. Twenty dollars an acre more than you could get on the open market, the way things are for farmers these days."

"Don't want to sell."

"You don't have a choice. The state has the legal right to come right through there with that highway. It's only a spur, really. I think you might squeeze them for a few dollars more. We could demand another five, maybe ten an acre. They would beat us in court, but it would hold them up. I can prepare a letter and see what happens. It would help if you would list it with a real estate broker at the price we want."

"Don't want no goddamn broker. Don't want their goddamn money. I want my farm. It's my farm. Born there. Lived there all my goddamn life. My folks is buried there. Wife, too."

"Well, you can still live there," Leftwich glanced at a fancy, black-faced clock on his desk. "They won't touch the house."

"They're cutting it right in two. I don't see the need for it. That road's done just fine goin' up by the bridge. Just who the hell wants a paved road through my farm anyway?"

Leftwich leaned back and tented his fingers. "You know as well as I do about the new development out at Pumpkin Center."

"*Pun*kin Center," Walker P. corrected. "Never was no pumpkins there. Named for folks named Punkin. My daddy knew them." Goddamn city people, he thought. Come out here, mess up everything. Ran half the town now, maybe all of it. Sure as hell ran the county.

"It's a five-mile drive up to the highway bridge and then into town. This spur'll make it a straight, three-mile shot." He pursed his lips and then reached out and adjusted the clock. "You know also that every farmer in Texas thinks it's his God-given right to have a paved road running right up to his front door. You probably voted for the men who passed this law."

"Ain't no farmers livin' in Punkin Center. Just a bunch of yahoo town people, bankers an' the like. Come out here 'cause they've already screwed up things where they was. Buildin' a country-club an' a lake an' sittin' 'round on their asses listenin' to the TV. I'm a farmer. That's my farm they're cuttin' up."

"You have a whole section. This isn't going to take up that much of it."

"They're going to fence off the whole damned place. Can't run no stock, got to take the tractor the long way 'round. Can't get combines into my fields. Half what I got is overrun with goddamn mesquite an' fire ants anyhow. They're going to ruin what I got left."

"Well, maybe it's time you thought about retiring. They're going to pay you a considerable amount. Why not sell out, lock, stock, and barrel? You could relax, take it easy. How old are you, anyway, Mr. Sloan?"

"None of your goddamn business."

"You're over seventy. You're a widower. You have no children to care for you."

"I got Mickey."

Leftwich frowned. "You ought to look at one of the rooming houses in town. There are several that cater to men your age. Your friends, farmers like yourself who've retired. They get together and have a great time. Uncle Buddy's living in one," he added hopefully.

"Sit 'round on their goddamn butts an' drool on each other. I been there. I seen them."

"They're your friends."

"My friends is all dead." He clenched his fists. "Look, I'm a healthy workin' man. I got all my teeth, don't take no tonic or pills. My heart's good, an' I think clear. See things clear, too. I can see they're stealin' my farm from me, an' I come to see ol' Buddy for help. Now, you tell me Buddy's over yonder pissin' on his boots, so I guess it's up to you."

"There's nothing I can do. I'm sorry. I have another appointment. I'll write the letter asking for more money, and I'll let you know—"

"Ol' Buddy'd never let them sons-of-bitches take my farm. That's a good farm. It makes its way. I never had to borrow extra on it, always paid my bills. I got money in the goddamn bank to carry it. They got no right to take it."

Leftwich rose. "They have the right. It's the law. And, I say again, they're not taking your farm, just running a highway through it." He looked hard at Walker P., but the old man saw only saw the pity in Leftwich's eyes. It infuriated him. It saddened him.

The lawyer stuck out his hand. "I urge you to remember that. They're not taking your farm, just cutting through it. There's nothing you can do to stop that highway."

"No," Walker P. came to his feet and stuck his gnarled hands into his overalls' pockets. "I guess they ain't."

"That's the way. Look at it positively. I mean, in the final analysis, you'll be better off. What have you really lost?"

"Etta's Pond," he said. "Sons-of-bitches'll ruin Etta's Pond."

***

It was really Walker P. who made the decision to ruin Etta's Pond. He had little choice. Clyde Dayton came into the house, sat down, and ignored the mug of reheated ebony bile which Walker P. put in front of him. Walker P. was no happier about the man's presence than the engineer was about how bitter the coffee was, but Etta had never turned away any person from her kitchen without some kind of refreshment, and the left-over breakfast coffee was handy.

Dayton didn't even take off his hat. He spread a map out on the oilcloth of the kitchen table and used a silver pen as a pointer.

Walker P. tried to listen, to understand, but the map looked like nothing he had ever seen before. It had swirls and lines going in circles. No landmarks were identified, only elevations, geographical problems, geological faults. Dayton lit a cigarette and continued to talk, sweeping his pen out toward the walls of the room in different directions, oblivious to the old farmer's confusion.

"So, we'll leave it up to you after this point," he said. Walker P. peered down to see the pen's point resting between a maelstrom of wavy lines. The name "Sloan" had been penciled inside a tiny circle a few inches away. Walker P. decided that was his farm. "We have three choices: We can go straight-away, which would run right through the house, here. We can cut to the north or south of it. We try not to take a man's house if we can avoid it. Costs too much." He winked. "So in this case, either route is fine. We'll just curve away in whichever direction you think is best for you."

Dayton went on about how they would erect fences along the right of way to protect the house and fields they were interrupting, suggested ways of moving the road coming up to the house to improve Walker P.'s access, and discussed the number of gates they would be required to place in the fence. Walker P. wasn't listening any more.

"So, which is it to be? North or south? It really doesn't matter to us." He walked out onto the porch. Walker P. followed. "I can come back next week, if you want to think about it. But we'll need an answer, soon. The road crews are already to the cut-off on Grangerford's place where the old road ties in. Surveyors will need to go to work here, soon."

What Dayton was saying finally registered in Walker P.'s mind. "Which away you want to go?"

Dayton patiently outlined the alternative routes once more. The rolled map substituted for the pen as he pointed north of the house, toward the knoll where Etta's grave was. Walker P. felt a chill in the summer air. She hadn't been in the ground but a few months. It was where she wanted to be, said so to him a million times. Now, this Yankee import was sent from Austin to build a road right over it.

"No goddamn way," he said. "There's a grave up there, cemetery. My daddy's up there. My mama, too." He paused. "My wife's up there."

Dayton studied Walker P. "Well, we can go south. It'll cut closer to the house, right across that tank. But if that's what you want."

"Ain't a tank, it's a pond," Walker P. corrected automatically. It was a common mistake. "Natural spring."

"Well, it's that or the cemetery. Which?"

"Can't you cut south of the pond. Maybe way over yonder someplace?"

"Nope," Dayton lit another smoke and shook his head. "Soil's unstable down in there. We did a preliminary shoot last month. Seismograph readings say it's almost a swamp. And if we go over to the north, we have to blast through solid rock. This is the only route."

Walker P. went in to see Buddy at that point. But Buddy wasn't there. Leftwich was, and was no help. When he saw Dayton again, he told him it would have to be the pond. Etta's Pond.

***

While Mickey finished the breakfast dishes, Walker P. went out on the porch with his coffee. He set it carefully on a rusty metal table and rolled a cigarette. For more than forty years, he had smoked four hand-rolled cigarettes a day: one after each meal, one right before bedtime. With the last one of an evening, it was also his habit to take a sip or two of whiskey from a pint bottle he kept under the kitchen sink.

Etta hated strong drink, but she never complained about that. In their forty years together, she complained about very little.

Looking out over the gray surface of the roadway, he observed morning traffic passing. There were plenty of pickups, some heavier vehicles, Suburbans, Broncos, Blazers, a variety of Japanese utility vehicles, some big cars. Mostly they were spanking new and driven by men and women dressed for office jobs. He doubted any of the vehicles would ever be worked the way he worked his old Ford truck or I-H tractor. He doubted that any of the drivers had ever really worked at all.

For a while after the highway was completed, motorists waved to him when they saw him sitting and sipping his coffee. The road was close to the house, too close, and they could see him clearly. He never waved back, and soon they stopped. He never drove or walked on the asphalt surface, except to cross it, either. When he went to town, he took the old county road by the bridge, which, he could see, they were letting go.

He hadn't planted any crops the spring they built the highway. He intended to, and the wheat was already up by the time they started, but instead of putting in alfalfa and soy beans, he spent the mornings watching them ruin the pond. He stayed on the porch every day until mid-May. Then, he left only to supervise the wheaties who took the grain from his fields. It was a good year, first in a long time that hail or excess rain hadn't ruined at least part of the golden crop before he got it out. Prices were high, too. It was a chance to replace worn out equipment, fix up the house and outbuildings. But he hadn't. His heart wasn't in it.

The year before Etta had still been alive. Ten inches of rain in two weeks washed the wheat down and rotted it in the fields. What he got out didn't get to the elevator for weighing until the price fell.

"Maybe next year," she said. She said that almost every year. When next year came, she was gone.

He banked the money and watched the workers destroy the pond. Butch and Mickey sat with him. The only work they did was essential chores: the cow, the chickens, the hogs. When they had the pond all filled in but a few thousand square feet out in the middle, they tossed in some dynamite and killed all the fish. Perch, channel cat, small-mouthed bass floated to the surface, stunned, dead. The construction workers gathered them up and put them in plastic coolers. They brought a mess up to the porch where Walker P. sat and offered them to him: his own fish. He told them to go to hell, and they stayed away from him after that.

Butch didn't even like them. He ran up and down the new fence they put up and barked at them constantly when they were working near the house. It was a wonder he didn't have a heart-attack, Walker P. told Mickey. He ran and yelped for hours: Etta's dog, protecting Etta's pond.

***

Walker P. met Etta just after his youngest sister married and left home. It was at the State Fair. He had a prize mule that year, and friends urged him to enter it. She was the last working mule he would ever own, he realized, and it seemed a good thing to do. It was his only trip to the Dallas event in his life, and he met Etta in the neighboring swine exhibit. He strolled over to admire the hogs, and she smiled at him and introduced herself.

"Name's Etta," she said. "For Etta Place. Know who she was?"

Walker P. acknowledged his ignorance.

"She was the Sundance Kid's sweetheart. He was an outlaw. My granddaddy was conductor on a railroad they held up. Always said she was the prettiest girl he'd ever seen, made my folks name me for her. Said he didn't want me to be an outlaw, but he was sure I'd turn out pretty. What do you think? Am I pretty?"

Walker P. admitted she was.

She was a farm girl from down along the coast, lived right on the ocean, she said, place called High Island where her daddy ran cattle, and she continued her Four-H work with hog-breeding long after she was too old for the club. They talked for hours, and when he got back to West Texas, he wrote to her. Four letters later, he proposed, and she accepted by telegram. He was impressed, and she *was* pretty. They were married at her aunt's house in Waco, about half-way between. She told him on their honeymoon night that she knew they would get married the minute she saw him. He was glad. He had felt the same way.

She took well to farm life in the arid climate, kept breeding hogs, the only husbandry he continued to practice after she died aside from keeping chickens and one good heifer for milk. Cheerful always, happy to be Walker P.'s wife, she asked him for very little he didn't provide and paid him back by becoming more beautiful every year. Her main oral expression of regret was that she missed seeing water.

"You live on the ocean all your life, you come to miss it. I never look out the kitchen window, I don't miss seeing a body of water," she told him once. Once was enough.

The next day he hired a dozer to come and dredge out the spring's creek and build a small earthen dam: the pond was born. That was when he stopped farming cotton. Irrigation was now possible from the run-off, and he sank three wells elsewhere on his property and began growing wheat, alfalfa, soy beans, even watermelon and cantaloupe. They planted a peach orchard alongside the graves where his parents were buried, had pecans along the old dry bed where it meandered off toward Blind Man's Creek and into the copper breaks, and they planted grass and flowerbeds in the house's yard where Sean Sloan grew cotton years before. Etta revived his mother's vegetable garden as well.

The pond was popular. Four-H and FFA boys who lived in town and needed a place to raise their livestock projects came out to swim and fish in the summer while they tended and pampered their animals which occupied pastures and pens Walker P. provided without charge. It was they who named it "Etta's Pond." They also provided a bit of labor around the house—mending things, chopping weeds, mowing grass—sometimes even taking a turn on the tractor when the wheat stubble needed plowing or hay needed baling in return for the farm's hospitality. Often, Etta would ask them to crank up a freezer of ice-cream she made to go with some fried chicken for an impromptu picnic along the banks. Eventually, they even built some rickety tables and benches to set out there. Some of them spent more time on the Sloan farm than they did at home. Some said they would rather be no place else in the world.

"It gives me such a warm feeling to see those kids out there," Etta always said. They were five years married then, and two doctors had confirmed that the Sloans would never have children of their own.

The best part of the pond, though, was the way he and Etta used it. In the heat of summer, when he would come in at dusk, filthy with soil and grease from the implements he had wrestled around all day, he wouldn't even go to the house. In the twilight, out among the crickets and bullfrogs, he would strip off his grimy overalls and swim out to the middle. Etta pretended to be outraged to see her naked husband cavorting in her pond, but after a few pretended scoldings, she, too, would respond to his calls, undress, and enter the cool, healing water, swim out to him, and they would splash and play until full dark.

"Don't need no bath when you got the pond," Walker P. would tell her when they came shivering into the house for supper. "Can't fill a tub with nothing as good as what we got right out there."

***

Walker P.'s coffee had gone cold, though he had barely sipped it. Mickey seemed to sense the problem, and before the old man splashed the black liquid into the dead flowerbeds alongside the porch, he emerged with the pot.

"We goin' to work today?" he asked.

"No more'n usual," Walker P. said.

"Thought I might go find some flowers to plant on ol' Butch's grave."

"It's too early for flowers."

"They's some daisies out yonder," Mickey said. He pointed off toward a north pasture. "I could dig up the roots while they're dead. See if they'd seed out. It'd be real pretty come summer."

Walker P. doubted it would work. They were more likely sunflowers than daisies. He sipped the scalding coffee and nodded. "Go ahead on," he nodded. "Get back 'fore dark. Tend them hogs." Etta's hogs, he amended. He hadn't been able to bring himself to sell or kill one since she died, and they had grown fat, lazy, and plentiful in their pen. It was all he could do to cut the boars in time to keep a new litter from appearing.

The boy scampered off.

Boy, Walker P. thought. He was nearing thirty, maybe. "Put some on Etta's grave, too," he shouted. Mickey stopped and turned.

"Miss Etta always did like flowers," Mickey grinned. He waved his gimme hat and took off at a dead run. Didn't even take a shovel, Walker P. thought. He'll be back in a spell.

***

Walker P. watched the roadbed grow to a completed highway. In a way, he told himself day after day as the trucks and machines worked in the increasingly hot afternoons, it's worse than if they had gone over the cemetery. It was almost as if they were burying all those kids who came out here. But then, it was worse than that, too. The kids were long grown and gone, and Walker P. and Etta were only old people, dim memories to them. By July, the workers had moved on, out of sight. Only a distant noise told the farmer that they had passed beyond the boundaries of his property and were now cutting up someone else's: Dutch Cummings', he reminded himself, but then he remembered that Dutch Cummings died. No one had lived on the Cummings place in ten years.

A group of people named The Sandhill Grain Syndicate farmed it now. They'd sent him letters from Dallas asking if he was interested in selling out to them. They offered him "top dollar," they said. He wondered if it was as much as the state paid. But he didn't wonder long. He burned their letters with the rest of the trash.

When the bright yellow truck came down painting stripes in the middle of the gray asphalt, it was over. The fence was up and sang in the summer wind, and cars and pickups were soon speeding past, hauling people from town to Punkin Center and the swimming pool and golf course they had put in alongside a small, man-made lake built for the exclusive use of the wealthy residents who lived there. Of an evening, when the wind lay, Walker P. could hear the high whine of their speed boats. Sometimes they reminded him of Etta's humming when it came across the fields.

He continued to go out to the porch and sit the rest of the summer. Only the greatest of effort forced him away from the rocker to gather his crops. The melons mostly rotted in the fields. He didn't have the energy to harvest them regularly.

The next year he did better. He put in his winter wheat, also planted in the spring, and did fairly well with all his crops, made money for the second year in a row. Mickey worked with him, but Mickey was little help at all. He never could master the intricate gears of the old tractor, and he didn't move a plow or handle anything more complicated than a hoe without hurting himself or destroying the implements. He couldn't even milk properly. It was only through the greatest effort he taught the boy to swim. In the pond. But Etta had loved him. Just as she had loved Butch. So Walker P. never complained or scolded him. He gave him chores to do that he knew he could do, saw to his needs, and let him alone.

***

One September noon almost fifteen years before, Walker came up from the fields for dinner and found Mickey sitting on the porch eating left-over stew. He gave the farmer a wide, dirty-faced grin when Walker P. stripped off his shirt and boots, stomped barefoot past him into the kitchen. It wasn't that unusual for Etta to feed a drifter, although in those days, drifters weren't as common as they had once been. It aggravated Walker P. nonetheless.

"They're like cats when they're that young," he said. His skin was milky where the sun hadn't touched it. His neck and hands were dark brown, almost mahogany from heat and dry wind. Bare-chested, he looked twenty years younger than he did in his sunbaked overalls and workshirts. "Feed them, an' they'll never leave."

"He was hungry," she said before he could go on. "He's going to clean out the henhouse after dinner. Says his name is Mickey. Don't say anything else."

"He'll be here a week if he's here a hour."

He was there all day, Walker P. discovered when he came in at dark. He had a plate of chicken and dumplings balanced on his ragged trousers and a huge tumbler of iced tea next to him on the porch. Walker P. noted that his shoes were bound together with strips of tape. He had no suitcase, no bindlestiff, nothing in the way of belongings besides what he was wearing.

"He's just like that goddamn dog," Walter P. growled over supper.

"Hush," Etta warned him. "And watch your language. He's just a boy."

Normally, Walker P. knew, drifters liked nothing better than eating but talking. Starved for company, they would sit and talk about their lives for hours: where they had been, where they were heading, what big things they planned to do. This boy was different. When Walker P. came out after supper for his smoke, the boy sat quietly and stared out over the pond.

"There any fish in there?" he asked.

"There's fish."

That was it. They sat silently in the darkness until Etta came out with a lantern, apologizing good-naturedly about Walker P.'s continued failure to wire the porch for electricity, and then sat next to her husband and pretended to crochet a baby blanket for a newborn grandniece they would never see.

When he was still there two days later, they questioned Mickey closely. He didn't know his last name—or wouldn't give it, Walker P. suspected—or exactly how old he was. He claimed to have finished eighth grade, but he couldn't remember—or wouldn't say—where. In fact, he said he didn't know where he was from, where he had been, exactly, or where in the world he was going. He slept in the barn. The next morning, they put him in the back of the pickup and took him to town.

Doc Pritchard told them he was mentally retarded: not "crazy," as Walker P. suggested, just "slow." He sent them to Sheriff Newsome for advice. Newsome told them he would make some calls, see if anyone had reported him missing. In the meantime, they could take him home. Two days later he drove out and told them that there was no record of

Mickey that he could find anywhere. He would keep looking. He suggested that they let him take Mickey back into town, call a social worker from Wichita Falls.

"What happens then?" Etta asked.

"Well, if they can't find his folks, I reckon he'll have to go down to Austin or maybe somewhere else. There's places for boys with his problems."

"You mean an asylum, don't you?" Etta asked. Her hands were bunched in her apron.

"Well," Newsome shifted his weight. "They don't call them that. But yes."

"Where you reckon he come from? Where's his folks?"

The sheriff looked down the old county road as it trailed dusty into the distance. "Sometimes, people just can't handle boys like that. They just dump them. Let somebody else worry about it," he said. "It's not pretty, but it happens."

"I know," Etta said thoughtfully. "That's how we come by Butch."

Walker P. walked away and went down to the barn. He knew that Mickey wasn't going with the sheriff. He wasn't going any place.

They bought him new clothes and enrolled him in school for one term, but he was too far behind to catch up, too slow-witted to follow much of anything. Other boys picked on him, even those half his size and years younger than he sent him home with a bloody nose or black eye. He didn't even have the sense to be ashamed of it. Doc Pritchard filled out a form saying that he was seventeen, old enough to quit school if he wanted, and he stayed on the farm, played with Butch, and helped Etta out with chores. He was less good than Butch as a hand, but he could do a few things, and he made Etta happy. She called him an "angel unawares," and that would have to be enough for Walker P.

When he had been there five years, they talked of putting him into a special school that was starting in Wichita Falls, maybe help him learn a trade. "Something to do with himself when we're gone," she said. She never considered his leaving before then, though Walker P. often wished he would. She wrote off for information twice. The principal at the high school in town said he would help arrange things. Walker P. never saw the need for it. "Good money after bad," he told her. "We feed him, give him a bed. If he wants more, let him go after it."

"He don't know his name, not even what day it is," she said. "He's God's gift to us. Just like that pond out there. Just like you and me are to each other."

"We'll see when the time comes," Walker P. promised. He then pointed out that Michey's going away might mean his staying away. That put an end to the argument. To Etta he was like the pond, like Butch, like Walker P. and the farm: her life.

***

To his surprise, it was afternoon when Walker P. finally rose from the porch and moved into the kitchen. He ought to make some dinner, but he knew that Mickey, wherever he was, wouldn't come back until he spotted his shadow long on the ground and saw that it was getting dark. Etta gave him a watch one Christmas, but he never mastered telling time. He didn't even cry at her funeral, Walter P. recalled. But then, neither had Walter P.

The old farmer didn't grieve for Etta, never had. She was a woman with a good heart, and one day, the heart just quit: like a piece of land that would grow fat crops year after year, then just quit. She wore out. Walter P. didn't begrudge God for taking her. In a way, he thought she was relieved to go. Farming was hard on a woman. Hard on a man, too. He missed her, but he never resented her leaving him behind.

He went into the kitchen, got some ham from the refrigerator, and made himself a sandwich, boiling up a new pot of coffee to go with it. There was a bucket of scraps by the sink, and he whistled and called Butch to come eat the bacon rind. He was out on the porch before he remembered. A car sped past to remind him.

Sometimes, he had trouble remembering exactly where the pond was. Now, as his eyes roamed over the highway and fence line, he couldn't recall it ever being there. There had been a stand of hackberry trees next to the spring, but they were gone. There was nothing left to mark where it had been.

Butch never forgot. Like Walter P. and Etta, he loved to swim in the pond, would go down on his own and cool off when the weather was hot and prowl the banks, barking at migrating ducks when they stopped over. After the highway went in, he'd roam the blacktop like it was a blanket covering a buried bone, sniffing at the ground and looking lost and quizzical when he couldn't figure out where the water was. Walter P. stood on the porch and realized that he had marked the pond's boundaries by Butch's antics, much as they aggravated him and made him fear for the dog's safety. Now Butch was gone. So was the pond.

For years, of an evening when the season didn't demand constant, daylight to dark labor, neighbors would come by and sit on the porch, sip iced tea or coffee, and look out over the pond, watch Butch or the boys from town swimming out there. Once in a while, they would take one of the cane poles Walker P. kept stacked by the barn and put a few grasshoppers out on the water. It didn't matter if they caught anything, it was the company that counted. On hot summer evenings, they would sometimes sit and watch the water rippling in the heat. From time to time a fish would jump, and through the cicadaes' buzzing the sound of that cool splash was the next best thing to an early norther.

More than once, when Etta was in town buying groceries or something, the pond was full of naked farmers, playing like school boys in the blue water. She wouldn't have minded, Walter P. thought. The pond was for friends, neighbors. It was for her and her life there.

Now, there were no more friends, no more neighbors. The county agent told Walker P. just before the highway was put in that he was only one of four resident farmers left in that end of the county. The rest had moved into town long ago. Or died. The farm had died, too. He wouldn't fool with the gates Dayton's people put up, and he leased out the fields and pastures across the highway. Last year, he had leased out all but the twenty-five acres immediately surrounding the house. It was still good land, mesquite and ant infested as it was. People were glad to have the use of it.

Walker P. looked around the yard. Rusty equipment, a falling down hog-wire fence, some broken pens greeted his eyes. Everything needed paint. Wind had almost pushed the barn over. The tractor hadn't been started in a year, probably wouldn't. Weeds choked the flowerbeds, and a failure to water had killed the grass last summer. Large bare patches of dusty ground spotted the yard. Etta's—his mother's—vegetable garden was overgrown with Johnson grass and tumbleweeds. There was a trash heap next to some sixty-gallon oil drums. He needed to do some burning, another chore he didn't trust Mickey with, and probably there were snakes under the henhouse. The weather was warming: they'd be out and after the chicks and eggs soon.

He went back inside and discovered the coffee pot boiling over. When he reached out his hand to grab it, the black liquid spilled out and scalded him.

"Goddamn!" he cried, turning and flinging the coffee pot across the room. Grounds splattered across the cracked linoleum. "Goddamn, goddamn!" He stepped to the sink and ran cold water over the burned area. That made it hurt even worse, and he jerked his hand away. "Son-of-a-bitch!" he hissed.

"Etta," he called, "Etta! I burned myself, goddamnit." She would be mad about his swearing, he thought. Can't be helped: A man has to swear out the pain. "Etta!"

His voice came back to him in a slight echo, and he remembered. The kitchen seemed to close in on him. Outside he heard the fence keening in the wind. Corner shadows raced toward him and made his head swim. He shook it, cleared his mind.

"Damned old fool," he said. "Not worth a good goddamn to nobody."

He stalked through the house back to the bathroom. It was an add-on, something Sean had not seen the need for when he constructed the house. And it was modern. Etta insisted on the best plumbing they could afford, and they had it. A well provided the water, and they had a Culligan softening system. He entered and opened the medicine cabinet.

An array of ointments and creams were stacked on the top shelf. Some had been left open and dried up. Others were hard to the touch, and he wasn't sure which ones were right. It was the first time he had hurt himself seriously since she died, and except for having to put a band-aid here or a corn plaster there, he hadn't needed any of the household first aid she always took care of. He almost yelled her name again before his mind jerked him back.

He fussed with several tubes and jars before losing patience and dumping them all into the trash can by the toilet. He ran more cold water over the burn, which was now red and puckering slightly, smeared some Vaseline on it, wrapped some gauze bandage around it, and tied it all up with a handkerchief.

"Have to do," he muttered. "Can't help it. Goddamn stupid old man."

When he passed through the house again, he realized that in all the years he had lived there, it was one of the few times since his childhood he had been anywhere but the kitchen or bathroom during the day. The house seemed small, tiny as he walked through the rooms. The livingroom appeared behind a curtain of dusty sunlight streaming in from the screens and Venetian blinds. The furniture looked moldy, used, and covered with dirt. The front door hadn't been opened since Etta's funeral. There was probably a good half-acre of soil on every table, he thought. Lying on Etta's secretary were the brochures from the special school in Wichita Falls. Like everything else, they were dusty, brittle to the touch.

The guncase in the corner was also dirty, unused. A rifle, two shotguns and a pistol, Walker made a mental inventory. He never went in for hunting. He suddenly remembered Dutch Cummings again. Widowed, ignored by his children, eat up with cancer, wheat hailed out two years running, Walter ticked off Cummings's problems. Now his oldest boy had come home, ran an insurance office in town and farmed his daddy's place when he felt like it. Walker P. wondered idly if Cummings had used a rifle or shotgun. Maybe a pistol, he thought: handier. Etta went to the house, Walker P. handled the funeral. He shook his head in the dusty sunlight and left the livingroom.

The bedrooms—two open, the rest closed off for years—were in better shape. He glanced into Mickey's neat room. The boy kept it spic and span: everything organized, in its place. At his own door he stopped. The furniture was old. Most of it belonged to Etta's folks. When they died, she had it shipped there to replace the more worn-out pieces bequeathed to Walker P. by his own parents. She shoved that into the spare bedrooms and shut the doors. The only strikingly modern piece was a console color TV—one of two sets they owned. It sat at the end of the bed, raised up on a crude platform of four by fours so they could watch it before they went to sleep. It had been broken for years and never picked up but two channels through the antenna mounted on top of the house. The radio in the kitchen gave Walker P. the farm and weather reports. He had never had a yen for any music he couldn't hear on the wind.

Etta's small black and white, which she kept in the kitchen for soap operas and game shows to keep her company while she worked, was now in Mickey's room. If he ever watched it, Walker P. didn't know it.

The house seemed strange, quiet, smaller and more empty than it ever had, and Walker P.'s odd feelings swam around him with the dust bugs he raised when he walked through the rooms.

"Need to clean this place up," he said. He vowed to set Mickey to work with mop and dust rag tomorrow.

He returned to the kitchen, cleaned up the spilled coffee, and ate his sandwich. His hand hurt, but somehow it felt like a proper retribution for how foolish he had been acting. He could hear a clock ticking somewhere, and he tried to remember where there was a clock in the house that ticked that loud. But he couldn't. He started to go and see, but he didn't. The house's interior, away from the familiar kitchen, seemed ominous suddenly. He could feel Etta there, sense her presence. It seemed a violation of something to go banging around back there during the day.

***

It was late, and he was burning the trash when Mickey came up, dirty from his face down. His arms bundled around a huge bunch of dead plants, their roots intact.

"Forgot the shovel," he said matter-of-factly. "But I'll need one to put these in up there."

Walker P. stood away from the trash fire. Boxes, cans, and bottles were visible in the flames. He used to burn trash once a week. Etta insisted that if he didn't, they'd have rats, snakes, other varmits poking around.

"Surest way to kill chickens," she said, "is to leave a bunch of trash lyin' 'round."

He had let it go this time for too long. But it was still early spring. No evidence of animals was about. He and Mickey didn't eat that much, anyway. Food scraps went to the hogs and Butch. It wasn't so bad to wait a while.

"It's gettin' late. You need to tend to the chickens an' hogs. I need to start supper," he said. "Them things won't grow."

Mickey looked abashed. Walker P. reminded himself that the boy had been out in the pasture all day, scraping these weeds out of the ground with his bare hands, all for the love of a dog. And Etta. He changed his tone. "Not without water, they won't. How you goin' to water them?"

Mickey looked up at the knoll. The gravesites were in deep shade now. The sun was declining rapidly. Cars and trucks whisked by on the highway. Quitting time in town, Walker P. thought with a sneer curling his lip. Get out to the goddamn lake, play a round of golf 'fore supper. Drive right through a man's land. Kill his dog.

"Well, I reckoned I could haul some up there. In a bucket." Mickey's dirty brow furrowed.

"I tell you what," Walker P. said suddenly. "There's some lengths of old hose in the barn. I don't think it leaks. I used it when we had to pump out that well few years back. More'n a five hundred, maybe eight hundred feet. You take one end, put it down in the pond. Get it out to the middle, way out. Then you take th'other end an' run it downhill here by the house. Ought to stretch a good ways. Then you suck real hard on it. One section at a time. Get it flowin' good, then hook up another section, and go do it again. Work your way uphill. Bet you can siphon water half way up there. Save you a lot of hard work. Give it a try. But don't suck no water inside you. Don't drink no pond water."

Mickey looked at him, then away at the highway. "I can't—"

"Course, if you'd rather haul water in a bucket, that's your lookout."

Mickey looked at him again. "I'll go get a shovel," he said. "Plant 'em first."

"Go on, then. But remember that hose. That'll work, if you suck real hard."

"What happened to your hand?"

"Burned it. Spilled hot coffee on it. Always be careful handlin' hot stuff like that. Take a lesson, Boy."

Mickey nodded.

"Now, go on. You got your chores. If you're goin' to water them things, you need to be quick about it."

Mickey left, and Walker P. used his rake to stir the fire. It was dying out, most of the garbage was reduced to cindery ash and black coal. His face was hot from it. It made his hand burn, and he thought again of the pond. When he lifted his head and looked over toward it, he froze.

It was there, he insisted. When he told the boy about the hose, he had glanced that way, and he saw it: just as it was, shimmering in the spring twilight. He had even seen a fish jump. He was sure of it.

Now, though, he only saw the gray, flat pavement. The fence and mesquite were as they had been for almost five years. The pond was gone: plowed up by huge machines, buried under fill dirt, gravel, and asphalt. A big car raced by, its headlights on against the gathering shadows.

Walker P. dropped the rake and walked slowly over to the fence. His boots were heavy, and his arms hung to his sides as if they carried huge weights. From the fence line, he surveyed the old dimensions of the pond in his mind. Just for a moment, he thought he could make out in between the gaps in the crickets' songs the sounds of boys splashing in the water, the shouts of fishermen who had bent a pole over a big one. He could smell the freshness of the water, see the cattails lining the banks, hear the bullfrogs calling from the shallows.

He turned to look at the house. The trash fire still smoked from an orange flame at its center. The barn and henhouse, hog pen and corrals seemed to stand more straight than they were before. They had fresh paint, and there was grass and flowers everywhere. Etta's garden was in full bloom. The corn waved in the breeze, beans climbed trellises. The old tractor still had an intact umbrella unfurled. He saw the kitchen lights were on, golden beacons streaming from the house. A shadow moved behind a screen, and there was a figure sitting in the rocking chair on the porch: he felt his heart stop.

A doolie pulling a gooseneck horse trailer sped by, a diesel. Its noise and exhaust hung in the evening atmosphere. Walker P. turned and watched its taillights disappear, and when he looked again at the house, it was dark. No lights appeared at the windows. The shapes of the buildings showed the sway wind and disrepair forced on them. The garden was a weedy ruin, the tractor rusty and cold. The house's exterior was gray, peeling, in need of washing and painting, and on the porch, the old rocker sat empty. But on the wind, he heard the distinct tones of a hymn being hummed.

Walker P. pulled up the top strand of barbed-wire and stepped through the opening. A loud rip when his overalls had caught on a sharp point didn't slow him down.

"It ain't fair," he said. "It ain't goddamn fair. I'm a old man. I don't deserve this. I always seen things clear."

His fists beat the air as he walked deliberately out to the middle of the highway. He put his boots on either side of the stripe and looked up. A cloud bank was coming in from the north. Cool front, he thought, we ain't done with winter yet. But the wind was warm on his face. He felt hot, sweaty, grimy from work he hadn't done.

He looked again at the house, and again the image transformed. The lights were on, the shapes erect and well cared for. The figure was still in the rocker, and his wife's shadow moved inside the kitchen, fixing supper, humming along with a memorized hymn. There was no fence, no ditch full of weeds and mesquite scrub between him and the farm. Instead, he seemed to be wet. He looked down, and saw that his boots were awash in the blue water of Etta's Pond. He knelt, scooped up two handfuls of the clear, cold water and splashed his face. The bandage disappeared. The moisture felt good on his burned hand. He was sinking up to his neck, floating, now swimming. His overalls fell away, and he was naked, bobbing. He filled his mouth and spouted like a whale. He felt free, clean, renewed. All around him the sights, smells, sounds of the pond and the farm lifted him up and made him buoyant. His hair matted on his forehead, and he could feel himself diving and writhing in the water.

"No bath tonight, Etta," he called. "Can't fill a tub with nothing as good as what we got right out here!" He flounced on his back and stroked away. "C'mon out! What're you scared of? Won't nobody see us way out here." The kitchen door opened.

***

The screaming protest of rubber on asphalt pierced the gray darkness and matched the high whine of an engine straining to wind down from highway speed to a dead stop.

"Are you crazy?" a voice shouted when the dust and dirt settled. A bright red Suburban was in the ditch opposite the Sloan farm, and a well-dressed young man was rushing up out of the Johnson grass and onto the blacktop. "Are you nuts?" he repeated. "I damn near ran right over you!"

Walker P. Sloan sat in the middle of the highway, his hips, clothed and dry and squarely on the white stripe. He blinked at the man's approach.

"Jesus Christ! Mr. Sloan, is that you? Are you all right?"

The man reached Walker P. and put hands on him.

"Are you all right? What happened? Did you fall down or something?"

"Who're you?" Walker P. allowed the young man to pull him up. He brushed away the hands. "Quit pawin' at me. Who'n hell're you an' what'd'you want?"

"I almost killed you. Almost ran right over you. What's wrong? Are you sick? What's going on here? You're in the middle of the road."

James David Leftwich. The name came to Walker P.: Lawyer, smart-alec little son-of-a-bitch. Billed him two hundred dollars to write that letter getting me five dollars more an acre than the state originally offered.

"Must of fell down," Walker P. said, backing up from the lawyer. "Some son-of-a-bitch run over my dog."

The lawyer looked around. It was now almost completely dark. Walker P. could see there were other people in the truck.

"James David?" a woman's voice called. "Is he all right? Do I need to call somebody?"

"Are you all right?" Leftwich asked.

"Yeah, I'm all right. Where're you goin' in such a goddamn hurry?"

"Home," Leftwich answered. "I live out here. Pumpkin Center. Go by here every day." He looked up and down the highway, remembered, then his tone softened. "I've been meaning to stop by. Say hello."

"You run over my dog?"

"Me? No! Never ran over a dog in my life. Knock wood."

"Well, somebody did. Been meaning to find out who. Owes me money. That was a good dog. Been lookin' for him."

"I think you'd do better not to do it in the middle of the highway."

Walker P. looked at him, back at the house. It was completely dark now. The only light was in the henhouse. Mickey was about his chores.

"Yeah, well, what the hell," he said. "'Bliged to you for stoppin'."

"You stay out of the road, now. Hear?"

He left the lawyer in the middle of the pavement, made his way through the Johnson grass, crossed the fence and walked up to the house. When his boots hit the porch, he heard the Suburban start, back up, then drive off, more slowly now.

"Prissy little dipshit son-of-a-bitch," Walker P. said. He went in to start supper.

***

It was ten o'clock, later than Walker P. had stayed up in years. Clouds covered the stars. Supper finished, dishes washed, chores done, he and Mickey sat out on the porch and watched the occasional car or pickup race by. Exhaust odors mixed with noise on the night air. Walker P. was half-way through a new pint, more than he usually drank, and he had rolled his third cigarette since sitting there.

"You get all them flowers planted?"

"Water'd 'em too. Just like you said."

Walker P. winced, sipped the whiskey.

"I put six on Butch's grave, six on Miss Etta's."

Walker P. rocked and nodded.

"I put six on your mama's grave, too. Thought she'd like that."

"Likely," Walker P. said. "Mama always liked flowers. Never had none, though. Daddy said where flowers'd grow, cotton'd grow. That was that." They sat and looked at the night a while. "Chill in the air. Might sleet, maybe snow. Rain for sure. My toe aches." His hand hurt, too. But he took another sip of whiskey and ignored it.

"Good for the wheat." Mickey sat on the edge of the porch and rocked his body in imitation of the old farmer. "Walker P.," he asked finally, "if you was to die, what'd become of me?" Same question as before, Walter thought.

"I don't know, Boy. Reckon you'd get on, somehow. You did before. You will again."

"Think?"

"Likely."

Again he rocked in silence. He heard Etta's voice—in his memory this time, not in any vision or nightmare of the past. It didn't chide or scold. It only reminded him. The time had come. He wondered what the selling price for prime field and pasture was. Tomorrow, he said to himself, he would go into town and find out.

"What'd you think 'bout moving into town, maybe goin' to school over to Wichita Falls?"

"I'd hate that. I hate school."

"Some schools is different from others. I think it's time you thought 'bout that. Seems to me like you already have."

Mickey said nothing. "I'll do what you want me to, Walker P. Whatever you say. You been good to me. You an' Miss Etta give me a place."

"Angel unawares," he heard Etta's voice say. He sipped the whiskey again. He enjoyed the way it burned going down.

"You know, Walker P., when I watered them flowers, I had to use the bucket. Made four trips. The pond ain't there no more. You know that, don't you?"

Walker P. looked out over the blackness of the highway. Just for a moment all the sights and sounds and sensations he felt before welled up inside him. He could feel it, smell it beneath the asphalt.

Just like Butch.
"Well, Mickey," he said. "That's where you're wrong. Etta's pond is there. It'll always be there. Now, it's time to go to bed. We got a early day tomorrow."
"We got a early day every day."
"Yeah, well, what the hell."
Out of the darkness headlights cut a path down the highway. The car zoomed past toward town, and in the quiet that settled in its wake, the two men sat in the shadows of the porch and rocked.

The Pool

David Ray

Let's plan again the decade
that's past, the one
I'm most fond of. This time
parking our trailer
in the nudist camp,
making lots of new
naked friends, enthralled
now and then by that landscape
out the window as if all
we had lost ever were there,
cavorting, heedless
of our dark thoughts,
our grief. And now and then
we too would put
our bodies where our hopes were—
flinging them up, golden
as a volleyball—or plunging
them into those blue waters
long since dispersed to skies
we ourselves flew through.
Thus now and then we gave
our bodies to heaven,
knifing air just as we parted
the waters of day, earth
of night, the fire
of our worst hour, praying then
as to this moment
that we may yet somehow achieve
the quaint and enviable
pride of believable angels.

Alzheimer's

David Ray

I send him a gift such as a boy
might wear with delight—a bola—
pendent to place around his neck,
sporting turquoise, a blue stone
with fissures like those
of the brain or the parched earth
or a clay marble held by a boy's thumb
—for he no longer wears that black bowtie
which was always his emblem
when he circled the barbershop chair
like Samson at his millwheel
and the curls went falling everywhere
as the eager boy went sweeping, sweeping.

He will look down and toy
with this stone, hold it up
as if it were a timepiece, again
be told who sent it, mutter my name
like a stranger, not recall
the son who once wrote from a near
deathbed to say he had begged
for bread, got a stone. Even then
there had been no response—
another stone in the mouth, survival
not blessed as it might have been.

I send him stone, cracked like the sky
full of tornadoes, where lightning raged
and earth had gone withered and dust storms
darkened his eyes. He too in that season
before he learned a new trade and moved into town,
plowed up nothing but stones, earth hard as stone.

And a visit—chance to gaze into blank eyes,
hunger anew? I have not half the courage to try,
and therefore across a great desert send stone.

Errancies, Anomalies, Promiscuities

James Drake

They are the pan-pipes for storms of desire,
these celebrities rebounding from success—
their rope-entangled dangling out of the ring,
love agglomerations, then a free-fall of grief—
and as I get in line for the cashier and stare,
I hear a goat-cry rising from the population
that invokes all primeval forces
plus a malign smile at their pain.
Yet they leave something to be desired
as they squint both sideways and downward,
and it is this diagonal yellowing
that makes an opera of the American Dream:
the soprano sings about her dildo;
on her flanks are sets of biting teeth.

Nature on Television

James Drake

Endlessly figurative, this blood red cantata
enacts the disfigured liberation of contrite barbarians
(we just can't get enough of being our own worst enemy).
Then apes, in half-glimpses, mock Time's gimpy gallop
with frivolous chromosomes and kamikazi mutations.
Next is God's longing for ogres, a promenade of furies,
featureless beasts that scream at community sings.
This keeps us yoked to a storm at sea.
Toiling with spasms, it creates a lithe necessity
from a menacing twilight and what is outwardly blind:
re the shark's mouth, purposively down under,
a rain of crumbs to keep it from overeating.
But how Australian are we? Large hops of greenness
burst their blazing edges. Spaces leap up amid the trees.

The Vacuum Lady

Ken Waldman

A woman with a vacuum
cleaner knocked and asked
if she could. She had
swimmer's shoulders
and a moustache. How much,
I asked her. She shook
her head and wheeled
the Hoover inside, the end
of the cord dragging
like a tail. Then she plugged
the machine in, running it
over the rug, the furniture,
me. When I got sucked through
the crack, through the ugly,
hairy rollers, I died,
and my death was like my life.
Everywhere, the grinding. Everything,
dark and soft. An invisible,
dirty wind. Trapped,
miserable inside a bag
of beat-up furniture, of filth
and litter, I had no idea
who to blame. The vacuum lady?
But that was impossible.
She was only doing her job.
As I was doing mine.

The Minimalist

Julian Silva

"I'm making a will. What would you like?"
Rodney's voice was brusque, but it always is on the telephone. Like one following a prescribed outline, he does not wish to be distracted by irrelevancies. Though he calls regularly, at least twice a month, he never calls just for a chat. He says what *he* has to say and the rest is usually silence.

My first reaction was one of shocked surprise. At sixty-one I have already made three wills, the last one after Zelda's death made all others inoperative.

"I thought you made one after your accident," I said.

"Well, I didn't."

Since he is fond of lecturing me on my financial irresponsibility, I could not refrain from a personal gibe:

"But if you'd broken your neck rather than a rib, your sister would have gotten everything. And better the SPCA than an unloved relative."

"Yes, yes, I know. But don't scold." There was a touch of pathos in the plea. "I'm rectifying that now. So you must tell me what you want."

I laughed. "Well, aside from a hundred thousand dollars. . . ."

"What money there is goes to Harvard." The voice was prissily dismissive.

"I was joking, Rodney."

"Well, don't."

"All right. The Kellys, then. And George, of course. If that isn't being greedy?"

"No, no. Are you sure there isn't anything else?" Though the intent of the words seemed clearly affectionate, the manner remained chillingly businesslike. "Once it's made, that's it. I'm only going to do it once."

"I don't know, Rodney—" I was beginning to feel uneasy. "Why don't *you* choose something a bit more personal."

There was a pause and I could picture him looking about his sterilely tasteful abode for something, anything, that might remotely be labeled personal. And to my surprise he hit upon the perfect solution.

"What about the carriage clock? It was my first serious purchase— almost a century ago, it seems. It used to sit on my mantlepiece at Harvard," he added, and for the first time there was a hint of something warmly personal struggling to break through the icy surface.

"I'd love the carriage clock. But is something the matter?"

"No, no." The thin cracks froze over again. "We'll discuss it on your visit. Have you made up your mind, by the way, when you're coming down?"

"I was thinking about next week, if that's all right with you?"

"The week after would be better."

"Then the week after it is."

"Good. I look forward to seeing you." And before there was a chance for me to respond, he had hung up.

***

Although a great believer in wills, I would not dream of discussing my own will with anyone except my attorney—or possibly my executor, who has a sealed envelope with certain grim, if necessary, instructions. Part of the fun of making a will—and, yes, the word is deliberate— comes from deciding on one's own what would best suit whom, then plotting those surprise bequests to one's secret loves, to say nothing of the surprise omissions; to act, in short, as playwright to the final scene of one's own life, a scene we trust will be a long time reaching the stage. It is an exercise almost every sensible person over fifty has at sometime or other indulged in.

But one tends to assume that one's contemporaries are as indestructible as oneself (Zelda, five years my junior, was a statistical fluke, a tragic exception), and since we will all probably stumble into our eighties together, which of one's friends is going to get what becomes purely academic. I have only to look at my own mother, a bitter, lonely, querulous eighty-five, to know how little possessions mean to one of that age. She has already given away virtually all of her "treasures" and would far rather be offered an invitation to bridge, which she can surprisingly still play, than a diamond necklace. A game of bridge would help pass an afternoon, while the diamonds would merely add a new burden to an already burdensome existence by giving her one more thing to hide from her paid companions, two estimable and extremely trustworthy women, whom she, unfortunately, does not trust.

There is also, I fear, a flagrantly acquisitive part to my nature. Though I would fain deny it, like any other lust, it is apt to be intensified by every effort at repression. Thus I would prefer *not* to know what is to be bequeathed to me. One does not tease an alcoholic with promises of champagne suppers. Certainly I treasure my friends more than my possessions, yet Rodney's strange call left me for a few uneasy moments wondering where, in the unlikely event they should indeed become mine, I would hang the Kellys—five large Ellsworth Kelly prints in a Matissean mode and as handsome as any prints made in America—or where I would place George—a slightly over-life-size marble bust of our last king, the late, though scarcely lamented, George III. Like a shy lecher lurking about some porno-emporium, I furtively roamed my own house de-accessioning less worthy pictures and moving furniture to accommodate a rather large and somber piece of marble. It was not one of my proudest moments.

***

Rodney and I have known each other close to forty years, yet never, in all that time, have I been tempted to call him Rod. The most private of all my friends, he has never invited intimacy. What little I know of that distant time before our meeting I have culled from hints dropped over the years, intentionally or unintentionally, one can never be sure which. But people are, I decided long ago, what they are and had best be accepted as such or not at all. I would no more dream of trying to batter down his reserves than I would of robbing him. For my part, there has always been a refreshing lack of tension in a relationship that can stimulate one intellectually and at the same time makes so few demands upon one's emotions.

With equal measures of grit and intelligence, he crawled out of the quagmire of some obscure midwestern town during the Depression to the dizzy heights of a Harvard Ph.D. Even the state of his birth I cannot swear to. I am sure that he has sometime or other mentioned it, but with so little emphasis it did not register. He has surely never revisited the place since his mother's death some thirty years ago and lives under the delusion that because he has written *it* off, it has returned the compliment and left no visible traces upon his present character.

All that I can surmise of his family background is that both parents were of German Lutheran stock and their marriage so rancorous it permanently stunted his emotional growth. Even the almost unconscious and often affectionate bickering that any two people who live together invariably indulge in rouses such agonies of social unease that almost all his friends are, like myself, solitaries. He does among his acquaintances have a few idealized marriages, couples of such exquisite good taste and placid temperaments they have somehow contrived to paint for him a kind of upper-class Norman Rockwell vision of what married life at its best might be—a state in which good taste outranks love and passion is the ultimate vulgarity. They are invariably well-bred and well-educated (Back Bay Harvard wed to Mainline Bryn Mawr) and their children invariably beautiful and preferably blond. These paragons are also kept at a safe remove and his infrequent visits so well staged as to preclude disillusionment. Yet they form an essential part of his life: they represent the heaven from which he has been forever barred by some primordial sin of his parents, and though he may be damned, they serve to keep his faith alive.

An unmitigated snob, he makes no pretense at being anything less. His parents' peasant origins he readily acknowledges with something akin to pride, but that is scarcely cause for any Rousseauistic glorification of the primitive. Whatever he is, he is for having become, all on his own, what they were not. Like the convert who is more Catholic than the Pope, he is far more staunchly Republican than any of the denizens of Newport or Southhampton and looks upon my addiction to liberal causes and the Democratic Party as an affectation to be deplored when it cannot be ignored.

During Rodney's adolescence his father abandoned the family. Rancor then was replaced, on his mother's part, by a bitter self-pity, of which Rodney received the brunt since his older sister made her escape by marrying the first man to make himself available—an escape that apparently proved no escape at all since her marriage very quickly began to duplicate that of her parents and only further reenforced her brother's aversion to all emotional commitments.

Rodney made his escape during the Second World War with a three-year stint in the army. It is a period of his life he discusses even less frequently than his childhood, though unlike the latter, it seems to have left few if any scars, either physical or emotional. It was, one gathers from his dismissive tone, simply an experience too painfully boring to inflict upon anyone else.

It did, however, present him with an entree into a world he had always longed but lacked the means to join. The G.I. Bill made the impossible possible by paying for a Harvard education. Almost instantly the school became for him his true home, emotionally as well as intellectually, both adored mother and respected father, and he has, as his proposed will indicates, proved a more than loyal son.

He was still a graduate student in the school of architecture when we first met. He had fallen ill while travelling in Mexico, and cutting short his trip, decided to end his summer in San Francisco, well out of the reach of the terrible Montezuma. Since I had just moved into my first apartment, a bright, sunny place in the Polk Gulch with a spare bed, a classmate of his and old friend of mine asked me to put him up—which I did, and despite the vast differences in our temperaments, we became friends.

It was a relationship solidified some years later, in 1956, to be precise, when I joined him during his Fulbright year for a tour of the Greek islands. The trip proved a magical experience for both of us, and its memory remains sufficiently strong to counter the many strains our friendship has since been subjected to—none of which, however, quite prepared me for those I was about to encounter.

***

My first reaction upon meeting him at the airport was that he had become suddenly an old man. Since he is my senior by only a few years, it was a disconcerting observation. Nature catches me up occasionally, but I adamantly refuse to think of myself in such terms. Old begins currently at—say—around seventy-five.

It was difficult to pin down precisely what about him had aged. His hair was far less gray than my own, his body still apparently robust. But something in the way the skin seemed to fall away from the face, a mask working its way loose from the skull, suggested a lost resilience—though I could not, at the time, decide whether the matter was physiological, psychological, or both.

He greeted me with his customary half-hearted embrace. Nor was the avoidance of eye contact significant. Demonstrations of affection have always been for him more a matter of duty than inclination. One is pleased that he recognizes the duty, but even more pleased when the duty is over, so clumsy are his attempts at good fellowship.

He was, I noticed after I had collected my baggage, limping.

"What's with the leg?" I asked, my concern somewhat unfocused, for the brilliant San Diego light assaulted us as soon as we stepped through the sliding doors, and after a particularly gray summer in San Francisco, I was more than prepared to be ravished.

"Oh, that," he answered, as if he had for the first time noticed the anomaly. "My knee's been playing tricks. But we're not going to talk about it now."

Though the "now" had a portentous ring, his words were clearly a command to change the subject. So we talked about the weather instead. A balmy eighty, that could hardly have been less controversial. He was dressed in a Brooks Brothers button-down shirt, regimental tie, and light-weight dark gray flannels—precisely the same costume with which he might have strolled across Harvard Yard some forty years earlier, even down to the scuffed tennis shoes so fashionable at the time as an antidote to the austere chic.

After nearly two decades in the state he still suffers from a mind-set as well as a time-set. He has remained obstinately New England in outlook. Deep in his heart California is still the cloud-cuckoo-land of the eastern press where one barters one's soul for sunshine and high salaries; and his Protestant nature has never absolved him of the guilt he suffers for having passed up a position at Amherst for twice the pay and half the prestige.

A Harvard education can be a blessing or a curse, but it seldom leaves the recipient unmarked. Three of my closest friends have graduated from the college. Unable to live up to the great expectations spawned by his degree, poor James committed suicide at twenty-seven; the erratically brilliant Sheldon (who first introduced me to Rodney, a fact they would both just as soon forget) has never held any job for longer than three years and for the last fifteen has been, for all practical purposes, unemployable. Of the three, Rodney alone has made what the world might consider a success of his life: a deanship at a state university and a number of eminently respectable publications from eminently reputable presses. But all three, even the suicidal James, had a way of looking down upon the rest of us poor blighted creatures for leading deprived lives. We went to schools in Berkeley or Los Angeles or wherever; they were *educated* at Harvard. And we are condemned, alas, forever to be outcasts from that magical kingdom.

As a fourth-generation Californian I smile tolerantly at the condescension and keep my own counsel.

Certainly Rodney has made efforts to adapt to his new environment, but they have proved no more heartfelt or successful than his awkward embrace. Christened Rodney William Leudtke, he has become to his Southern California friends simple Bill Lucky. Though he retains the original spelling of his name, he has, without any sense of the implied irony, simplified its pronunciation. There are only a few of us who have known him since his student days who still think of him as Rodney Leudtke. To us the Bill Lucky known to his current students and colleagues is a fictional character in some cinematic western, a stranger so bland as to be virtually unrecognizable.

***

The drive to his home some fifteen miles up the coast was not, despite the light and the landscape, a pleasant one. Since he had for months been contemplating a trip to Europe the last two weeks of September, I asked him if he had yet made his reservations and was hardly surprised to learn he had not.

For as long as I have known him he has only with the greatest difficulty ever been able to force a moment to its crisis. He plans and plans, revises his revisions of his former plans, and then invariably defers action. It took him ten years from first plans to functional reality to remodel his kitchen. Even his will is typical. He had, some two years before, shortly after his car had turned over during a sudden rainstorm of tropical proportions and given him his first serious brush with mortality, discussed a will, yet he had never gotten beyond talking about it, as he had never gotten beyond talking about his last two prospective trips, one to Japan, the other to England.

"If you're not careful," I chided, since it was already the last week of July, "you'll find yourself arriving in Paris with no place to stay."

"Oh, there'll always be *some* place."
"Yes, but why settle for 'some' place when you might have the best? For the money of course."
"Oh, what does it matter?" His response was unexpectedly churlish. "Paris will still be Paris. That's all that counts. Not one's hotel. I don't, after all, mean to do anything more than sleep in it. And quite alone," he added gratuitously.

We were obviously no longer travellers of an ilk. So I tried to make the discussion more general:
"Where else beside Paris are you going?"
"Copenhagen. To see an old friend. Inga. Then Stuttgart. To look at some new buildings."
"I'm not very fond of Germany," I interjected irrelevantly, for I had ceased any longer to believe in his trip.
"Well, frankly, I don't much care *what* you think about Germany," he responded testily, his eyes fixed grimly on the road before him, his pedal foot pumping erratically so that the car kept lurching. "I thought we were discussing *my* plans."
"Sor-ree. . . ."
"Sorry is all very well," he retorted, "but you have an infuriating way of turning everything round to yourself. You aren't the center of the universe, you know."

So sharp and bitter was his reaction to my innocuous remark, I knew something must be troubling him; but I also knew well enough not to probe, particularly in his present foul mood. So we rode on in silence for a few minutes. It was a ponderous silence broken by an even more ponderous question:
"What do you know about Parkinson's Disease?"
I studied him intently. "Not you, I hope?"
"No, no. An old friend of mine in Minneapolis. The mother of the couple I mean to leave my house to. His mother, that is. A lovely old thing. She took charge of me when I first went to teach there."
"An old teacher of mine had it," I answered, somewhat relieved, if puzzled by so casual a reference to his heirs. Was his life, I wondered, so short of drama he had to turn something so prosaic as the making of a will into a five-act production? "I used to see him on the bus, shaking and drooling like a mindless baby. But he wasn't mindless. That's the worst of it. Only the body falls apart. The mind, apparently, remains sharp enough to register each fresh indignity."

We were both silent for a minute before I added:
"There are infinitely worse things than an early death, and that's one of them."
"Well, I won't argue with you there. . . . Your friend in London—what was her name?"

A sudden chill froze my voice so that I could scarcely get the word out, though it had been sitting there on the tip of my tongue:

"Zelda," I answered. It was not a name one easily forgot. Still, after almost two years, the hurt was too deep for probing. And in all that time, except for whatever regrets could be squeezed into a single embarrassed sentence immediately after my return from London for her burial, he had never before alluded to her. Which was the way I preferred it; he was not someone I particularly wanted to share her with.

"How long had she had cancer?" he asked.

"Ten years."

"And she had to live with the knowledge all that time!"

With that his secret was out. There was such a sense of heavy wonder in his voice, he could clearly be thinking of no one but himself. I remembered vaguely some months back his mentioning a small lump on his chest and my dismissing it with some light reference to the minimal risks of breast cancer in men. But what connection there could be between the lump on his chest and the limp I could not imagine. It didn't matter. He was demanding comfort and I gave what comfort I had.

"She thought she had beaten it. And then, she did have ten mostly good years between that first little mole on her arm and her death."

I turned to look out the window so that he could not read the hurt in my eyes. Of all my friends he was the last who could understand what she had meant to me, and my grief must seem to him, more than a mystery, a solecism. Yet his very detachment made it, oddly, that much easier for me to talk about her, and without any encouragement from him more overt than an obvious willingness to listen, I continued:

"It wasn't even the cancer that killed her, finally, but the cure. Too much chemotherapy. Or the wrong kind. But even that, I suppose, was something of a blessing. The autopsy revealed cancer cells already in the brain. . . ."

Almost compelled by his continued silence to continue talking, I went on:

"She wasn't ever in any real pain. She was an actress, and a damn fine one, but the greatest actress in the world couldn't have hidden that from me. All she ever complained about was exhaustion. But 'complain' is too strong a word. She never complained about anything. Her exhaustion was simply a fact that could no longer be ignored. And oddly," I continued, for now I *wanted* to talk about her, to resurrect her, and not simply to shame him out of any self pity by the example of her smiling courage, "she never looked more beautiful than she did three months before her death. She'd lost all that puffy fat that comes with middle age and a good appetite. Wherever we went her trim little figure turned any number of heads. And don't think she didn't take note of every one of them. She was onstage and loving every minute. Until the final curtain fell, if you'll excuse the cliché. At fifty-five," I couldn't help adding with a bitterness so personal he must have taken note of the near-decade

advantage he already had on her. For by now I felt he must be made to pay something for reopening those wounds.
And that pretty much brought an end to all conversation until we arrived at his home.

***

His condominium sits in a white-washed cluster of stucco buildings reminiscent of some Greek island village—Mykonos on a grand scale. The stark whiteness of the exterior is offset by lush cascades of bougainvillaea, but the color stops at the front door. Inside, the ascetic air of a monk's cell predominates: the chapel at Vence stripped of its glorious windows. Except for an occasional bouquet, everything is black, white, gray, or brown, including the single decorative object, a dramatic, large, brown-toned Navajo pot standing on a slender rectangular plinth and hiding a spotlight, which even Rodney admits— disparagingly—is a bit too much like something out of the glossy pages of *Architectural Digest*.

Early on at Harvard he became a disciple of Mies and he has carried his master's famous dictum, Less is More, to almost absurd lengths. My own taste he once, in his student days, cavalierly dismissed as Whorehouse Baroque, not without a modicum of justification. Though my penchant for the baroque has persisted, it has become over the years considerably more chaste, but as far from Mies as Bernini is from Brancusi.

Fortunately I can admire the play of wit and the sleek beauty of a Brancusi as he can do the same for Bernini. In defiance of all principle— and indicative, perhaps, of a secret hankering of his own for the tinsel glories of the bordello—Rome is his favorite city and THE SPLENDOR OF THE BAROQUE stands out in box letters on the bookshelves of his bedroom/study. Here also, in the far corner, George holds court, brooding like a middle-aged Lear over the black-leather-topped Mies desk, the white marble of the bust dulled and streaked by the elements, for his previous owners obviously found him too ponderously somber for any place but the garden, where time took its toll, oddly adding to the pathos of a most uncourtly portrait in which the incipient madness is all too evident. Pomp that has already overdosed on physik.

Rodney's home is seen at its best in the entrance hall, a two-story white shaft rising from a black-slate floor. Four perpendicular black-and-white Kelly prints in stainless steel frames form a welcoming wedge—a pear, a camellia bud, a cyclamen, and a fig branch—the stark elegance relieved by a lush cluster of shining green spathyphylum in a terracotta pot. The fifth and handsomest of the Kelly's, a horizontal branch of tulip magnolia, hangs at the top of the stairwell and is the single picture visible from the living room area—a large irregularly-ceilinged space, dazzlingly bright despite the thin metal blinds that filter, but scarcely dim, the light. It is all bleakly impressive.

***

There were changes since my last visit. The single comfortable piece of furniture, an easy chair, had been moved to the downstairs study and replaced by the two extra chrome-and-leather Mies dining chairs. The other four ringed a large circular gray-marble slab held up by four chrome legs—a "grammatical" error according to the Miesean canon, since the flat metal legs of the chairs should never, as Rodney woefully admits, be mixed with the tubular ones that support the table—an anomaly that troubles no one but him and perhaps a few of his more fanatical architectural buddies. But trouble him it does. For strive as he may, perfection always seems to elude him.

At least eight years before, I had helped him install the two large speakers that flank the fireplace, one of which has, from the first day, tilted at a disturbingly noticeable angle that would drive me up the wall within a week; but he accepts the irregularity with placid resignation since the speaker, though crooked, is precisely where it should be and offends no sacred architectural canon, only the eye. Not long after, the raw boards that ceiling the stairwell were stained a pale driftwood color as far as the roller would reach without a ladder, and because he was less than pleased with the result, he has left it unfinished ever since, and the far side remains still blushingly raw.

By far the most important change was the kitchen. After years of work and great expense, much of it wasted on second thoughts (two different sinks, one porcelain and its replacement stainless) it has finally been finished, white cabinets and black counters as richly austere as a MOMA showroom. Form and function, however, are not perfectly mated. The central faucet, for example, an elegant stainless-steel stem, turns to the right for cold, to the left for hot, and then lifts for the flow—but instead of flowing, the water either trickles or gushes.

He is a touchingly impractical man, Rodney is. Thank God. Otherwise he might, should his minimalist dream ever be realized, prove unbearable. Despite its many imperfections, the upstairs living area, judged as pure space and an arrangement of plastic forms, is impressive. One is always and everywhere conscious of a disciplined intellect at work. What depresses is the total failure to consider the human element. The closest concession made to comfort is the thin flannel-covered cushions and somewhat fuller pillows that cover the low shelves which form an L-shaped wedge and act as seating areas and all-purpose tables, including space for a discreetly small black-and-white television set. But far worse, to my Latin nature, is the absence of color. A single bouquet of asters on the dining table, though lovely, seemed too calculated and altogether inadequate to perform the job demanded of it. The walls cried out for a splash of red, the floors for some garishly-dyed carpet. Even the hardiest Bedouin brightens his desert with his woven garden.

***

As I sank back with my scotch onto the flannel cushion—too low for anything but reclining—the tulip-magnolia print caught my eye. It seemed in its stark setting more beautiful than ever, the black lines sensual in their undulations.

"The Kellys," I said, "get better every time I see them. It's hard to believe anything so pure can be so sexy. But they are."

He turned with his glass of white wine to admire his picture. "They do hold up, don't they?"

Then I remembered the damn will and hoped he wasn't thinking I was already salivating to have them. So he had cancer. So Zelda lived for ten years with it. So he'd die in his mid-seventies instead of his mid-eighties—which, considering my mother's sad state and his friend with Parkinson's, was not the worst possible scenario.

"Don't you think it's time we got it all out in the open and cleared the air?" I tried but failed to meet his eye.

Though my pronoun had no obvious antecedent, we both knew what it referred to. But he was having none of it.

"Not now. Before you leave, I promise. But I'm not up to it just yet."

He obviously had a game-plan and was determined to follow it, despite the consequences. But it was his life—or death, as the case might be. It was not my place to drag the terrible word out into the open.

"The closer you come to your ideal," I said, turning from him to his home and a more general topic, though everything I said seemed to be festooned with crepe, "the gloomier your place becomes. This room is about as cheerful as a mausoleum. When are you going to give it a touch of color?"

"That is something we can do while you're here. Look at rugs. I've been meaning to get one for years."

"Nothing I like better than shopping with other people's money," I responded with real enthusiasm.

"Maybe tomorrow."

And tomorrow it was. Certainly the pleasantest few hours of my five-day stay. Armed with minimum and maximum measurements, we explored San Diego's antique rug markets and very soon hit upon a Turkish kilim as near to perfect as he had any right to expect. Now, I thought, resigned to his quirks, comes the agonizing round of decision and indecision, but to my surprise and delight, with scarcely a demur, and not so much as a murmur about the price, he took the rug on approval, and almost immediately after laying it on the floor decided to keep it. And for the first time the room seemed a proper vessel for living, the gorgeous colors pulsating in the brilliant light, infecting both of us with their glow.

"Oh, I *do* like it!" Like a child before a gift-laden Christmas tree, he was scarcely able to contain his delight. "I'm so glad you came. I need someone to force me to be more decisive."

"You see," I boasted, only half joking, "I bring color into your life."

***

The purchase served also to lessen my apprehension. Certainly a man facing imminent death would not bother with so inconsequential an indulgence. Then I remembered Zelda. As her cancer grew, her need to shop kept pace with it, as if each new possession were one more confirmation of her continued survival. Even as she lay dead in the Marsden Hospital, her most recent purchases—two splendid and expensive kilims, oddly enough—lay still folded with their price tags in her Onslow Square flat.

But no two people could have been more different than Zelda and Rodney and one indulgence hardly constituted compulsion. There was nothing to link them in my imagination except my conviction that he too had cancer. Why else his abiding curiosity about her travails?

Although I found it at first difficult to talk about her, with each fresh revival of some old memory I grew ever more voluble, until eventually, I relished the chance to give her an airing, taking her out of the closet where I had kept her too long.

"The one thing she was truly terrified of," I said in response to one of his queries, "was losing her wig in public. I don't think she thought much about dying. She certainly never talked about it, except for an occasional sardonic aside. It was the loss of her wig that preoccupied her."

"Why," he wanted to know, "was she wearing a wig?"

"The chemotherapy had made her bald."

"Ah. . . ." He seemed to be contemplating his own future baldness.

"But she'd already been wearing one for years," I hastily added. "For no good reason, really, except that she'd convinced herself her own hair was woefully inadequate, and she wanted to look like some pre-Raphaelite heroine. Do you know Hunt's 'Lady of Shallot'?"

"I've never considered the pre-Raphaelites worthy of notice," he answered haughtily. He could be infuriatingly priggish when he put his mind to it.

"Well, I'm not particularly keen on them either, except as campy curiosities. But I thought we were talking about Zelda. You too," I could not resist adding with a sly thrust, "have a curious way of directing the conversation back to your own prejudices."

"Touché," he answered with a touch of chagrin. "But go on."

"If you don't know the picture, it doesn't matter."

"But I do know the picture."

So unsettling did I find his admission, for the first time during my visit I became truly angry. "Why in hell couldn't you have said so then? Without having to make some value judgment about the pre-Raphaelites.

We're not discussing art history, for God's sake. We're talking about a dead friend of mine."

His reaction was sudden and drastic, his high color like that of a child who has just been publicly reprimanded. I even feared for an instant he might cry or run from the room.

"*Any*way," I continued, quickly, to cover the embarrassment, mine as well as his. "I think she thought of the picture as a kind of Platonic ideal. Her dream self. And that's why the wig. That's all.

"But I'm glad it was there to worry about. The wig," I added. "It shielded us from all those other terrors neither of us wanted to face."

"Why," he asked, as if the most obvious of truths were some profound puzzle in search of a sphinx, "do we keep returning to the same subject?"

Because, I wanted to answer, but lacked the heart, you won't bring the obvious out into the open so we can stop talking in circles.

***

But talk in circles we continued to. When he was done with Zelda, he dragged his mother out of the closet. Or coffin, if you prefer. We were in Balboa Park waiting for a performance of *Coriolanus* to start when he said, unexpectedly:

"My mother died at sixty. She'd been such a miserably unhappy woman I couldn't feel anything at the time but relief. I'd been helping support her. Even on my Fulbright," he continued, the resentment still vibrant, "when we were in Greece, I had to send her part of my pittance. Otherwise she would have starved. Or so she led me to believe. My sister was having her own problems. So it was all up to me. And if she hadn't so conveniently died when she did, I never would have been able to make my start. So you see, I took it as a stroke of luck. And there was no use pretending I loved her. Because I didn't. Does that shock you?"

"Hardly. If it comes right down to that," I answered, "I don't suppose I really love my own mother. I loved my grandmother far more. And my father—though that took some time coming round to."

"You're lucky." He spoke without looking at me, his voice flat and impersonal. "I don't think I've ever loved anyone."

His desolate words were soon dissipated in the luxuriant shadows of palms and eucalyptus which looked in the artificial light more like props for some operatic extravaganza than the real thing.

"Well, that's a pity," I answered, sincerely, but unwilling to explore so bleak a confession further. "What did your mother die of?"

"Cancer."

The word hung in the air as heavy as the scent of the nearby angels' trumpets, so tropically sweet it was one step removed from decay.

So it wasn't the lack of feeling for her death that was troubling him, but their shared genes.

***

When we weren't talking about death and disease, we seemed to alternate between quarreling and pouting. But quarreling isn't the word, for a quarrel requires two, and his churlishness generally found in me a silent partner. As my stay wore on, virtually everything I said or did seemed to annoy him. Though I knew it was not I that was the true bone of contention, but my abundant good health, which there was no forgiving, my tolerance soon stretched to the snapping point.

Pick, pick, pick—he kept probing in search of fresh matter to vent his testiness upon. Nothing was too trivial or impersonal to rouse his ire. Even my refusal to give up my subscription to the *San Francisco Chronicle* for *The New York Times*, he seemed to take as a personal affront.

Here I did rise to a mild defense.

"I'm quite willing to concede the vast superiority of *The New York Times*. Unfortunately it doesn't tell me what's playing at the local cinema."

"A truly stupid reason for taking a newspaper!" he countered with something close to real venom in his voice.

"Not at all, if it's a movie you're interested in. And sometimes, believe it or not, that's all I'm interested in. Not the in's and out's of our Central-American policy."

"And you dare to pose as an intellectual!"

"Oh, Rodney, come off it! I don't pose as anything of the sort. But if it's intellectual fare you're after, why not curl up with the *Dialogues of Plato*? Not *The New York Times*."

He ended the discussion with a snort and a request:

"Lean over and press the FM button, will you."

We were at the dinner table finishing an altogether unsuccessful meal, a mutual friend's recipe for giant shrimp that I was, apparently, responsible for having ruined by going too easy on the tabasco, though I made no claim to ever having mastered this or any other recipe.

"Kathleen Battle," the announcer came on in the rather fruity tones of one trying to give the impression he might have been schooled at the BBC.

"Ah, I like Miss Battle," I was quick to respond, hoping we had finally reached neutral ground.

". . . will now sing 'Juliet's Waltz Song.'"

"Though I'd rather hear her do something other than Gounod," I added, and the explosion was instantaneous.

"Like Mozart, I suppose," he fairly screamed.

I shrugged, but there was no deflecting his rage.

"If you could only hear yourself! Why can't you ever be satisfied with what's offered without looking for something else? What's *wrong* with Gounod? So he isn't Mozart. So what? Music doesn't

begin and end with Mozart. . . . ."
And so on and so forth, the honeyed voice of Miss Battle tripping and trilling her way through the saccharine strains of a Frenchified Juliet as an ironic accompaniment to his bitter tirade, until his whole body shook, his loose-skinned face sagging from what looked like nothing so much as the weight of repressed hatred; he rose, turned off the radio, and stalked into the kitchen.

It was a reaction so grossly intemperate, it clearly had nothing to do with a defense of French camp and everything to do with his own secret terrors. Yet so genuine had the look of hatred been, I could answer it only with rigid silence.

***

What most concerned me once I got back to my room was why I was putting up with his unconscionable behavior. Perhaps I too had fallen victim to his trap of snobbery. For despite my many disclaimers, I *was* impressed with his Harvard education. Not the education so much as the whole world of Cambridge—Lowell House, Harvard Yard, and the Brattle Theater—experiences and places denied to me and the sense of exclusivity they suggested, being a part of the brightest and the best. And yes, I *was* impressed—indeed, envious—that he had been invited by MIT Press to do yet another book on Frank Lloyd Wright, though baffled as to what there could possibly be left to say about the man that he or somebody else had not already said. I had even come to accept his authoritative and sometimes brutal manner as a justified reproach to my own often infuriating passivity. He had convictions on everything, from social welfare to Post-Modernism, and though they sometimes verged on the fanatical, he was not, like myself, a child of doubt, paying court to good manners and common sense and the other man's point of view. Everything in the world I most admired was the product of single-minded and often fanatical devotion to something or other: Flaubert's fixation upon *le mot juste*; Cézanne's preoccupation with *Mont Sainte-Victoire* and all those apples so tirelessly and obsessively brought to stunning life stroke by tiny stroke. Even my capacity for pity (and why else had I stayed so long?) was a kind of weakness. The strong were too busy being strong to weep over the fallen.

Well, I would show him. I would move up my departure date and leave on the morrow.

But the next morning his expression was so hangdog, his manner so solicitous, I decided—old wishy-washy—to stick it out. Was it pity that kept me? Since his pain was transparent I could not decide. Perhaps I merely wished to avoid the inevitable scene a change of plans would entail. Certainly at this point I felt nothing that could be called affection. Our friendship, such as it had now become, was mere habit, easier to continue than to break off, so strong is my aversion to violence.

My manner remained too distantly cool to give him cause for another outburst. We were like two rival business associates trapped at some conference we would both just as soon escape, but neither dares abandon for fear of giving the other an advantage. The mornings were mine to do with as I wished as he went off to the post office and what I was led to believe was his gym. To avoid another culinary disaster I took him out to dinner. It was an innocuous meal with French pretensions that *he* seemed to enjoy, perhaps because he had suggested the restaurant. The conversation never got more personal than a discussion, without enthusiasm on either side, about the logistics of his prospective trip: how best to get from Stockholm to Paris by way of Copenhagen and Stuttgart.

On our way to the car, he put his arm around my shoulder and gave it a little squeeze. Like all his attempts at intimacy, it seemed far more awkwardly contrived than genuinely affectionate. Yet I did credit him with trying.

"I am glad you came," he said in his gentlest voice, obviously intended to counterbalance the animosity of the previous evening.

Then why, I wanted to ask, but refrained, have you been behaving like such a shit?

Since I couldn't say what I wanted to, I said nothing, letting his declaration hang in the air as incense burnt before an empty altar. I meant to reserve all judgment until after the promised talk. Only then would I decide whether I too was glad I had come.

***

But our last evening together passed without a talk of any kind, both of us retiring early, at his suggestion, to read. More baffled than ever, I remained stubbornly determined I would not again initiate the subject of his health. If he wanted to talk, I was there to listen, but I would not force out of him any intimate details he was not prepared to share of his own volition. At this point, I decided, I no longer cared enough to want to know.

The following morning I was ready to credit him with one full day of good behavior. The hatred I had read on his face I was willing to downgrade, in retrospect, to mere contempt. But the sting endured to keep me on my guard. My flight was at three, which would give us time for a leisurely lunch and ride to the airport. That left only the last half of the morning to get through, after his customary visit to the post office and the gym.

While we were lounging on his low-slung bench admiring his new rug—since all other topics seemed far too volatile to risk—I was struck suddenly with the solution to his fireplace wall, which, like his floor, had since he bought the place been nakedly awaiting the perfect object.

Why not, I suggested, one of the Kellys, which together rather overwhelmed the tiny entrance hall? The size and the shape were perfect and the picture would also complement the tulip magnolia in the lightwell.

To my surprise the suggestion met with almost instant approval. But which Kelly? The camellia bud we both agreed was the strongest of the perpendiculars. I must get it for him immediately. His limp, I had already noticed, was more pronounced and it seemed tacitly agreed I do all the fetching. We took turns, however, holding it in place for each other's inspection.

Yes, he agreed, it was striking.

"Then let's hang it," I urged.

I wanted action—something, anything to dispel the gloom that had crippled my entire stay; some visible sign, besides the rug, to mark my visit.

But no, he thought, his enthusiasm just as suddenly dissipating. Perhaps after lunch. Before I left. But not now.

He had returned to his old indecisiveness, I thought, and was trapped once again in a paralysis of inaction. The rug had been a mere fluke; the picture, I knew, would never be hung. So I set it beside the fireplace, my spirits cast down with it. I longed to be home, or at the very least, airborne. For despite the vibrant colors of the rug, the place had once again assumed the character of a mausoleum.

***

Lunch consisted of salad, cheese, and succulent vine-ripened tomatoes, both red and yellow, from the Japanese farm up the Via de la Valle. The meal looked as good as it tasted, a feast for the eyes as well as the palate. Yet something was missing. Though the strain of the previous evening had somewhat relaxed there was still no sense of camaraderie. In fact, the only times during the five days we had truly connected were when we had talked about Zelda, his mother, or his friend with Parkinson's. Death and disease had been our sole bond.

I was still sipping the last of my wine when, without forewarning, his head sank to the table. He was tired, I thought, if I thought anything. Though napping at the table seemed odd, any other explanation seemed altogether too odd to credit. It must have taken one full startled minute to register what was happening: he was crying. His head hidden from view, he was shaking with sobs.

Momentarily paralyzed, I was transfixed before the unprecedented spectacle. Then somehow I rose. Standing behind him and too horrified for any emotion so trivial as embarrassment, I massaged his shoulders, aware suddenly of my own physical awkwardness, for he failed to respond to my touch. I might have been kneading a lump of clay.

"I've got cancer. I'm going to die."

The ugly words were blurted out, and like the lancing of a boil, the very voicing of them was, though gross, therapeutic.

"The first I'd already guessed," I said, releasing my hold of his shoulders and resuming my seat now that he had once again found his voice. "About the rest—get hold of yourself and let's talk. Though I don't understand," I could not help adding, "why you couldn't have spoken sooner."

"I didn't want to spoil your trip." He turned to me a face I scarcely recognized. Like one of those strange Chinese dogs with far too much skin to fit their tiny skulls, a sharpei, he seemed lost in his own sagging flesh.

Not wish to spoil my trip! And just what did he think his silence had done! He had not only spoiled my stay, he had in the process made a mockery of our long friendship.

But his pain was too naked now for reproach.

"I'm sorry." He wiped his face with both hands as if attempting to fit the skin back in place. "I lost control. It won't happen again. . . . I meant to wait until I was driving you to the airport," he added abjectly.

"Oh, great," I said, my repressed anger finding an innocuous outlet. "You'd probably have killed us both. Now why don't you catch your breath. Then start at the beginning."

"Well, you know I had that little lump on my chest. I told you about it." He looked at me for confirmation, as if my nod were necessary to make him believe in the reality of his own account. His face was already reshaping itself, his voice for a moment steady. "At first the doctor seemed to think it might be nothing more serious than a cyst. But when it got bigger, he decided to cut it out. In his office. It didn't even take five minutes. Then he arranged a CATscan."

Once again his face seemed to fall apart and he broke down, sobbing; but this time he quickly caught his breath, and squaring his shoulders like a good soldier, once again apologized.

"When I went back for the report," he continued, once he had regained control, "there were three doctors—my own, an oncologist, and an x-ray technician. The first thing they said—it must have been my own doctor, I don't even remember—was that I'd better get my affairs in order. I might live till Christmas. Or I might—if I was lucky—live another year."

I was incredulous. "How could so small a lump have moved so fast?"

"That was only the first manifestation. I've apparently got something called asymptomatic cancer. It attaches itself to a non-vital organ, and you don't find out about it until it's too late. It started on my kidney. But it's already moved to the lower spine. That explains the limp. And my chest, of course. So you see, it's well beyond surgery."

His smile seemed almost apologetic, as if he had breached decorum by allowing himself to be caught in so hopeless a predicament, one from which no gentlemanly code could possibly extricate him.

"It wasn't anything I did. Or failed to do," he added, obviously still stunned and rankled by the injustice. "Like smoking or indiscriminate sex."

"What about chemotherapy?"

"They've dismissed that. For the time being, anyway. I've been getting radium treatments every morning." He looked sheepish. "That's why I've taken so long to get my mail and do the shopping."

"You mean you've been getting radium the whole time I was here and you didn't tell me!"

I found his silence on so crucial a matter harder to accept than his impending death. Here was an opportunity—perhaps the last we'd ever have—to become more than intimate strangers tricked by time and habit into a mockery of friendship. For what more did our friendship consist of than a shared sense of values—the taste, intelligence, and yes, class, that gave us a common frame of reference? We had remained such friends as we were, mostly, I suppose, because we remembered each other's youths and that magical summer when we first discovered the Greek islands.

Zelda had proven the depth of her love by welcoming me into her sickbed with her and allowing me to help her to her grave with as much loving laughter and precious silence as we could mine from the bleak landscape of her foreshortened future. While Rodney had never even peeked into the corner of my heart, had, in fact, until this recent visit, always made it abundantly clear that any interjection of my most personal life upon his consciousness would be viewed as an unwarranted intrusion. He had always wanted to be spared the messy emotions of other people's lives. And love is almost always messy.

As is dying.

Well, I would give the poor bastard what help I could, but without a heart that too would be mere form. He had cheated me as well as himself.

I moved from the dining table to the flannel-covered bench, my hands cupping my head as I stared aimlessly at the Kelly print standing beside the fireplace. He had not hung it, I understood now, because he had not wanted to mar the clean wall with a nail hole so that the couple getting his place would be free to make their own decisions. He had taken his doctor quite literally and was already packing his bags. And the picture itself, cruelly beautiful now, I also understood, was meant, along with its companions, to be a kind of bribe, as were all his announced bequests, rather like my mother distributing her treasures to buy the affection she had been too selfish to earn.

Behind me he stopped on the stairway to clasp my arm. And ironically, it was the first time a touch of his had not seemed clumsily misplaced.

"Don't brood," he said. "*I* don't mean to—now it's all out in the open."

"I have been here before," I answered, "so I know the territory," and without turning to look at him, I placed my hand on his. It seemed, curiously, warmly, even intensely, alive. Oh, I would play the game to the end. We would be two Jamesian heroes performing a ritual dance about a sickbed that was more metaphor than reality. Intimate strangers, as we had always been. For there was no way I could ever make him understand, it was not his death I was brooding over, but that bleak and colorless landscape that had been his life.

Miniatures

Floyd Skloot

The oak bar in our living
room had a door filled
with miniature bottles
of rye whiskey and gin.
I loved to open it slowly
enough to keep my parents
in their bedroom, take out
the miniatures and line
them up like soldiers
in the ice trenches,
hide them behind shot
glass boulders suddenly
dark in my mind, see them die
in a salvo of swizzle sticks.

It was almost too much
to keep to myself, this
army my friends never dreamt
of, stuck with their molded
plastic toys. But in my dreams,
there was always Father
coming in his hairy armor
to rip off their heads
and drink their blood.

Spanish Revival

Floyd Skloot

What did my parents know
about living in a house?
What did we know about
tides, about island life?

Imagine: gutters and downspouts!
Imagine: laurel hedge!
There were leaves on window sills!
There were pruning shears
hung on a hook by the door!

What did we know about separate
rooms, no one above, no one
below? Think of fighting
at night, louder than ever,
and not disturbing anyone!

Milky stucco walls flaked
in my hands, a red tile
roof bled beneath the eaves.

There was no one to call for
help with the heat, no one
to patch a leak. There were
bees. There was a porch with black
iron fencing above a private garage.

What did we know about
walking the beach in the eye
of a hurricane? What did we
know about new beginnings?

My father was gone by dawn.
My father was gone till dead
of night, gone six days
a week. What did we know
about Sundays at the seashore?

A Clean Poem

Floyd Skloot

This is a clean poem. It is handsome
and manly, dressed in a well-fitting tux,
with short hair freshly trimmed. It has just come
from the club, looking like a million bucks

and ready to waltz. This is a married
poem searching the room to find its wife.
She was to have arrived first but, harried
by their croupy child, is late. Such is life.

This poem does not worry in the least
over her whereabouts; she is just late.
A sonnet, this poem long ago ceased
to think bad thoughts. It is happy to wait

all night, if need be, and will neither think
of other women nor long for a drink.

American Lit: Witter Bynner

Harold Witt

"Your skill moves through the stanzas like a breeze . . ."
Witter Bynner wrote from Mexico
when—in Reno—I was needing praise,
writing at night and crunching through the snow
to answer where the johns were and check out
romance to ladies coming in in furs;
after a while of which you start to doubt
if even teaching freshmen could be worse—
but I'd said no to that, and there I was,
now and then appearing here and there
in Journals and in Quarterly Reviews
and out of the mailbox in that bright air
plucking approval from a famous name:
"how very much I like your 'Veil of Perfume.'"

Watching the Ax Fall

Gary Short

I heard the wood crack—

the sound delayed,
unlike now when first the leaves rattle,
a door slams shut somewhere in the house
& then I feel the wind.

Nothing is completed, not even thought.
Starlings swirl
& climb a spiral of air,
then as one body & at a certain tilt
    disappear.

This morning there were new tulips abruptly red,
vestment red, & morning glories

blossoming. Snowflakes in my father's hair
when he walked that winter out to the woodpile
behind the barn.
In a photograph on the end table,
he's in uniform. Once he told me
about Paris after the war
& a carousel of brightly painted cows.

Sunfall, a blade of light slices the Sierra.
My father, small & afraid, in his hospital bed.
The cold rails of the bed. The wind.

The cows all face the flesh sun.
The horse is eating dropped fruit in the orchard
where century trees bend.
The eyes of the cattle reflect
what is outside them. If you looked you would see
the night falling against the barn
collapsed on itself.

Photograph

Gary Short

We didn't know, but now
we can see a balance has tipped
against him. And now that we see it,
there will never be a time
when we will not see it. His face,
ill-fitting, a mask
rising away from bone. As a result
his dark brown eyes become a voice,
a moment of recognition. . .

> *It's come to this. I have*
> *a new language. In four months*
> *the doctors will open the book*
> *of my body, read its last pages.*

In this photograph, the clock
a remark on the wall.
Outside, the sky falls like seconds,
the rain a consecration. My brother's face
will blur as he turns toward the window
to look beyond the bare maple, beyond
what I do not know.

A Foil Girl

Peter LaSalle

Sometimes the days stalled completely in a blur of the soft rust red and the soft buff yellow they seemed to have reduced everything to in the sprawling new building that wasn't even called a building, but a complex. Though now it was Wednesday afternoon, fourth-period English class after lunch, and for Mia it was the best time of the week at Austin High. By Wednesday afternoon she knew she had indeed made it through the worst of the week, and Mrs. Dietz in her jogging sneakers, tropical slacks, and golf shirt seemed to like to listen to herself talk so much (she had been to New England the summer before and they were doing Robert Frost; now it was as if she alone knew the details about piling up those stones for fence mending at the farms there, she alone knew the real dope on birch trees and how you could ride them), yes, she liked her own talk so much that she wasn't about to bother you, put you on the spot. Usually.

"How could one do worse than be a swinger of birches?" Mrs. Dietz asked.

Nobody said a thing.

"Mark?" A square-jawed baseball player with a deep chin dimple that some girls thought was unbelievably cute. He wore a white Texas Longhorns sweatshirt. He had no idea and flatly admitted it.

"Andrea? How about you? How could one do worse in this life, as he says in the poem?" Andrea was Hispanic and in this eleventh-grade class only since the beginning of the term, bussed from East Austin and probably not aware, in her shyness, of how really pretty her olive skin was; those eyes, like almonds, Mia thought.

"I'm not sure, Mrs. Dietz. I am sorry."

"Mia, how about you, Mia?"

And Mia herself felt a little dizzying rush, and she looked at her long fingers on which the nails were nibbled to the quick, shifted her legs under the formica-topped desk—then was passed.

"George?"

No, Mrs. Dietz didn't put anybody on the spot for too long, and seeing Mia had written the essay on "freedom" that was selected by Mrs. Dietz as one of the school's entries to the contest on the youth page of the Austin *American-Statesman* on the subject, Mrs. Dietz only smiled with Mia. The essay won an honorable mention and was printed in the Saturday edition along with the winner. Mia was surprised. Of course, English had always been easy for her, maybe because her mother, a psychologist, had taught her to read even before she started school and had made sure that she read so much as a kid. But what she put down about freedom was nothing more than what anybody had heard about a billion times before in civics classes from about the fourth grade onward, stuff about the right to chose, the right to differ, certainly nothing new. That it had received even the honorable mention was simply proof of what a joke the whole contest was, as far as Mia was concerned.

Mia now just looked out the window. The complex of the school sat in a parklike stretch, and on this side the second-floor classrooms overlooked the graveled hike-and-bike trail. The trail ran through the sunny city right along Town Lake, which was really more like a wide blue river at this stretch, before the pocket of highrises downtown. It was late March, balmy spring, and the skinny little fruit trees planted on the grassy banks puffed their petals, like pink popcorn maybe. Even on a weekday afternoon such as this a couple of the rented miniature sailboats were out there. The sails planted white triangles on the surface that sparkled as if truly dusted with diamonds, and though you couldn't be sure of it from here, Mia knew that up close those boats were like toys, scaled-down yachts with varnished decks, so small that you didn't sit on a seat in them, but just stretched out, the tiller rope in your hands, as if you were relaxing on a chaise lounge. Up beyond arched the bridge for Lamar Boulevard, and beyond that the bigger one for Interstate 35. Staring, and not so much as making an attempt to listen to Mrs. Dietz now, Mia wondered about what she had been wondering about a lot lately. What she had seen on Channel Seven news a few days before concerning the "transient" population in the city. The newscaster under his high-pomped hair had explained how there were so many of the ragged men in Austin because of the good climate, plus vagrancy laws that were some of the easiest in the state. Clips showed them, not very old, drunk in the afternoon over at the little alley of crafts sellers called Renaissance Market across from the university; clips showed them off on their own with trashbags slung over their shoulders Santa Claus style, going from dumpster to dumpster searching for aluminum cans, or just waiting at dawn as the trucks from the farms outside town pulled up at the red sign for the Salvation Army center on Fifth Street. But what struck Mia, what she remembered most, was the clip showing how they had set up almost little households for themselves on the streamlined concrete ledges underneath that bridge for the interstate: salvaged mattresses, sterno stoves, pictures from glossy magazines stuck up for homeyness. So cozy, and right there beyond all the leafy trees and down the blue a bit, where the cars now sped over the six lanes, which Mia could just about see from the classroom.

After English, with one more class to go that afternoon, Mia ran into Davey in the corridor. He had just left the advanced placement chemistry lab, she knew, and in the rush of traffic along the yellow linoleum that the janitors must have buffed and buffed for such a shine, they both stopped. They got out of the noisy flow.

"If it isn't the foil girl," he said.

He had had a haircut, she noticed. She always noticed when he had a haircut, when the blond curls weren't as thick at his neck anymore. They had known each other since grade school, old pals. She wished he hadn't said that, especially that way. She didn't like that.

"I'm not a foil girl," she said.

"You could have fooled me. And all your Westlake friends."

"Excuse me." And she just left him there. Sure, she was a foil girl, she had to admit it. And she would be one again that Friday. She just didn't like being called that, especially by Davey. The way his smokey gray eyes had stared right at her, accusingly. Two more classes to go, and Wednesday was over.

***

The last bell on Friday afternoon came like something you weren't quite sure of, something you seemed to have dreamt about, but the dream itself was dissolving like maybe one of those Polaroid shots in reverse development.

Mia had her father's car for the day. It seemed a mile to get to the designated no-permit student day parking, Area G. The car was a Ford Taurus station wagon, white. Her father was an architect, and he had thought that by buying this particular car he had somehow been in the avant-garde. Far from a station wagon type, he had driven a variety of sportscars in the past. And when Mia was a kid there had been a restored Triumph two-seater, a convertible that he used to let her "drive" sitting smack on his lap on the farm-to-market roads when they took spins on Sunday afternoon. But when Ford took the chance and came out with the sleek-shaped new line of supposedly European-styled bullets, the Taurus, he was sure they wouldn't catch on with an American driving public who liked their huge chrome-trimmed boxes. He would be making a statement by daring to go with that futuristic shape on an American car, and he thought the design was even more pronounced, "purer" as he said, on the station wagon. Yet as it turned out, the Taurus caught on immediately, and everybody seemed to have the same wagon. Her father was maybe stung by that, and handsome and even boyish at forty, he had that soft side to him, which he jokingly covered by saying that at least he hadn't been stupid enough to buy it in silver; if the car proved popular in general, the silver was more popular in particular.

Turning into the shaded drive at their house, Mia thought that the deal with the car was somehow like that with the house itself and what her mother often said about it. Her mother called it his "architect's pipe dream," and though she laughed about the name for the poured-concrete place that her father had, in fact, designed himself, it did suggest that it was true that her father never did too well in the firm. It suggested that her father had to show what he was capable of on the only thing that anybody would let him show it—his own home.

The reason Mia had the car that Friday was so she could drive over to the nursing home and bring her grandmother a gift for her birthday. She was her mother's mom, and the wrapped package, an Irish-knit cardigan sweater, Mia knew, was on the kitchen table. Her mother must have returned from her office sometime during the day, because the note hadn't been there when Mia and her father had their English muffins together that morning, after her mother had already left and before Mia dropped her father off at his office.

Give Gran a big birthday kiss for me,
And be sure to ask about the television.
—Love, Mom

The kitchen was airy, at the rear of the house. It opened, with long windows, onto the back patio, where the sun sifted through the high, gnarled live oaks and planted puzzle patterns of honey on the blue slate paving stones. There was an island counter for the built-in stove and the built-in sink, and above it hung the big Swiss cooking pans, even a couple of bona fide cauldrons, all copper and mirroring. Mia went to the refrigerator, took a Diet Pepsi, and she found the jalapeño potato chips her father liked behind the last of the white cupboard doors on the far wall. Snacking like that at the table, she thought about calling her mother and asking her what she was supposed to do if the color television in her grandmother's room still wasn't there. But Mia knew that her mother had a full day of it, and her mother got so nervous on full days that there was no sense in bothering her. Her mother's career, maybe unlike her father's, was starting to take off. Her mother was a slim woman who had once actually been a University of Texas football cheerleader. After a graduate degree, she landed a safe-enough job as the resident psychologist for one of the big new high-tech companies, a place of green-tinted glass up near Route 183. Then she decided, just a couple of years before, to try to give it a go on her own, first just doing general advising work for the same kind of high-tech places, and now seeing her own patients—"clients" as she called them—in an office where she had already hired another Ph.D. to handle the overflow of counseling. But again, it wasn't easy on her, and that she had managed to even slip over to the department store to buy the gift, never mind deliver it, was an accomplishment in itself.

Parents.

***

"Just go on and open it, I guess, Gran."
"Open it?" the old woman asked, vacantly.
"Sure, that's the idea."
"For me?"
"It's your birthday present, from Mom and Dad and me."

Mia was with her grandmother in the room in the nursing home. She watched as her grandmother's freckled hands and bony fingers worked on the bow, green, and then the paper, little white pin dots on cheery yellow. The woman sat in the one chair in the white-walled cubicle, a chrome-legged thing upholstered with gray Naugahyde, and Mia sat on the edge of the bed, one of those high contraptions you could crank up; the pink blanket and the white sheet and pillowcase were all tucked in at stark angles with almost military precision. But then her grandmother wanted Mia to open it. She handed it to Mia. The old woman was skinny to the point of near nothingness, and the way that the hairdresser here at the home had permed her gray-white hair in a tuft of neat ringlets wasn't at all the way Mia remembered her when she still lived in the big house with pillars out front, overlooking Pease Park, for years after Mia's grandfather died. But her smile was Gran's, the seawater blue eyes as well.

"For you," the old woman said.
"No, it's for you, Gran."

Mia was used to these shifts. They were reversals that came as her grandmother, with that whispery voice, didn't seem to follow what was going on at all; yes, for a minute it seemed that her grandmother was trying to give Mia the present.

"It's for you, Gran. From us."
"I know that. But we should save the paper." And so maybe Mia was wrong. And Mia somehow liked the idea that her grandmother remained practical herself, thinking that it would be good to save the paper for use on possibly another gift given to somebody else. Of course, it wouldn't be saved for anybody, and according to the strict rules of the private home, a patient was allowed to keep only as much in personal belongings as could fit into that tiny dresser and in the tiny closet with its door no wider than a plank; the paper would be tossed away. But it was like the old Gran indeed to do something like that, and it was good to see. Mia peeled off the yellow paper, gingerly, and Mia carefully folded back the tissue paper and took out the sweater for her. It was quite heavy, with

knit cables and plastic bone buttons.
"A sweater," the grandmother said. "A sweater for you. Because you said the air-conditioning got so cold here. It's heavy, from Ireland."
"And it's pink. My blanket is pink."
"You like it?"
"Yes, it is a very beautiful sweater. And it's from Ireland."

Mia helped her try it on, and she helped her stand so she could look at herself in the mirror above the dresser. Eventually, halfway though her stay, Mia brought up the matter of the missing television. She got the answer from her grandmother that the TV was gone for good, and she had given it away. Mia suspected as much, and her grandmother had been giving away little things (handkerchiefs, belts) for the last six months or so. But a television, a color set with remote control that Mia's father had just bought only a month before to replace her old black-and-white model that had finally conked out.

"You *gave* it away?" Mia asked her, a bit stunned.
"I don't like television." The old woman grinned.
"Wow, I can't believe that, Gran. Just like that. Gave it away."

And for some reason that struck Mia as about the funniest thing in the world then, and for a while the two of them laughed and laughed about it. That was like the old Gran too, and soon they were laughing about a lot of things. Though when Mia recognized that smell of the cooking— no matter what it was, always like instant mashed potatoes—from the open corridor, she knew she better get going. She wanted to stop over at the Eckerd drugstore on Guadalupe on her way back home and buy some of that Atune shampoo she liked so much, to wash her hair before she had to pick up her father in the station wagon at five-thirty. Tonight was Friday night.

She gave her grandmother a big hug, and a kiss.
"And here's another kiss, from Mom."
"Is she still in the lounge?" the old woman asked.
"Gran, Mom was never here today. It was just me. I'm giving you a kiss from her."

This wasn't like the old Gran Mia once knew; she was Out There again.

No sooner did Mia get into the house than the phone rang. She was sure it was going to be Kristen calling her, telling her exactly what time she would pick her up that night, give her the word on what the pack of them would be doing later when they all went out together to Sixth Street. But it was only Mary Hughes.

Mary Hughes lived in the same neighborhood. Her family had moved there from California. She went to St. Stephen's, an Episcopal day school out in a suburb, where some of Mia's friends from grade school and junior high themselves went now. But while they didn't make much of an effort to see Mia anymore and Mia made no effort to see them,

Mary Hughes was always calling Mia to ask if she wanted to play tennis in the afternoon, or to see if she wanted to come over to her house and play tapes. Both which usually meant the same thing. And that was listening to Mary Hughes go on and on about colleges she would apply to next year. Prettily freckled and making cheeriness almost a full-time occupation, Mary Hughes wasn't so bad; it was just that it wasn't any good to play tennis and listen to her talk about how Cornell was better than Brown, and it wasn't any good to sit around her room and play tapes and listen to her talk about how possibly Stanford was better than any Ivy, anyway, as the glossy-paged college catalogues (did all those places have walks of brick laid like herringbone? did everybody wear turtlenecks in the dining halls?) from all over the country were inevitably brought out. Mia sometimes wondered if Mary Hughes only wanted Mia as company because she actually believed that Mia was the kind of girl who shared her interests. There was no convincing Mary Hughes that she wanted to volley a tennis ball and not think about *anything*, to listen to music and not think about *anything*. Mary Hughes was convinced, however, that Mia did have college on her mind, and getting into a "top-notch" school would probably be no problem for Mia. Even though Mia repeatedly assured her that her own grades were merely low B's. Mary Hughes even found the proverbial silver lining there, saying that if Mia got B's doing as little as she did, imagine what a performance she could turn in to convince those admissions officers in her senior year, if she simply made half an effort—imagine how high she was bound to score on the SAT's when they both took them the following fall. Mary Hughes could have been more impressed than even Mrs. Dietz about Mia taking honorable mention in that *American-Statesman* essay contest; "Can you imagine what a *great* writing sample you'll be able to turn out when it comes time?" In fact, Mia might have had an easier time convincing somebody like Mrs. Dietz what a joke that contest was than Mary Hughes. Mary Hughes was like school away from school.

"I'd like to play, Mary. But I'm going to wash my hair, then I have to hustle to pick up my dad. I used his car today."

"We'll have to play this weekend."

"Sure."

***

Mia sometimes wondered: would it have been better if her father's career and not her mother's career had turned out so well? Would her father be more the way he was when she was a kid, more, well, confident and not having to drink as much as he did before dinner? And would her mother be more the way she was when Mia was a kid, less nervous, and not so constantly worried that there weren't just enough clock-ticking minutes in the hurried day for everything?

***

The trouble didn't really begin until Mia was nearly on her way out. Maybe only ten minutes before Kristen was supposed to show up at nine.

As it turned out, there wasn't a chance for showering and washing her hair before she had to pick up her father. When they got home, she helped him make a salad (lots of tomatoes, plus the spinach instead of lettuce, his favorite) to add to the frozen lasagna that her mother would bring from the Italian restaurant in a small mall near her office; it sold the frozen bricks of supposedly special stuff (four stars for the restaurant, according to *Texas Monthly*'s listing) for ready microwaving. Mia's father joked, sipping another scotch. They ate at about seven. Mia's mother asked about Mia's visit to the nursing home that day, and Mia finally had to admit, when asked about it specifically, that the grandmother had apparently given away the television set, to whom she had no idea. Her mother shook her head, but didn't seem upset by it. She only concluded that it was bound to happen, and she predicted that the sweater would probably last about a week before the same fate befell it. To which Mia's father answered that it wasn't all that great a TV anyway, and he had been concerned ever since he first brought it to the home and the woman didn't vaguely understand the business of the tiny press tabs, rather than the usual knobs, for everything from changing the station to simple volume control. Sure, the meal was easy enough, and to keep the situation smooth, Mia even got up before everybody else to set the yellow plates and the second-best stainless-steel silverware into the sink in the island, for a rinse before packing the dishwasher. Her mother thanked her; her mother said she herself had had a day of it indeed.

Upstairs, Mia took a long shower. She lathered her hair once with the Atune, rinsed it, and lathered it fully again, when you knew it was really clean. She stepped out of the shower, dripping, and shaved her legs over the bathtub, then got in the shower again. She eventually used one of the giant towels still smelling of the perfumey fabric softener, then put on her white terry cloth robe. In her own room, she turned on the radio, and, standing in front of the mirror on the closet door, dried her hair with the big red Conair blower, keeping it on the "medium" setting because it was true that with fine hair like hers, blasting away with the drier on "high" could only invite damage. The song on the radio was that Lisa Lisa thing, "Lost in Emotion," which Mia liked. Something about the way the girl's voice in it blended so right with the slow, heavy snare drum for the basic beat. She walked over to the mirror again. Mia had big green eyes and whiskey-colored hair, wispy now after the washing and pushed back from her forehead. She wondered if she *was* pretty. For a long time she had no reason to even ask that, because she was sure she was destined to be the way she had always been—skinny, goofy, as far as she was concerned. But now it seemed that suddenly boys were starting to pay attention to her. But she wasn't sure. The green eyes looked back at her; they, most of all, weren't sure at all.

She wore the gold miniskirt and the red dress flats that night. It was like a lamé, that gold. She wore a baggy white T-shirt, nothing on it and tucked in, and she looped a gold shell earring on each lobe. She used some eyeliner, Merle Norman, not much, and she glossed her lips with the true red, Merle Norman too. The whole trick was to look dressy, some effect of the formal earrings and the shimmery gold skirt, and to look casual too, the obvious effect of the T-shirt, on which she now rolled a couple of big cuffs on the baggy sleeves. She put on her worn blue jean jacket. Her plan was to simply go out through the living room when she heard Kristen beep her horn, to tell her parents that she would be back by twelve from the party she had lied to them that she was going to—and get out of the house as quickly as possible. But she made the mistake of venturing into the kitchen for a Diet Pepsi to take back to her room while she waited, and her mother, unpacking the dishwasher, started it. At first it was but a matter of her mother saying that she wished Mia wouldn't wear that ridiculous skirt, and with pretty eyes like hers there was no need for what she called "that eyeliner gunk"; and then it turned more complicated. She wanted Mia to assure her that she was going to a party in Westlake Hills and not going to Sixth Street downtown, about which there had been an article in the paper only a month or so before; it told of teenage girls hanging around the rock clubs there, dressed just like that. So-called foil girls, though her mother didn't use the phrase.

"Mom, everybody wears stuff like this skirt. I'm just going to a party. Call the parents, if you want." Which she knew her mother wouldn't do. For her mother it was probably enough that though she hadn't met Kristen or any of the other girls Mia herself had only met through friends of friends, Kristen's father was a well-known doctor and they did live in the posh neighborhood of Westlake. Then it turned even more complicated, and that was what saved Mia in the end. Her mother started on what had surely been bothering her ever since dinner, the fact that Mia hadn't at least made an effort to ask around, to the home's attendants or even to the director, if anybody had any idea what happened to her grandmother's color television: "You weren't supposed to just waltz in there and waltz out again." Mia told her she couldn't *believe* she was blaming her for that, and her mother finally agreed, maybe feeling so bad about burdening Mia with any guilt—the psychologist in her, Mia had long ago learned—that she backed off quickly.

The horn sounded. And Mia was out in the little red Mazda Kristen had gotten for her seventeenth birthday. They were going to pick up some of the other girls, then head right down to those clubs on Sixth Street.

***

The cars were crazy.

The Mexican boys from the East Side pulled up to the lights on Sixth Street in their customized low-riders, so cool that they could have been dry-iced. Four lanes, Sixth Street was one way for this pocket of what must have been rough-and-tumble feed stores and the like in Austin's Wild West days, and now was just one reconditioned pink brick or reconditioned white limestone building after another, each with a club. The sidewalks were packed, alive, and under the big inky sky in which the stars hung as close as matches flickering on this balmy night, the handsome fraternity boys from the university traveled in bunches, smelling of their aftershave, the chic sorority girls too traveled in bunches, smelling of their perfume. There must have been a formal dance later on at one of the ritzy old hotels, like the Driskill or the Stephen F. Austin, because of all the men in black tie and the women in jewelry and dressy sheaths. The flower sellers did their tricks, one famous for being able to twirl on the tip of a finger one of the long greenstemmed roses he peddled. Everything was bright neon, and the flashing chrome and glass from the jammed traffic. The music coming out of the open French doors, which most of the clubs had, was enough to thump away inside your rib cage, which Mia always thought was something that people only said figuratively, something that really didn't happen, until she got to Sixth Street. And the low-riders just kept coming, working their way past the half dozen lights as if they were on parade. Mother-of-pearl finishes sometimes, popsicle blue or popsicle green and the way sometimes they trimmed the back windows with a little fringe of jiggling balls, the way sometimes the cars themselves had whitewalls as wide as the palm of your hand. And with the signal turned red, and with an audience on the street of everybody from the guys with the little quilted aluminum fajita carts under Carta Blanca umbrellas, to the young cops on foot patrol (men and women) who looked as caught up in it all as anybody else in their open-necked light-blue uniform shirts and dark-blue baseball caps, a boy pulled up in a long sixties Chevy, glossy black and its grill somehow rigged up with lights for a continuously undulating rainbow. The giant engine gargled lowly, echoingly in its idle, through perforated chrome pipes below the door panels, and the whole ark rode no more than six inches off the velvety asphalt. Everybody waited, and a cigarette unlit in his mouth and some Phil Collins from the living-room-sized speakers on the rear deck, he paid no attention to any of the attention, finally flicking a switch somewhere under the dash to send the hydraulic charge into gear, to pumpingly jerk the thing up and down a good foot a few times—amazingly so. But, again, for the sleepy-eyed boy it was as boring as church, just a chore he had to do—or so he wanted to make it seem. That was always the best part for Mia. He eased off with the glowing green.

There were six girls. As Kristen had told Mia when she picked her up, "I wasn't even going to wear this blouse"—she had on the silver lamé, foil—"but ever since that article, we're, well, kind of famous." Not that they were the only foil girls, and Mia knew that so many of the high-schoolers like themselves were known as foil girls long before the newspaper got hold of it. But, anyway, it was fun. Sixth Street was fun. Besides Mia and Kristen, there were other girls from Westlake. Liz and Anne (the twins) and Sue. And then there was Rennie, who wasn't from Westlake and its high school in those fancy hills, but from LBJ, plain old Johnson High, there within the Austin limits on the flat other side of town near the airport. There was no questioning of whether or not Rennie was pretty, or even beautiful. Kristen and Sue maybe attracted attention by the way they had their hair frosted and elegantly teased like that; they were hairdos right out of "Dynasty" or "Falcon Crest," nicely so, Mia thought. The twins got second looks when together because they were picture-perfect reproductions of each other, with their cute snubbed noses and their cute, and gummily toothy, smiles. Once, in one of the clubs, the girls all agreed they would just *die* if another guy came up to the twins with that same line that was the refrain from the Doublemint commercial, the one about "doubling your pleasure"; immediately they were confronted by another fraternity guy using it, and they giggled so much that Mia thought she was going to melt. But for Rennie, everything worked: her pinched figure, even if she wasn't very tall, was perfect; her lips were full and perpetually bruised looking, perfect; and her skin was milky and almost babyish, perfect. She spoke kind of sexy, raspy, when she got around guys, and guys were always saying that she looked and sounded French, even though she talked and talked quite differently, loud and laughing, when she was with only the crew of girls. Rennie really liked cocaine.

Since the drinking age had been raised to twenty-one again at the clubs, the setup was usually to have a section of the place separated (streamlined chrome railings in one, simply the way they arranged the big gray-velvet sitting chairs facing inward in another), and in that area no alcohol could be served. Which was all close to a joke, everybody knew. It was just a matter of having guys buy drinks for you, which they were always doing, or buying them yourself on the way up to dance or to the ladies room. The latter never posed much of a problem, and if somebody actually did ask to see your driver's license, you moved on to another club.

They went to a lot of them. At the 606 there was a band called Blue Mist, kind of funk. And upstairs at Maggie Mae's there was a band called The Beet Meters, kind of punk. At Baxter's, usually a jazz club, there was a band called Steel Power, and they were just that, a steel drum band with black musicians in knit reggae toques and mirror sunglasses playing hollow, jangling fare that could make you think that you really were in some place with shag-topped coconut palms and a big, never-ending crescent of a bright white beach. Some fraternity guys—there were so many fraternity guys, the casual button-down shirts and pressed jeans their uniform—brought them all a round of frozen margaritas, and the keyboard man, taking a break on his own while the rest of the band played on, asked Mia to dance. Which she did. Right up front in the moving mass, next to those drums that were more like big cymbals pressed out convex, and it was amazing how the flickering sticks, almost giant Q-tips with such cottony ends, moved up and down and all around the disks for what almost sounded like a xylophone, Mia thought. Back at the table, Mia listened as the girls said how "cool" she was about it, cool when he asked her and cool as she went hand-in-hand with him right up to the front to dance like that. The fraternity boys were sitting with them, and they just grinned. But the girls didn't stay there. On a group trip to the ladies room, loudly tiled in pink and black for maybe a fifties revival motif, Rennie announced that they had to escape.

She could make it sound like a true adventure.

"I think they've ordered another round of drinks for us," Kristen said.

"Believe me," Rennie said, "they're all insurance agents in former lives. Bo-ring. That big one is close to salivating all over what I want to try to keep as a clean blouse."

In truth, Mia thought they were nice. Plus, she was suddenly so tired after that third drink. She had never had three drinks before, she now realized. But Rennie said that she had told some guy they would all meet him at Wylie's, a club a couple of doors down, at ten-thirty on the dot. And this guy was the one who owned his own record studio in town, the one she had been telling them about all night.

"We can't just walk out on them," Kristen said.

"Like hell we can't," Rennie said. "Listen, here's the plan."

Which was, return to the table, normal as can be. Sit at the table, normal as can be, and nonchalantly put away as much as each of them could of one of the Slurpee-thick margaritas, topped with a cherry and the glass's rim edged with big grains of salt. Then all pretend, en masse and far from normal, that they spotted somebody outside who they just had to see—and with that they would bolt out (not forgetting their bags, or the gold foil clutches the twins had) as fast as they could.

"I'll say Delores," Rennie said.

"Who's Delores?" Anne, a twin, asked. She was the one with the mole right on the tip of her nose.

"Who knows. All I know is whoever she is, she's going to deliver us from these dweebs. I'll say 'Delores!,' wave like I see her on the sidewalk, maybe, then everybody just starts shouting 'Delores!' and we're history here."

They giggled about it, and they giggled more when a heavy woman in what had to be a blonde wig came into that pink-and-blackness, the fluorescent light so strange, and went behind the shut door of the single pink stall to clatteringly lower herself onto the porcelain; *if* she ended up there at all. The escape back in the club proper when it came was actually more pure confusion than anything else. And there was a moment out on that moving sidewalk and out of breath when one of the twins, Liz, thought that the other one, Anne, had, in fact, grabbed just *one* of the gold clutches from the seat of the empty chair beside her, and not the *two* she was supposed to; but, after all, she did have it, having forgotten (thank God!) that she had stuffed it in the pocket of her own jean jacket when the "Delores" alarm sounded.

It was all crazy.

***

Settled at last at Wylie's. They had to go up Trinity Street in their dash and use the side door there for Wylie's, rather than the front door and be anywhere near to Baxter's and those fraternity guys. They must have put out close to twenty dollars for that second round of margaritas and now were left sitting solo.

"We stiffed them, I guess," Kristen said.

"I wouldn't say that," Rennie said. "They were plenty stiffed before they sat down with us, and they were just looking for some unstiffening."

They laughed. They were in the back room at Wylie's, the narrow setup which was open air, a white trellis spilling red-blossoming vines between them and Trinity. There was no music here, and Mia was grateful for the relative quiet. They watched a pretty drunk guy, obviously, in a yellow Mercedes on Trinity manage to wedge himself in a nonexistent parking space. First he rammed the car behind him, a light Honda, back about a foot or so; then he tried to ram the car in front of him, a much bigger American job, with the same technique. It didn't work, but that extra foot had tempted him on the Honda, which he slammed a couple of more times, earning still another foot. After which he parallel-parked so slow and law-abidingly that he could have been auditioning for a driver's ed instructional film. Across the street, the sign for the 606 Club sat atop the single-story building, its white neon script almost floating into the night sky; inside the place looked pretty deserted, and seeing it was one of the clubs that offered that section for nonalcoholic drinkers, it emptied earlier than the others. Mia knew it was getting late.

They talked about music. They talked about that guy who did the Church Lady character on "Saturday Night Live." The twins and Kristen and Sue—all Westlake girls—talked about other girls at Westlake High. Then about the boys. Rennie talked about the boys at "sorry" LBJ High, and how most of them were so bad that they still wore cowboy boots and Western shirts, which *nobody* wore anymore. Rennie talked too about this guy who was supposed to show, the one with the record studio, how she had met him the week before, and how she just knew that he was really interested in her. "He's got a ski boat that he keeps down at that place called Boat Town. You know, off Enfield. I mean, I was just sitting there at that little dock they have, trying to get some sun, and he and these four other guys, musicians, kept cruising by me. I was kind of hoping they'd ask me to ski."

"You were just sitting there," Kristen said. "Likely story."

"Well, sitting there," Rennie said, "in that string bikini I can put in an envelope, the one I got at By George. Remember?"

They laughed some more. When there came some talk about Mia, and some asking about what the kids were like at Austin High, Mia didn't have much to say. Then Kristen told the others about Davey.

"There is that one boy," Kristen said. "The one with the curls, who was over at your house that day. What's his name?"

"Who?"

"You know who."

"Davey. Davey is just a friend. Come on. I've known him since I was about zero years old."

"I can't believe it's eleven!" Anne, one of the twins, almost screamed that, jumping up as if stung by electricity. With that the twins were simply up and gone. They were living with their father since their parents' divorce, and though he often didn't even show up till dawn when he went out with one of his own girlfriends, when he was home and it came to his setting a time to be in for his daughters, he was as strict as that Church Lady they had been giggling about. And then somehow—Mia never should have had those three drinks, she was so dizzy—Rennie had decided to phone this guy who was supposed to meet her; and within five minutes she had Mia aside to say that she needed just one other girl for the little party her friend was having, at, could you believe it, the Driskill Hotel. And somehow Sue and Kristen were soon gone too, and the guy was reportedly on his way, in, could you believe it, a rented limo.

***

   ... yes, how those so-called transients had set up little households for themselves on the concrete ledges of the underside for that bridge for the interstate, so cozy, and. ...

***

But what was the reason for the limousines. Maybe no reason, as Stu himself admitted. He had only needed it earlier to bring "some people" over to the big concrete drum of the university's Erwin Center, where a group of his was one of the openers for the famous band. Mia recognized the name of the band from the oldies stations, but she wasn't sure she could actually name a song of theirs. Or maybe her father had one of their albums, and that was where she had seen it, in that collection of old LP's of his now packed in a couple of Sunkist Orange boxes out in the garage. This Stu was back from that errand, and he had just happened to stop at his condominium when Rennie called. She surely was lucky to catch him there before he set out again, and she surely knew that he had forgotten altogether about meeting her at Wylie's, as originally arranged after she water-skied with him and his friends the Wednesday afternoon before. Rennie's voice turned raspy now, not the way she had talked with the girls. Slower, and, well, sexy. Maybe why everybody thought her French.

"I bet you weren't going to call," she told him.

"You're my sweet little thing." He leaned over and kissed her on the back of her hair. "Of course I was going to call." He looked across to Mia, on the end of the swallowing blue leather seat of the limo, so soft; he reached over and put his hand on her knee. "And you're a sweet little thing too. What's your name, ah. . . ."

"Mia," she said softly.

"Yeah, Mia. You are a sweet one too." He still hadn't removed his hand. He had dark eyebrows, and his dark hair was thinning some; he was a *lot* older than those fraternity boys. His eyes were very dark, or maybe it was just how dark everything seemed inside that giant stretched-out car. Because the tinted windows made all outside look dim and blurred, the streetlights passing slow, like fuzzily haloed moons. He had on a red-and-gray Hawaiian sportshirt, gray slacks, and gray leather shoes—Mia had noticed his shoes—that reminded her of a little girl's Maryjanes, criss-crossing leather over the toe and a buckle strap. He stared at her for what seemed forever, then finally took his hand away.

"Oh yeah, a sweet one too."

"How does this TV work, anyway?" Rennie asked. She leaned to adjust it.

"TV?" he said. "Let me show you how easy that is, sugar. What do you girls like. I'll bet there are some videos on. You girls are crazy about videos, aren't you."

He fiddled with the chrome knobs on the set built into the mahogany on the back of the front seat. The car just hummed along, as cushiony as a dream, and Mia found herself looking at his hand now lit by the flickering flow of TV light that was too green. Black hair blanketed the back of that hand, the hand that was just on Mia's knee.

"You know why you girls are going to like the Driskill?" he asked.

"Why," Rennie said, pouty.

"Because you girls are so-oo sweet, and I've got a suite up there. A suite for the sweet."

"I hate puns," Rennie said, still prettily pouting.

"Rennie and Mia," he said. It was as if he were talking to himself, testing the names on his palate—and he liked them.

He offered to make drinks from the little fold-out bar set into that mahogany, next to the television. Rennie said she couldn't believe the limo, and he joked that he had to admit he made the mistake of not getting the one with the frozen margarita machine this time; nevertheless, he knew what they would like. The car, almost like a ship continued to nudge easily around the corners, and they must have been circling the same block over and over. He managed to balance the glasses as he poured. One of the girls from "The Cosby Show," the oldest daughter in the TV family, hosted the "Friday Night Videos," though none of it was very clear, either the picture that still showed almost that x-ray greenness on the color unit no bigger than a lunchbox, or the sound that came scratchily through the dozen speakers that must have been hidden away everywhere in the fragrant blue leather of it all. The streetlights were still those passing moons out there; the guy who was driving—a chauffeur? because he did have one of those hats—was a silhouette, so far away he seemed very distant, somebody you weren't quite sure of.

"It's good," Rennie said. She lifted the glass again to her full lips, like a kid with a mug of hot chocolate. "Real go-ood. What is this, anyway?"

"Rum and collins."

"Sweet," Rennie said.

"What did I tell you, sugar," he said.

"You-ooo," Rennie said. "You tricked me into saying that."

"You like it too, Mia?" he asked. Why did he stare and stare at her. Mia sipped a bit, and it was sugary, the aromatic smack of the rum almost a cologne.

"Sure, it's good. We're going to the Driskill?"

"The Driskill it is," he said. "Only the best. You know where the Driskill is?"

"Sure," Mia said.

"You girls like that gold stuff, don't you. Gold or silver." He was looking at Mia's shimmery miniskirt. She felt undressed. "What do you call that?"

"Foil, I guess," Rennie said. She maybe didn't like the way she was being left out, if only for a minute.

"The Driskill," Mia said to herself.

"The Driskill Hotel," Stu said.

Mia didn't want anything more to drink. She possibly never wanted to think of any variety of alcohol again, but she took another sip of that rum and collins.

"I want to know the stars who come to your studio," Rennie said.

"Where do I begin, honey," Stu said.

Yet Mia didn't seem to hear much of that talk. Because the Driskill was a big old hotel from the turn of the century. A brownstone rise with arches and turrets and gables, further down Sixth Street. The offices for her father's firm were originally downtown, and when he went there on Saturday afternoon Mia would sometimes go with him. With the dark graphite pencils and the colored markers, she would draw at one of the plywood tilt desks, while he did whatever work he had to catch up on then. For a break, her father would take her for a long walk on Congress

Avenue, the pink granite statehouse at its top. Over to the lunch counter of the old Woolworth's (a highrise stood there now), and sitting at the chrome-stemmed stools with their red vinyl seats—Mia liked to spin on hers—they would order a tall iced tea for him and a strawberry ice cream soda for her. Walking back she would tell him, "There's the castle," and at that age she had been convinced that the Driskill truly was just that. And what else was there, now that she thought about it? Up along the top of the building, under the eaves of the gables, were carved into the stone all kinds of strange details, big as platters: a Texas star, maybe; a Texas cactus, maybe; a Texas longhorn steer, maybe. And then right in the center, beneath the highest peak of the three- or four-story place, was the statue of a stern, bearded man, a bust in an old-fashioned frock coat and high starched collar looking out from his perch. And that, naturally, was Colonel Driskill. He was the original proprietor who named the operation after himself in a time not long after Texas lost its independent republic status. Her father would call up to him with a line like, "How's the weather up there, Colonel?" Or Mia would ask her father to ask him if he could see different Texas cities. They were names she had learned in grade school and liked to say herself. "Ask him if he can see Fort Worth, Dad." And her father would call up and come back with the answer himself. "Yes, he can see Fort Worth, even the stockyards, clear as a bell." Ask him if he can see Corpus Christi, El Paso, Houston, or Big Spring. No matter if there were clouds, Colonel Driskill could always see them all.

So, with Stu this night, who knows what it was or how it happened after they got up to his rooms on the top floor. (After having driven around in the limousine for maybe a half hour, despite the hotel being only a few blocks from where they had originally met, at Wylie's.) The place had icy blue brocade furniture and fresh orange flowers in a vase on the coffee table. There were other people, a few older girls truly beautiful enough to have been models, and there was Stu's friend Will, graying and wearing a tissue-thin black leather jacket, the guy who Mia had been brought to meet, and there was a tape playing the music of the group that Stu handled and that had opened for the famous band at the Erwin Center earlier, and there was cocaine set out in lines on the coffee table's glass top. And again, who knows what it was, but Mia was just sitting on a chair so big it felt like a throne to her, and that guy Will had left her for a minute to make a call. It could have been looking at Rennie taking another long sniff of the coke, then slouching into the sofa. Rennie leaned her head back, and next to her, Stu had his hand, that black-haired hand, under Rennie's skirt, which was really nothing more than a wide band around her thighs, and he was whisperingly asking her again why she never wore panties—he wanted to hear it again—and she was whisperingly saying again that she didn't because it felt so "go-ood" not to . . . or it could have only been thinking of going downtown with her father when she was a kid—about a billion years before. In any case,

Mia started crying, and once she began she couldn't stop; she just cried and cried and cried. She cried for nothing in particular, she cried for a lot of things. And nobody knew how to stop her, and Stu asked Rennie to try to "shut her the fuck up," that he had had enough problems with the management of this hotel already, and then he started to shout loudly at her himself, which only made her cry more, and there was nothing else to do for Mia but to leave, run out, because she didn't want to be there, and she couldn't stop crying, and. . . .

***

"Do you think they really live up there?" Mia asked Davey, softly.
"Who?" Davey said.
"You know, those people, the transients, or whatever they call them."
"You're really big on that, aren't you," he said.
"No, it's just something I've been thinking about."
"Well, I guess if they showed it in those clips on TV, those little nooks with the mattresses they set up, right, then I guess it's true."
"I think it is. I hope it is, anyway."
They were in Davey's father's Oldsmobile. He had come downtown to pick her up. It was all she could think of doing after she ran down the fire stairway from the Driskill's top floor, then to the second floor, where she spilled into the empty ballroom. Big tables blanketed with white cloths pushed off to the side of the room, black marble pillars, gold frills along the top of the walls that were genuine red silk. Out on Congress Avenue there were cabs, but Mia had only ten dollars in her purse. Or the five, three ones, and the change she counted. Plus, she had no idea how you even negotiated for a cab, how you paid the cab driver or what the eventual cost would be. Although she and Davey hadn't been getting along too smoothly lately, Davey and his brother had a "children's phone" in their bedroom over their garage. Davey wouldn't mind; Davey was like that.

He wore shorts and a gray sweatshirt, and the big unlaced basketball shoes. He obviously hadn't combed his hair before he hurriedly left. The windows were down. They passed the Austin Electric plant, its red neon lightning bolts on either side of the door framed with glass bricks, and continued on South First along the river. Then they got on the MoPac expressway, which was virtually empty.

"Do you have another one of those Lifesavers?" she asked him. "Take the whole pack," he said. He hadn't combed his hair, but he had remembered to rummage through his desk for the mints, knowing surely that Mia had been drinking and would need the camouflage. Davey was like that.

"I really appreciate this, you know that, Davey."
"Oh, don't worry," he said, tapping his nails on the gray vinyl dash, "I'll think of some way to make you pay." It was his put-on horror movie

voice. And if Davey would corner her again in the high school corridor sometime, or come over to her house when he saw she was home from school one afternoon and tell her that she got what she deserved for hanging around with those Westlake girls, maybe even call her a foil girl again, so accusingly, like he did before, she knew that for now he would be content to think that he had rescued her. He could bask in his chivalry, which, honestly, she was thankful for. Along with the fact, amazingly, according to her yellow Swatch watch, its face like graph paper, it was only twenty-past-twelve, and she had managed to get home on time. Or close to it.

She talked for a couple of minutes to her parents in the darkness of their bedroom. She assured them she had had fun at the party. But then, in her own room, she got sadder than before, and she started crying again. By the time she had changed into her sleeping T-shirt and washed and washed her face in cold water, however, that had gone. She tried to tell herself that things with her parents could only get better, maybe things at Austin High too.

She was so tired. And it was good to at least know that somewhere in all the blue shadows out there those grumbling transients were climbing up to their mattresses under the hissing traffic, that somewhere in all the blue shadows too her grandmother herself was already asleep and dreaming, her hair that ringleted tuft on her pillow and the pink sweater folded carefully in the drawer of that little white chest—for a while, anyway. Yes, somewhere in all those blue shadows.

***

As it turned out, not even Rennie held what happened at the Driskill against Mia. Rennie herself said that Stu and his friends were "dweebs," and on other nights on Sixth Street, Mia just laughed with the girls about the whole escapade at the Driskill. Maybe, however, it did happen that Friday, or maybe it was just that particular Friday that Mia would look back on as the turning point. Whatever, she knew that she wasn't a kid anymore, and it was a whole new world now.

Blood-Red History

David Sumner

In the blood-red history of man,
it is an old story: the oppressed
become oppressors, the conquerors
are conquered, the grass rises from
their bones, and the weeds become
totems.

The archaeologist of mounds
studies the seven horizons of death
and discovers endless repetition,
civilizations wearing out
their plumes and dying
under tin cans:
a shoe in the ashes,
a set of false teeth,
a shattered hand, a cistern full
of heads from broken athletes
and forgotten film stars.

Here in Portland I let the rain
wash away my rotting self,
the rubble of what I was,
the thick deepness of silence within
the ruins, the seven layers of
abandonment that no archaeologist
will ever read.

At Your Side

David Sumner

Your forehead feels hot to the back of my hand
now familiar with the normal temperature
of your soft skin beneath the damp thatch
of hair covering your fevered brow.
The heat of your face is less than that found

in the crevices of your thigh, or belly,
or behind your knee. I cool your face
with a Disney fan, and bathe your hot skin:
this is how I pay homage to all that you are
to me. In this morning shallow in December,
the first deep snow falls and accumulates,
covering all that should not be seen.

Your God is chilling the world
to save your life; although I know
that isn't how it works. Your father sleeps
outside your door; he is ready
to take his shift by your side
because together we have risen above

many disasters. After you moan, I hold you
close to my heart. The sky turns clear,
and the sun is healing the world
with a different warmth. And while we cling
to each other, I think I feel you cooling
in my arms.

Children's Hospital, 1959
for Melody

Joseph Hutchison

I remember a room full of weak fall light.
Your blood's sick, they said; don't cut yourself
(you'll keep bleeding), and don't go barefoot
down the hall, or you'll bruise your soles.
There were purple blotches on my shoulders
where I'd slept hard against the bed's sidebars,
which they lowered only to bathe me. Baths
are what I remember best. Yes: water
warm in its sponge, then cool on my skin;
the palely freckled hands of the Irish nurse
and her voice like a tree full of June wind:
*Lift up your hip, please; relax, just relax,
don't pull away; how's that feel now?* It felt
soothing, safe, being so gently cared for—

the way you always make me feel: bathed
in beauty, lifted and healed, my heart
repeating the one good thing that illness
taught me: *Relax, just relax. Don't pull away.*

The Hagfish

P. H. Liotta

This is the sea's vicious achievement:
the head's swollen nacelle carries a brain-
case for some larger awareness: though
each sex is separate, he carries a part of her
vestigial organs with him, and she his:
it: this miracle of primitive evolution,
the slime eel as parasitic
amazement: lacks a sympathetic
nervous system, holds a huge heart,
the burning sun of its iris, circular
sucking mouth and rows of horny teeth:
blood, gorged in a weave of rubbery
outer skin, pools from the sinuses,
flows to swell the lower body: produces
mucous enough to fill a bucket:
frictionless: bores inside the larger body:
consumed by its devourer

it consumes its devourer
from within, suddenly
sheds itself of whatever it was, from
mouth to damascened flesh to
disappearing tail, dissolving itself
into fish, fish dissolving naturally
into its victim: the hagfish shifts:
a grinning void beneath the skin:
eats its way out, makes its living
to become other flesh, internal
organs, leaves only skin and skeleton:
mutilated by desire, the fish is given
over to absence, while the hagfish survives,
reëmerges, gorged, itself as it is:
it escapes, or merely
thrives in the alluvial silt
at the bottom of everything.

The Pub

Leigh Cross

Long before the real-estate boom and even before we moved to Cuerno Island ourselves, Jolly Jock Flannell founded the Cuerno Island Pub. Of course, in those days, the idea of a real-estate boom would have made the island's residents snort into their home-made beer. What fool would want to buy stump-ranches and swamps for inflated prices? Certainly not the one-hundred-forty odd locals. And I do mean odd. A few artistic folk moved on in the summer months to live simple organic lives eating home-grown vegetables and to dwell in quaint hovels thrown together from driftwood, previously-owned windows and fishnet; however, year-around islanders were plain-jane, backwoods fruitcakes who'd come to hide from the world until they died or got over whatever had driven them into hiding.

Jolly Jock Flannell wasn't a hider; he was a predator on hiders and anyone else who happened along. He'd acquired the Cuerno Island Motel as a dowry when he led the blushing and slightly over-mature White Mouse to the altar. (Semi-acquired, that is. It was the White Mouse's third marriage and Jock's fifth. She'd learned to temper passion with prudence and her name stayed on the title.)

What a courtship that had been! Even when we arrived three years later, it was still the best story going. In those days, television was a citified toy for the idle rich and we backwoods fruitcakes had to take our entertainment where we found it.

The White Mouse had been Mrs. White Mouse Karlholz. Colorless hair coiled in two ear-like buns, pink eyes shielded behind tinted glasses, she managed the island's only motel, in summer, a flypaper-like hostelry on which tourists stuck and buzzed while the White Mouse gnawed steadily away at their ready cash—genteelly, of course; she was nothing if not a "proper lydie." In the winter, when rain pissed down in buckets and salt spray lashed the thin walls and leaky windows of the motel cabins, the White Mouse put her gentility on the shelf in the linen closet with the summer blankets and catered cannily and mercilessly to those of the rock-bottom, rootless-feckless who could still cough up a weekly pittance for rent.

Mr. Karlholz operated an obsolete, one-man, commercial fishing boat of a model called a "Fraser River gill-netter," a banana shaped shell of dry-rot and fish-offal in whose rheumatic heart rattled a quirky Easthope engine. Such craft are now collector's items (being susceptible to fire, don't you know, especially when over-insured). Mr. Karlholz was—well—let's be charitable: "not overly imaginative," or "careful-spoken—" oh, what the hell; he was dull, dull, dull, and after he'd been away for a couple of months, the White Mouse was bored, bored, bored.

One Wednesday evening, fate seated her next to Jock Flannell at the weekly whist party in the Cuerno Island Community Hall. What started as accidental footsie during a friendly hand of cards progressed to tentative, questioning footsie, then serious, exploratory footsie, then impassioned footsie, then a torrid hand of ensconce the salami, conducted in one of the White Mouse's motel cabins—but not until late the following afternoon. The White Mouse wanted Jock to know that she was bloody well not easy, not by a long shot.

Meanwhile, who should unexpectedly chug his gill-netter into the harbor on the other side of the island but Mr. Karlholz. Now, peccadilloes have always flourished on Cuerno Island but, with only one harbour, one road, one motel, such infidelities are never secret. By the time Mr. Karlholz had methodically dickered with the fish-camp over his catch, carefully rinsed his net in fresh water, scrubbed the blood, dried guts and scales from the deck, washed and put away the dishes, swept the cabin, turned off the oil stove and snapped verdigrised brass padlocks on all the hatches, the word had spread like poison ivy, and knots of whispering, giggling islanders clotted behind moss-grown stumps on the knoll overlooking the motel, ready to take in the concert.

***

For the overture Karlholz threw open the door with a traditional fanfare: a shout of "Aha!" which identified the entertainment as a *Concerto Grossissimo*.

Right on cue the White Mouse shrieked: "Oh my God! It's my *husband!*" a charming flutter in the string section to balance the heavier brass and percussion of the fanfare.

Jolly Jock, ever the veteran performer, introduced the "A" theme by jumping out the window.

Around and around the cabin the two men stumbled, over mounds of

moldering fir-bark, a dead refrigerator, cases of beer bottles, even a soggy pile of disposable diapers under the bathroom window, (leftovers from a duet of dedicated fuckups who had passed their time in residence rearing their own replacements). Karlholz, still in his fisherman's oilskins, fired a shotgun in the air, Jock, in nothing at all, brandished a double bitted axe which he'd snatched from the woodpile during his first circuit.
"Where is he!" Jock shouted.
"Where is he!" Karlholz said.
"I'll kill him!" Jock snarled.
"I'll kill him!" Karlholz said.
With this simple but poignant thematic material, the two men improvised in *stretto* for a full half-hour—they'd have quit sooner but the guffaws from the voyeurs capering about on the knoll and slapping their thighs alerted the gladiators to an audience. And what a performance! It's not easy to chase someone around a cabin for half an hour without catching or even seeing your opponent but they managed, and all to a measured *continuo* from the White Mouse (in a charming state of dishabille) as she leaned from the open window (over the rancid pile of diapers) and screamed: "Stop them, somebody, stop them! They'll *kiiiilll* each other!"

Well, of course, they didn't "kiiiiillll" each other. Jolly Jock was ever a devout coward and Karlholz was too harmless to die and too dense to become a murderer of anything smarter than fish. After the islanders had finally separated the combatants, they held them face to face for a resounding recapitulation and coda:

"Hold me, somebody! Don't let me get near that axe! I can't control myself when I'm angry! I might do something I'd regret for the rest of my life!" Jock roared, struggling mightily to escape the feather-light grasp of an arthritic octogenarian, rendered even weaker by his wheezes of mirth.

"Lemme go, Goddammit! Gimme back my shotgun! I'll murder the lousy bastard!" Karlholz blubbered.

"Stop them, somebody! Stop them! They'll *kiiiiill* each other!" screamed the White Mouse, a rock-steady ostinato for the expressive and rubato performances of the two men. She still delivered from the open window, but she'd slipped on her flowered kimono.

One hell of a concert. After the curtain calls, Karlholz chugged away on his fishing boat, vowing never to return. And he didn't; perhaps from rancor but more likely he'd forgotten the name of the island. After the minimum period required by law, Jolly Jock Flannell changed Mrs. White Mouse Karlholz's name to Mrs. White Mouse Flannell in a double ring ceremony at the Community Hall.

Jock spent most of his honeymoon scheming. When Jock schemed, which was often, his eyes would soften and his face, usually twisted into a gargoyle leer, would relax and become almost symmetrical. Nothing triggered Jock's devious brain more than the sight of a naive young nickel trotting down the street in clean shorts, all bright-eyed, bushy-tailed and aching to be spent. Jock had observed that the island's few die-hard alcoholics were in the custom of squandering their pension cheques on sugar, yeast and malt with which they made beer in galvanized garbage-cans under their kitchen sinks. They rationed this nectar over the month, sipping it from coffee mugs, chipped enamelware dippers, mason-jars, hub-caps or whatever else happened to be concave and handy. Now Jock wanted those pension cheques for his very own, so, as soon as the White Mouse had installed him as manager of the motel, he started to build the Pub. He extended a bait-shack, which had also served as the motel office, out over the dock to create a long, low, sod-roofed structure surrounded with windows and perched on piling over the tide flats. From the ferry, it looked like a cross between a Haida sweat-lodge and a daddy-longlegs. He blackmailed a license out of the Liquor Control Board. The Pub was born.

In the winter, Jock would open on pension-cheque day and close when the financial well ran dry. The island drunks were delighted to abandon their home-brewing operations in favor of Jock's expensive draft beer and rye whisky: more than booze, drunks crave alcoholic camaraderie and the Yin-Yang of suffering and relief, punishment and forgiveness to drug their intellects until the bone-faced Publican with the scythe calls: "Time, Gentlemen!"

***

In the summer, during Cuerno Island's brief tourist season, Jock would rush to don his apron any time the dust of a strange car obscured the horizon, sometimes even sending one of his or the White Mouse's many children to lie down in the road and feign sunstroke. "By Jove, folks! I'm certainly glad you happened to see the poor little tyke—not that I would have the slightest idea who in the God damned hell the little asshole might happen to be, anyway, but a few moments more in the broiling sun and it would have been—well—curtains! Now, what that little sod needs is a cold beer—and, by the way, can I get you folks anything while I'm behind the bar?"

And a jolly good publican was Jock: always ready with the lopsided leer, the joke to make a stevedore blush. I'll never forget when Jock told his terminally disgusting "—and, splat! Her panties stuck to the wall!" joke to a United Church minister and his dear old mother. And Jock never extended credit, nor drank on the job, nor let the drunks sleep on the floor. And Jock kept a gimlet eye on the cash-register. And when Jock closed the bar, he double-locked everything securely.

During the twelve years Jock would run the Pub, Cuerno Island was "discovered" by more of the esthetic summer crowd. In the late sixties it began to attract year-round settlers of the mushroom-hatted, hand-woven-underweared, screw-the-war species. I should know. I was one of them, and in spite of our urbane ways we were just more typical islanders: plain-jane, backwoods fruitcakes who'd come to hide from the world until we died or recovered from whatever had driven us into hiding.

Of course, hillbilly xenophobia dictated that when there were more than ten newcomers, we had the Great Hippy War of 1969, a bloodless fiasco worthy of its own book and one that would tinge island relationships for years. The White Mouse chose sides and fought the war passionately: "What do those people want, anyway? They have a perfectly good country; why don't they go back where they came from?"

Although he'd been a primary instigator of the Great Hippy War, Jock remained neutral, played both sides against the middle, kept his eye on the cash-register, carefully separating business from warfare. The Pub flourished: the hippy-haters sat by the windows, we furry freaks around the pitted stone fireplace and the pool table. Whether the bush alcoholics had pension money or not, we furry freaks took up the slack and Jock was able to stay open every weekend throughout the winter.

Year-around population reached eight hundred, in summer, two thousand! Such a wellspring of ready cash so tickled Jock's greed that he expanded the Pub and redecorated with a fireplace of pock-marked stones and paneling of worm-eaten planks. He even renamed the joint "The Teredo Room." Appropriately enough: a teredo or shipworm is an animal that hides in the dark and chews his own home from wood, like Jock's clientele.

***

But furry freaks travel with furry freaquesses. Jock could have grown old, mellow and rich on Cuerno Island had it not been for one of these very freaquesses, Tanya the odalisque, who decided to leave her position with a *menage à cinq* as chopstick-scrubber and the one who organically tie-died (with onion-skins and baby-piss) the handwoven underwear for the group. All alone, Tanya moved into a derelict tar-paper shack and set up shop as a *femme fatale,* a transformation to the pure essence of carnality, from odalisque to *eau de letch* in one fluid leap. So successful was her change of lifestyle that it was only a matter of days until she'd driven those islanders susceptible to *femmes fatales* mad with lust, and of those susceptible, none was more so than Jock, a twenty-four-carat philanderer of the first water—but sly, sly! The White Mouse had always suspected the slippery rascal but could never catch him. However, Tanya so dazzled Jock's animal cunning that the island was treated to yet another performance of the old *Concerto Grossissimo* except this time it was the White Mouse who threw open the door with a shout of "Aha," Jock who clutched the bedclothes to his chin and said "Oh, my God, it's my wife," and Tanya who jumped out the window.

I don't think it was infidelity that bothered the White Mouse as much as treason. The White Mouse had taken the Great Hippy War seriously, and, to her, Tanya was an enemy, a sub-human, foul-mouthed witch from entirely another species, a practitioner of black arts (else how had she beguiled poor Jock?) and undoubtedly a walking culture-medium for dozens of loathsome oriental social diseases.

When the smoke cleared, the White Mouse shipped the concupiscent pair off into the sunset and repossessed the motel and bar.

***

A dollar is a dollar and an island real estate boom, a bonanza. The White Mouse put the Pub on the market for a price straight from the optimistic clouds of "creative accounting" and entirely out of touch with the cold douche of earnings. But the Pub sold quickly to the Vetos and their silent partner, the bank. And they paid list price!

Dave and Vivian Veto came from off-island, of course; what native could have deluded himself with visions of gaining riches locally? Does a duck give milk? Can a snake play hopscotch?

Dave Veto had energy to burn, at first, anyway. He was a spider-monkey, spot-before-your-eyes sort of a fellow: wherever you looked, there was Dave Veto making faces at you like a rubber pretzel while Vivian sat placidly in the corner, chuckling, shaking her head and wondering how long he could keep it up.

Well, she found out, as we all did.

Dave was determined to succeed this time (it wasn't for years that we discovered how many times he'd failed). He and Vivian stayed on the wagon for a week while the whole island came and sipped a drink or two to get the measure of these new residents. Then the Vetos fell off the wagon in a lazy, fluttering descent like two crisped maple leaves in autumn, a long, slow fall that would last six months. It was a tall wagon.

Now, by God, there was a party! No more spider-monkey stuff; you could look in any direction and Dave Veto *didn't* appear before your eyes like an electric pretzel; he was on the floor under a table making gorping noises while Vivian sat placidly in the same damned corner, speaking in tongues: "Wuzza-muzza 'i fobbe walla?" and gorping right along with Dave. We mixed our own drinks and made our own change from the till. Most of us made accurate drinks and correct change but there were enough cheats that, after those six magic months, the bank (no longer silent) turfed the still gorping Vetos out onto the road, nailed plywood over the windows and planted a sign saying: "For sale. Fabulous business potential for the handyman-entrepreneur" in the grass patch out front, right next to the stove-in skiff planted full of geraniums.

***

We'd begun to bind up the wounds of the Great Hippy War. The old-timers and the furry-freaks were speaking again, usually meeting in neutral ground. We'd park our trucks in the middle of the dirt road, get out and have a pow-wow. Three of us had formed a thrombosis in the mud track between the Coop Store and Chevvy Cove, discussing something significant—migration of codfish or the sexual deviations of the new school teacher, or that most momentous of Cuerno Island topics: "Who started the fire at the garbage dump?" We'd gotten down to cases when we were disturbed by strident automobile horns: somebody wanted to drive past on the public road and lacked both patience to wait a half hour for the bullshit to dissipate and the inclination to hop out and join in the debate. We moved our trucks over to the side of the road. Down the rutted crown drove not just somebody but a whole parade: first a black four-by-four pickup, not one of your cunning little oriental jobs either but a snorting bull of a crew-cabbed, American monster with a bellowing v-8 engine. We could only see the bottom half of the driver's head. He had a chin like a tugboat's bow-pudding, a schnozz like a rhino, and the arm that rested on the door would have made a Virginia ham look like a Colonel Sanders economy drumstick. This rhino gave us a smile and a wave; "Thanks, fellas," he bellowed. On the pickup door was lettered "Leon Buckler" in gold-leaf, tastefully outlined in maroon. The pickup pulled a boat trailer on which perched *Leon's Baby*, a neat outboard sport fisherman with a fighting chair aft and a cuddy cabin forward.

"Jesus Christ!" I said. "Isn't that something!"

Moonshine Mcintyre, the boat flake, hooked his thumbs in his blue-and-white striped bib overalls and wiped his wiry red hair back from his eyes for a better look. "I mean, man, like it was that—I mean, like wow! I mean like who the fuck was *that*!" he said, opening his eyes wide. It was the most I'd ever seen of Moonshine besides hair and beard. Anything nautical fascinated him. He collected cut-rate, documented hulks and had a fleet of leaky craft tied up in Chevvy Cove. Rumor was he fancied the documents more than the boats, wouldn't touch anything, even free, unless it was a fully registered vessel.

"Nice boat," said Barney. "Wish I had the money he spent on it." He reefed a tin of Copenhagen from his shirt pocket and packed a generous pinch under his upper lip.

Something was bothering me. "I know that guy from somewhere but I can't place him," I said. A nag was born that would drive me half nuts for a month until it was resolved.

We stood in the road and stared at the dwindling stern of *Leon's Baby*. Another horn blared. "Look out!" I said. "Here comes another."

Next in line rumbled a wallowing American station wagon, white, with skinny windows in the roof.

"Biggest station wagon I ever saw," I said.

"I mean, man! Like wow! Like a whale. Like you know what I mean?" said Moonshine.

"Yup. Beluga whale. White," said Barney.

"Like—a Beluga whale? Man, like what's a Beluga whale? Where do they live?" asked Moonshine Mcintyre.

"Up in the Artic. Fat fuckers. White, you know," Barney said. "The old lady and me, we went to Vancouver last year and we seen a couple Beluga whales in the aquarium. But fat."

The Beluga station-wagon's driver, a lady every bit a match for Leon, rolled down the window and, with a big smile on her big face, asked: "Pardon me, gentlemen, but this is the way to the development on Petrel Beach, no?" The entire back of the wagon was crammed with potted plants, some of them quite exotic, maybe extra-terrestrial. Plants from Mars, perhaps?

"Yes, ma'am," said Barney.

"I mean like you take your first good left, like the first real road, you know? Like it was that you can't miss it," said Moonshine.

"Going to live here?" I asked.

"You bet!" she said and stuck her right hand out the Beluga's window. We took turns shaking the hand, a big one, clean but powerful with short nails. "I'm Thelma Buckler," she said. "My husband, Leon, and I've bought the Pub."

"Oh yeah?" said Barney.

"Yeah?" I said.

"Man, like wow!" said Moonshine.

From behind the Beluga, a truck honked a series of impatient toots on an air horn.

"Well, I must be moving," said Thelma. "Can't hold up the parade, can we. We'll be seeing you in the bar, yes?"

"Sure," I said.

"Man, like wow," said Moonshine. "See you at the bar. Yeah. Wow."

On through the ruts wallowed the Beluga, tailgate plastered with stickers espousing labor unions and lost political causes. Next, a strange looking truck, one of those super-short trailer-movers, slithered past us, twin stacks belching diesel fumes. The windows were so filthy and the cab so choked with cigarette smoke, we couldn't see much of the truck driver except he was thin and dark, had sickle sideburns and, God knows, he smoked. We only saw him that one time.

"That guy, he's a real trailer person," said Barney. "Different from you or me. Moves around a lot, I'll bet. Next week, he'll be in Newfoundland, maybe, or the States, or jail, like." A drop of Copenhagen-stained slobber ran down his chin. "Man, like nobody-much ever sees the same trailer person more than once, huh?" said Moonshine, luxuriously scratching his balls inside his baggy overalls.

"Nobody much cares," I said.

"For sure I don't," said Barney. He wiped the drop off his chin with his sleeve.

Last came the trailer, an immense, chartreuse mobile home, complete with vinyl siding and glass patio doors. It passed quietly, only the occasional creak when the wheels hit a rock.

"Well, she's not going to see *me* at the bar," said Barney. "I used to drink, don't any more. Can't. I go plumb mesachi. That's Salish—bow-and-arrow, you know? Means ape-shit."

"I know," I said. "You've told me about that quite a few times."

"That's right, I did, didn't I," Barney said.

"That guy, Leon," I said, "I know him from someplace—"

"You already told *me* that. Just once. But enough," Barney said.

"Man, like I can't stay around here all day, listening to you guys tell each other the same things over and over to each other; like I got to go *pump*," Moonshine said. Though he had lousy taste in boats, necessity dictated excellent taste in bilge pumps. The back of his rickety pickup was full of them, well-used but well-maintained, all gassed up and ready to go.

The road-thrombosis dissolved and restored circulation to Chevvy Cove.

***

But what a hustle at the Pub! The Veto's long party hadn't left the joint in such swift shape: gorping and janitorial services don't go hand in hand. Take a room; get fifty people to drink, smoke, throw up and piss on the floor for six months without swamping it out, then lock it up tight for six weeks. When you open the door it's—well—interesting. For a week the Bucklers swept, mopped, scraped, painted and disinfected, murdering the regiments of lower animal life which replicated in every convenient crevice. In the latrines, maggots thrived in rotting piles of semi-gelatinous material while Jesus-bugs enthusiastically paddled their canoes in the urinals and toilet tanks. In the bowl of one toilet, a desperate but weakening rat still swam in circles, squeaking hoarsely while anaerobic rotifers spun malignantly in the depths, waiting to dine on the rat's emaciated body. Kindly Leon reefed the rat out by his tail. With his last strength, the waterlogged ingrate climbed up himself and gave kindly Leon a nasty bite on the thumb.

Such are rats.

With a curse, Leon dropped, stomped and flushed the rat.

Such are men.

In the septic tank, the rotifers worked their will on the rat's mangled remains and, had it not been for modern antibiotics, the rotifer's land-dwelling cousins, the corpse-worms, would have worked their will on the remains of Leon. The bite of a starved rat half drowned in sewage is no joke and Leon had to spend a few days on his face in bed while the island doctor injected monster doses of penicillin into his rump. Most of the bull work in the Pub had been done by the time Leon had his brush with death, and Thelma figured she could make the final feminine touches without Leon's help. She gave Leon three days off to go fishing.

***

When Leon arrived at the launching ramp, it happened that I was there. I'd been on a job for Moonshine Mcintyre who'd bought a fish-camp at a bankruptcy auction and tied her to the Pub's piling. Moonshine's new acquisition had such a burning desire to sink that she had to be pumped twenty-four hours a day. Moonshine had made a deal with Thelma to run an extension out of the window in the Pub's storeroom and I was to rig an electric bilge pump. "Man, like wow! Isn't she beautiful!" Moonshine said when I met him on the float.

We stood on the float and looked up at her: a rusted sheet-iron shed perched on a rotting wooden scow bathed in a miasma of fish-guts. "You're nuts, Moonshine," I said. "She's a marine catastrophe looking for a place to happen."

"Man, like no," Moonshine said. "I got her for fifty dollars and you should see her registration papers. *Man*, like *they're* what's beautiful. She's a hundred-twenty-ton, diesel fish-packer. I need a packer for my fleet of seiners."

I was in a mechanical mode and mechanics are allowed to be brusque. "Like I said, you're nuts. Don't believe everything you read in the papers, even registration papers. She's a hundred-twenty-ton nursery for baby codfish. Take her out in the channel and let her fulfill her destiny. A decent human being doesn't expose rotting corpses in public. Have a heart. Give her a proper burial. And that seiner fleet! Surely to God you don't, by any remote chance, mean that flotilla of worm-eaten hulks you got on life support down in the Cove?"

"Man, like maybe you don't believe everything you read in the papers and maybe I don't either, but, *man*, like *some people* do." Moonshine gave me a broadside of enthusiastic winks. What a total nut!

I shut my trap and went about rigging the electric bilge-pump. I mean, life is too short to argue with flakes and besides, when all was said and done, he was picking up the cheque for my time and the golden rule applied: "He who has the gold, makes the rules."

"Whatever you say, Moonshine," I muttered.

When the bilge pump was gushing a clear jet of frothing, tangy-green sea water—the more a boat leaks, the cleaner the bilges—we walked back up the ramp and past the windows of the Pub. Thelma looked up briefly and waved, then went back to haggling with a delivery truck driver over an invoice for frozen french-fries.

I had tossed my tool box in my truck and was about to go home when Leon drove up in his black pickup, towing his boat. I said to Moonshine:

"I know that guy from someplace."
"Yeah?" said Moonshine. "Man, like where?"
"I don't know and it's driving me crazy."
"Well, maaaaan! Like pipe Mr. Sanity!" said Moonshine nastily. I guess I *had* been razzing him a little hard about being a boat-flake.

Naturally we had to walk over to talk to Leon. There's no such thing as too much information on an island.

"Going fishing?" I asked.

"Yeah, I thought I'd spend a couple days out on the boat," Leon said. "I'll launch her when the ferry's unloaded." He pointed with his chin to the ferry landing where the current ham-handed klutz of a Government skipper bashed his way into the slip. Splinters flew; the tortured pilings groaned. "Pitiful. Just pitiful," Leon said with a shake of his head. "The poor clown couldn't hit a bull's ass with a banjo let alone a slip with a ferry boat."

"They say he was in the navy," I offered. We watched the ferry traffic drive by.

"Well, I wouldn't doubt it. Typical navy man," Leon said with all the civilian seaman's scorn for the military. "Never mind the gold braid and bosun's pipes, the poor bastard shouldn't be trusted with a Celluloid duck in a bathtub."

Now, ship handling is not your ordinary skill. Anyone with half an eye could see that the Government ferry skipper was hopeless, but as I watched Leon launch and cross-tie *Leon's Baby*, I could see that here was a man who'd not only been born knowing how to handle a ship but who'd spent a good part of his adult life perfecting his skill. The void in my memory tweaked. I almost had it when Moonshine tapped me on the shoulder. "Man, like who's that?" he said and pointed across the water at an approaching canoe.

"Damned if I know," I said.

A near-sighted anthropologist and his guppy-like, live-in girl-friend had rented a motel cabin from the White Mouse for the week. As Leon parked his truck and trailer, Moonshine and I watched the pair paddle toward us. Of course they didn't speak to us or even notice us, they were much too nice and sensitive. They stared down into the water as they paddled; the anthropologist explained the marine life, using long and complicated Latin names while she "Ooed" and "Ahed" at his erudition and asked intelligent questions.

Leon boarded his boat and busied himself getting everything ship-shape before he cast off. Anthropologist and girl-friend were so busy ignoring us and so intent on undersea marvels that they drove the bow of their canoe into the side of Leon's sport fisherman, making a small dent in the paint. "Sorry about that," said the anthropologist, bristling his red beard and smiling his best, passive-aggressive, peace-love-and-brotherhood smile.

"Oh yes," said the girl-friend, triumphantly. "Please *do* forgive us.

We're frightfully sorry."

"'Sorry!'" Leon bellowed. "I'll give you 'sorry!' You listen to me, Charlie! You don't learn how to steer that fuckin' little piss-ant turd-raft, I might have to take it away from you and shove it up your fat little red ass, paddles and all. You got me?"

"Man, like wow!" Moonshine murmured in admiration.

I had to admit I'd never heard a more professional and seaman-like dressing-down, and delivered in the correct voice: one that would carry through a bank vault during a hurricane but perhaps, in the quiet of the launching ramp on Cuerno Island, a bit of overkill, like setting a carpet tack with a pile driver. But then, I've never seen an anthropologist shut up and paddle faster.

It was the voice that did it. I remembered. A year or so before, I'd been working in a logging camp up in the inlets, only about a hundred miles as the crow flies from smiling, balmy Cuerno Island but the inlets are neither smiling nor balmy. Granite crags loom over freezing cold, bottomless fjords and only giant trees can thrive in the howling wind and cold rain. A tug arrived with a ramp-scow a good hundred-sixty feet long, on which perched some equipment for our job. The tug skipper strapped his two-thousand-horsepower, steel Goliath up beside that scow, gently kissed the ramp into a ledge we'd blasted from the cliff and held her there, rock steady, never mind the twenty-knot breeze and four knots of cross-tide while a bunch of owly, foul-mouthed loggers (myself among them) pulled straw-line and trotted about, speaking in vocal whistle signals and obscenity, and unloaded an eighty-ton steel spar, a couple of crummies, several thousand-gallon propane tanks, a D-8 cat and some bunkhouses on skids.

Our boom man cruised up in our yarding tug, a steel muffin of a mere two-hundred horsepower. "Hi there, skipper," shouted the boom man brashly. "How about I nose in and help you hold her against the tide?"

"Are you *kidding*, Charlie?" The voice from the tug's bridge carried clear as a bell over the twenty-knot breeze, the rumble of the tug's thundering diesel, the bellowing of logging equipment engines and clanking of treads—even over the blisteringly rancid obscenities of the loggers. "Any time I need help doing my job—particularly from a piss-ant turd-raft like that—I'll kiss your ass on the courthouse steps and give you twenty minutes to draw a crowd."

Yup. Same style, same voice. Must be the same man. It looked as if Cuerno Island had a tug skipper for a publican.

Moonshine and I watched Leon cast off, coil his lines and cruise away, a man as completely at home as a clam in the mud.

***

Thelma placed the plastic flowers on the tables and mounted the cute signs on the bar mirror: "This is a non-profit organization; we didn't plan it that way but—" "Keep your wife for a pet and eat here," and "We got a deal with the Bank: They don't sell booze, we don't cash cheques," and so on. Trucks arrived with fresh stock. Thelma wired fragrant, white urinal-cookies in all the appropriate bathroom facilities to keep Jesus-bugs, malignant rotifers and all their relatives at bay. By the time Leon got back, rested, happy and with a cooler full of fresh-caught salmon, the Pub was ready to open again.

Of course, everybody who was anybody came to take in the style of the new owners. Some hoped for a repetition of the Veto's six-month party, but the Bucklers were made of sterner stuff: *they* poured the drinks and *they* punched the register and I never heard them gorp, either. Yes, they drank, like desert-parched camels at an oasis, but their powerful, sack-like bodies threw off the alcohol as camels shake off flies.

Under the Bucklers the Pub blossomed—not into a rose or pansy but a giant technicolor bloom, not as besotted as under the Vetos, nor as canny as under Jock Flannell. Neither was it as homey as under some later owners or as trendy as under some others. But the laughs and music were louder; the arguments, fiercer and more political; the jokes, raunchier and the bar-romances were even more grotesque. Several interesting fights occurred in the parking lot: half an hour of obscenity and threats, three fast clouts, blood, doctors, bandages and days of enjoyable post-mortem conversation for the entire island population. But in the bar there was no fighting; throw one punch and you were out on your ear. Either Buckler could turn the trick but Leon usually did the honors and, while executing a classic bum's rush, would educate the miscreant with a plain-spoken critique of his lack of good taste: "Any time you can get away with that shit in my bar, Charlie, I'll kiss your ass on the courthouse steps and give you twenty minutes to draw a crowd."

And Leon closed the place with the same magnificent frankness: "Awright. Fuck off! Twelve o'clock. Everybody fuck off! Fuck off!"

And Thelma? Not only could she equal Leon at his own, plain-spoken, direct phrase but also, when she shot off her mouth, she did it with such a ponderous, grand-dame graciousness that the offender felt like a becalmed smuggler when a heavy cruiser steams up: crisp white bow wave, massive gun turrets swinging to bear and the skipper on the loud hailer: "Beg pardon sir, heave to and explain yourself or we'll blow you out of the water." Not that Thelma's graciousness had the slightest hint of aristocracy. Her *noblesse* gushed from pure proletarian springs: Thelma was a capital "R" Red of the old school, a true-blue disciple of *Das Kapital*. How many Saturday nights have I heard Thelma's voice ring out over the uproar like an old ship's bell: "Perhaps *here*, my friend, but I assure you that in a *properly* organized society . . . " Thelma's red credentials were so impeccable that her participation in such a bourgeois activity as running a Pub could be ignored. After all, had her late father not been a saint so red he glowed in the dark? Indeed. He'd been one of the Grand Old Men of the Founding-Father-Reds of Western Canada, an area world famous for pain-in-the-ass lumpen-proletariat. In the bush he'd organized loggers and miners; in the hotel, bellboys; in the street, taxi-drivers and meter maids; in court, the stenographers and in jail, he was assigned work in the cheese factory where he organized the mice. His only daughter, Thelma, showed her true colors early. While dad was away, Thelma was sent to a convent school by her Roman Catholic mother, who'd never have dared had the old man not been safely in the bucket. Within three months Thelma had organized the nuns and taken them out on strike. The Bishop was mad as hell, turfed Thelma out pronto and brought in scab nuns from Ireland. Didn't do him any good; the nuns stayed out. Nuns can be quick studies and they'd learned a lot from Thelma. Within a few days, the locals had subverted the Irish nuns and the whole flapping penguin flotilla was out on the line. The Irish even added quaint old-country touches: while the red-faced and frothing Bish stood on the sidewalk, screaming incoherently and shaking his cross at the pickets (fortunately, his driver was around the corner in a news-stand playing pin-ball), his Cadillac was blown to fiery atoms with " . . . just a bit of the old gel, don't you know."

The issue ended in a classic Mexican standoff. The Church excommunicated everybody right down to the weevils in the communion wafers. The nuns "painted" the whole convent, chapel and all, declared it "hot," told the Bishop to go "piss up a rope" and emigrated to Central America where they were welcomed by a Nicaraguan revolutionary order. The Church had to sell the convent to a boy's school that wasn't even Catholic. A bitter pill.

***

One hot summer Wednesday, I drove my old Dodge truck off the ferry and onto the island, truck-springs bent double under a load of pressure-treated fence-posts. Every time I'd hit a bump, a rear tire would chafe against the truck bed, bray, stink and give off a cloud of foul smoke. It had been a miserable trip and I needed a lift. I parked at the bar, entered and buried my nose in a cool pint of beer. The high tide rustled soothingly through the pilings below. Leon lazed behind the bar, gazing into the distance as he tranquilly picked his teeth with a plastic olive-sword. Thelma lounged against the jamb of the galley door and sucked down a cigarette like a combat soldier: keeping the butt chucked between thumb and two fingers to hide the glowing end in her cupped hand. Besides myself, there was only one other group in the bar, a quintet of wine-and-soda sipping tourists dressed in the type of peasant working clothes that cost a bundle.

"So?" Leon said. "What you got on your truck?"

"Fence-posts," I said. I studied the quintet out of the corner of my eye.

They looked like Californians, show folks, maybe. The two older men were possibly film producers: bearded, meticulously coiffed, synthetically hearty. Occasionally they'd beat each other jovially on the back, smiling a lot with their white teeth but not with their sad, piggy eyes. The two women were skinny, beautiful and madly in love with the world (I guess things must have been going their way). The fifth member of the group, a clever young Adonis in a purple sweat-suit, entertained them with *sotto voce* remarks, probably cutting ones, about the native customs. "Who're they?" I asked Leon.

"Don't know," he answered. "But they're spending money out the ass: Swampsinger wine one bottle after another and they wouldn't think of eating hamburgers or chips like you ordinary drunks neither. Thelma fixed 'em a platter of rye-crisps and carrots and celery—stuff like that. Soaked 'em plenty for it but they didn't bat an eye. And they pay in American bucks. What you going to do with the fence-posts?"

"Well, Leon," I said, "I'm going to stick 'em in the ground and string wire on them. Tell me, what do you do with fence-posts?"

Leon laughed. "'Ask a stupid question.' You get them pressure treated?"

"You bet," I said. "I should piss away my life stringing wire on untreated posts? Those, people—ah—where they staying?"

Leon said: "They've rented a house on the north side for a couple of months, but they like it best right here in the bar. And we like it best, too, don't think we don't. Few more like that bunch and we could pay off the mortgage."

"Quite the smartass, that kid," I said.

"Listen!" Leon said. "As long as they keep on throwing money at us, I'll laugh at their jokes and turn somersaults on the floor like Mickey Mouse."

"More fun than a barrel of monkeys! When are you going to do that, Leon. I want to watch," I said.

Leon snorted.

"I hope no cops come around," I mumbled.

"Cops?" barked Thelma from the galley door (few old-time reds are in love with the police). "Cops where? Why do you say 'cops'?"

"Well, it looks to me like that one is under-age." I pointed at the California youth with my chin.

"God damn if I don't think you're right," Leon said. "Can't have that stuff going on. I'd lose my license."

Normal bartender procedure dictates a discreet sidle across the floor and an apologetic murmur: "I'm sorry, sir. I'll have to see some identification." But not our Leon. Not only no, but hell no. Like a rhino from a dust-wallow, he lumbered from behind the bar, across the groaning floorboards, gathering steam in his cavernous lungs, put both hands flat on the offending party's table, lowered his stupendous rhino schnozz within an inch of the youth's Grecian proboscis and expended his accumulated vapor in a thunderous bellow: "What kind of fuckin' bullshit *is* this, anyhow?" There was no argument from the tourists; how could they argue when they'd been washed into the middle of the road on a tidal-wave of hot air? Leon returned behind the bar. "That takes care of that," he said, satisfied.

"I guess so!" I said. "How about your mortgage?"

"Oh well," Leon smiled ruefully, "guy *needs* a mortgage, don't he? Keeps him on his toes, eh? Better. Yeah."

Thelma expertly flipped her cigarette butt across the room and through a tiny crack in the bottom of a window to hiss into the salt-chuck eddying below. "Yeah. Better. Oh yeah. We *really need* that goddam mortgage," she said.

"Well, what else would you have me do?" Leon bellowed. "The kid was under legal drinking age."

"Just give me a minute, Leon," Thelma said, regally calm (but the powder room crew were sending up cartridges for the big guns). "I'll turn off the fire under the griddle and then I'll be glad to explain to you precisely what else you could have done." She backed into the galley to clear the decks for action.

Oh Jesus! A Rhinoceros-and-Heavy-Cruiser Fight! Fascinating! But not a safe place for wee furry folk like me. I guzzled my pint, paid and scurried for the door on my wee furry feet. "See you later, Leon," I squeaked.

"Maybe you will; maybe you won't," he rumbled. (His guts growled as his engine-room pumped adrenalin. Angry rhinos need a lot of steam.) I made it out the door one jump ahead of the Wednesday afternoon edition of *World War Three at the Cuerno Island Pub*.

I fired up the truck. Through the windshield I saw that a new boat had been tied alongside Moonshine's "hundred-twenty ton packer." What a mess! This particular marine disaster had probably started out in 1910 as a plumb-stemmed, wooden motor-yacht. As the decades rolled by and she got doggier and doggier, they must have gotten tired of caulking her because she'd been fiberglassed. And badly. I guess she'd done time as a cod-fisherman for the Vancouver trade because she'd once been fitted with a live fish hold. Chinese customers will pay a good premium to buy their fish alive and swimming. But then, who knows? She'd been fitted with spuds. What in hell does a cod-fisherman need with spuds? And that God-awful plywood deckhouse that overhung the hull like London Bridge! And the paint job! Someone had painted her orange, apparently with a whisk-broom. Even from the parking lot, I could hear the shipworms caroling merrily as they gnawed away at what few scraps were left of her ancient wooden frame. It had to be Moonshine's boat; that orange dog's-breakfast was something only he could have loved. And I suppose her papers said she was a tuna clipper or whale factory ship or maybe the *Queen Mary*.

Jesus!

Moonshine!
What a flake!

***

But Haley's Comet livens up the skies only once in most lifetimes. And how many days did Einstein piss away doing nothing brilliant whatsoever? And didn't the night arrive when Henry the Eighth could no longer get it up? And what gets accomplished on Sunday morning? Or January second? No, my friends, nobody lives in the fast lane forever, not even Leon and Thelma.

I wasn't in on the beginning, but I heard about it from the neighbors. It was Sunday. Back in those days, the pubs had to close on Sundays. Leon and Thelma had decided to spend their day of rest in their cozy trailer enjoying a pro football game on their giant tv. As the afternoon wore on, they lubricated their throats from a forty-pounder of mellow rye whiskey. Near the bottom of the bottle, they had a difference of opinion, at first friendly but it built as arguments fueled by whiskey are wont, oh, how it built! No one knows the subject, the neighbors weren't listening and of course Leon and Thelma have forgotten. But it must have been one of those earth-shakers like: "Who was the leader of the CCF in 1928?"; "From where does a cat sweat?"; or "Will a fart really burn if ignited correctly?" By the time the neighbors became aware, it had blossomed into the Sunday afternoon edition of *World War Three at Leon and Thelma's House*.

"What an asshole!" Thelma shrieked, as she winged plates like keening discuses at Leon's head. "I'll never understand why I wasted all those god-damned years on—"

"Shut up. Just shut the fuck up," Leon bellowed back, dodging the plates and twirling the crank handle on the boat trailer like an eggbeater to lower it onto the ball of his pickup. "I'm moving onto my boat and I'm gonna fuckin' stay there. Maybe get a little fuckin' peace and quiet for the first time in thirty fuckin' years." A plate skimmed Leon's Adam's apple and he caught it. Slowly he spread a wicked smile. He cocked his arm and winged the plate back at Thelma. The humming projectile might have ripped her head from her shoulders had a gust of wind not deflected it into a cold-frame that stood beside the trailer door. The glass shattered. A tiny, grotesque vegetable died miserably. Perhaps its soul returned to Mars?

If you criticize middle-aged ladies' children, they'll wonder if you might not be right. But God help you if you kill one of their plants. Thelma's rage waxed a thousand fold. "You unmitigated. Lousy. Miserable. Bourgeois. Bastard!" she squalled. "You *killed* my plant." She raised her arms, crooked her fingers and lumbered toward Leon like the Bride of Frankenstein.

"Aw, shit. What's the use," muttered Leon. He hopped in his truck and towed his boat away.

***

When Leon arrived, the ferry was pulling in. I was on board with the old Dodge truck, bringing back some dairy-ration and plastic irrigation pipe so I had a first class view of the boat launching ramp. Leon roared up in a cloud of dust and backed his boat trailer down the ramp and into the water. He must have been doing twenty miles an hour—by god, that man could drive. The trailer ran straight as a die, without a wiggle. After he'd launched the boat, he cross-tied her to the pilings and parked his pickup and trailer with more than his usual panache.

A mere twenty ounces of rye could never affect Leon's driving or ship-handling.

Only his memory.

He'd forgotten to replace the drain plug in his boat. The water bubbled up through the floorboards. She was sinking, and quickly.

Leon squalled, and started a whirlwind search for the plug.

The boat settled more.

Leon recollected he'd packed the plug in his suitcase.

With another cougar-like squall, Leon leaped from the boat and dashed to his truck, seized his suitcase and dumped the contents in the road. He pawed through a heap of gaunchies, shaving gear, paper-back westerns, a deck of condoms, dirty socks, a half-empty mickey of vodka—all the stuff a man is apt to carry when he packs in a hurry. He found the plug and dashed for his boat. Waist-deep in the bilges, he inserted the plug as the waters of Lambent Channel washed over the transom and sunk *Leon's Baby* in four feet of water. Up to his chest, Leon stood in deep contemplation as the guffawing, cheering crowds drove their vehicles over his suitcase and its contents.

It was a real wowser and I laughed so hard I had to park the truck, fall down, roll on the ground and even piss my pants.

When I could breathe again, I observed that another man had gotten out of a shiny, late-model car parked in the ferry lineup and sat on a road-post, also howling with laughter. At first I didn't recognize him but his laugh gave him away. It was Moonshine Mcintyre, shaved and bathed and dressed in a snappy chalk-striped suit and tie.

"Jesus. Moonshine, is that you?" I asked.

"Did you ever see anything like that?" he said.

Yes, it was indeed Moonshine. I said, "What's gotten into you? You're all spiffed up, and that car! What happened to your old pickup?"

"I rented the car," Moonshine said. "Got a little business in town."

The ferry crew raised the gate and turned on the green light. The off-island traffic started to load.

"I guess I'd better go," Moonshine said. He stuck his hand out to me. "Well, old man, it's been real. Maybe I'll see you someday."

I shook his hand. "But, Moonshine, where are you going? What do you mean 'someday?'"

"I mean someday," he said briefly. "I'm going abroad."

"Abroad! Where?"

"I'd prefer not to say," Moonshine said. "But give it a few days and you'll figure it out." He drove onto the ferry.

It wasn't until the ferry had pulled out that I realized he hadn't said anything resembling: "Man, like it was that—"

Thelma drove up in the Beluga. Leon was always able to appreciate a joke, even one on himself. When the shock of the cold water had worn off, he, too, roared with laughter, louder than any of us. When Thelma was sure Leon's laughter was genuine, not a shield for hurt pride, her guffaws outdid everyone, even as she pitched in and helped Leon beach and drain his boat.

There are those who say Leon's spirit was broken by the boat fiasco, but I don't believe it for a minute. I think the belly laugh reminded both Leon and Thelma how much fun life could be if they weren't busting their humps to pay off a bank. A few days later, I was having a quiet pint at the Pub. I was the only one seated close to the bar, all the rest were at the tables by the windows overlooking the water. Leon came over and sat down. "Well," he said, "we're going to pack it in."

"You're kidding!" I said.

"Nope. After we figured out how much money we were making, what with the mortgage and all, we're working for less than minimum wage. Me, I'd rather go fishing."

"I'll be damned!" I said. Thelma came out of the kitchen to suck down a cigarette. "Is this true, Thelma?" I called. "Are you guys really quitting?"

"You bet!" she said. "I can't wait to see the last of this hole. I got a book to write. Going to straighten out the political history of this God-damned Province."

***

A representative of the bank, one Daryl Griebe, came out to close up the Pub, or at least watch the bank's janitor do the job. This time they called me in to shut down the refrigeration machinery and the furnace and drain the pumps and plumbing. The furnace and pumps were right up my alley and maybe I'm not the best refrigeration man in the world but I could fake it. The janitor was all right, I guess. He nailed up the plywood and planted the "For Sale—Fabulous Business Opportunity for the Handyman/Entrepreneur" sign in the grass patch out front, right beside the stove-in skiff planted full of geraniums. I don't suppose the janitor could help working for the bank, I mean, a job's a job and probably his paychecks seldom bounced.

But that banker now, Daryl to his friends (if there were any), Mr. Griebe to me, he was something else.

"Hurry it up, will you?" Mr. Griebe said. "We're paying you by the hour and we're *not* made of *money*."

No mechanic can resist that kind of provocation so I slowed up about fifty percent and moved like cold molasses. I was working in the men's room. "Sorry, Mr. Griebe," I said. "I'm a poor dumb country boy and a job like this takes me a lot of time." I started to whistle the *Too Fat Polka*—drives 'em up the wall if you're cheerful.

Griebe delivered a whining soliloquy as I slowly drained the plumbing. "It's just *impossible* to do business with you island people. You've just got *no* sense of fiscal responsibility at all. Like these Buckler people, they just *don't* understand how to do business."

"Is that a fact?" I drawled. I used a lube gun to suck the water out of the traps and blow it into a bucket.

"We didn't take enough of a down payment from those Bucklers and it doesn't appear that they're actionable. They'll get out without it costing them hardly *anything*. And they had the *unmitigated gall* to tell me to 'shove this joint up your ass.' I ask you!"

"No shit?" I said. I picked up the bucket and my tool box, headed out of the men's room and into the woman's. Griebe followed me.

"If I'd had *my* way, we'd have made them sign over *everything* they *owned* when they first took on the contract." Griebe said. "Is that so?" I said. I started pumping the water out of the traps.

"Yes. That *is* so," Griebe snapped. "Why are you playing around with that squirt-gun?"

"I'm draining the traps, Mr. Griebe," I said. "You want the furnace turned off. If we get a freeze, the plumbing might get busted."

"Whatever," he said. "But snap it up, will you? I want to catch the *next* ferry."

"Roger, Mr. Griebe," I said. "But I'm already working as fast as I can." I slowed up another notch.

"It's absolutely *ridiculous*. I told the manager he should *demand* more collateral. If they'd listened to *me,* we'd be foreclosing on those Buckler people right now and taking everything they own. But I suppose there'd have been trouble, maybe even violence. People like that just don't understand banking. But perhaps I'm being too hard on you people, at least *some* of you are *real* businessmen."

"We are, huh?" I asked. "Like who, for instance?"

"Why, like Captain Mcintyre, of Mcintyre Fish Corporation, for instance."

"Captain Mcintyre!" I yelled. But Griebe didn't notice my amazement.

"Yes. When Captain Mcintyre moved his fishing fleet here from the East, he needed interim financing, about half a million dollars."

"HALF A MILLION DOLLARS!" I shouted. But Griebe still didn't notice. I doubt he'd have noticed if his dick was in a meat grinder unless you wrote him a letter.

"When I mentioned collateral, he didn't bat an eye," Griebe continued smugly. "As casually as you or I would light a cigarette, he tossed the registration papers for his *whole fleet* on the desk—worth ten or twenty *million* if it's worth a *penny*. 'Will that do?' he asked me—"

***

A couple of weeks later, Mr. Griebe telephoned me. Casually he asked if I'd seen "Captain Mcintyre."
"Not recently, Mr. Griebe," I said. "But he must be around somewhere."
"His boats—ah—they're still moored at the island, aren't they?" he asked.
"Oh yeah."
He sounded relieved. I didn't bother to tell him that all the boats had sunk and were firmly moored to the bottom. Why spoil his fun? Let him find out for himself.

***

It wasn't more than two weeks before the bank found another sucker to buy the Pub: a couple of would-be yuppies from Port Alberni. They went in for the trendy effect: long gingham dresses on the waitresses, quiches, potted plastic ivy and chilled white wine.
Of course, the Californians came back and wouldn't you know it? Their cheques began to bounce. The Royal Canadian Mounted Police came and dragged the two men away; they weren't producers, they were dope dealers. The two beautiful blonde women turned out to be transvestites from Medicine Hat, got in a cat-fight in the ladies room and left the island the next day without paying their bar bill. The Kid? The Adonis in the purple sweat-suit? Hell, he wasn't a kid at all, but a forty-eight-year-old ex-jockey with a lift on his face, a boyish rug on his head and also on the dodge from the law: statutory rape, bicycle theft, fraud, barratry, pandering, coinage, *lèse majesté*, pig-fucking—sort of a jack-of-all-trades, you might say, and he, too, was plucked from the island by the RCMP as easily as a hotel chef would scoop a poached egg from a pan of boiling water.

***

Some afternoons Leon and Thelma stop by the bar for a quickie. No regrets. They're happy to sit by the window and guzzle while Thelma talks bright-red politics and Leon watches the current ham-handed klutz of a Government ferry skipper bash his way into the slip.
Splinters fly; the tortured pilings groan.
"Pitiful. Just pitiful," Leon says and shakes his head. "Poor bastard couldn't handle a Celluloid duck in a bathtub let alone a piss-ant ferry in a calm sea. I'll tell you, Charlie, if I couldn't handle a boat any better than that, I'd kiss your ass on the courthouse steps and give you twenty minutes to draw a crowd."

Semejanzas

Graciela Guzmán

Te pregunté si alguna vez
tus alas se extendieron
para tropezar con el aire
que no respira la gente

si el despertador de la luz
era un diálogo entre palomas
o un agudo grito a la maldición
de encontrarte siempre de golpe
con otro día
de tiras color de ayer

si el hastio
no te ha destejido la piel
para anidar una eterna desespera

si las estrellas
nunca han besado
el azul de tus plumas

si tienes hijos
de la soledad

El silencio
me dio la respuesta
        eres un pájaro tan muerto
        como un cadáver desenterrado

Resemblances

Sandra Gail Teichmann - Translator
Graciela Guzmán - Poet

I ask you if some time
your wings extended
to collide with the air
which people do not breathe

if the awakener of the light
was a dialogue between pigeons
or a sharp cry to the curse
of always meeting you suddenly
with another day
of stripes, colored of yesterday

if the loathing
has not unknit your skin
for harboring an eternal despair

if the stars
have never kissed
the blue of your feathers

if you have sons
of solitude

The silence
gave me the answer
                you are a bird as dead
                as an unearthed corpse

At the Continental Divide

Diana Abu-Jaber

All the people he had ever loved came up to him laughing, telling him about betrayals they had committed against him. He had struck at them, trying to stop them from speaking. He was slapping his uncle and begging him, "Stop, please don't tell me! Don't tell me!"

Jamil is exhausted by this dream and for some minutes can only lie flat on his bed.

Aunt Helwa comes into the room and asks if he is sick. Since he has begun working she is sure that he will become ill.

"No, I'm fine, just fine," he says in Arabic.

Helwa, despite having lived in the United States for three years, speaks almost exclusively Arabic. She clicks in the back of her throat to her nephew. She knows that when you move to America things turn glassy, as if they were submerged in water. Among Americans, deprived of language, she loses her thoughts. She worries about this nephew of hers, her younger sister's child.

She has stood in the parking lot of the mall when the lights come on, turning the night to silver, standing among the dirty cars, looking at the sign seven feet tall, fifteen feet across that lights up the words: "Crossways Mall," the wattage passing through her.

She puts one hand on Jamil's arm.

"Auntie! Enough!" he says. "Leave me alone now. I have to get dressed for work."

She looks at him. "Such an American now, Jamil, I'm not allowed to see your body! Listen, I stood you in my sink and bathed you."

He waits until she leaves the room and resumes dressing. He likes buttoning his white dress shirt up, feeling the boiled cotton, full cuffs, one button against his trachea.

He likes his new job, his first, to which the train spirits him away. The New York-suburban sky. Hurtling over the elevated platform from Old Westbury to Crossways, the light comes through shutter slats and chain-links, through the maple, oak, and near- hysterical sparrows, cardinals, and piercing blue jays. All this in the morning, pressed in a car in the perfume of American business suits, grey flannel and navy pinstripe.

He goes to this work as joyfully as a lover to his tryst, crossing foggy streets, the bite of air heightening his ardor. From the office window, adjacent to his station on the sixth floor, men's sportswear, Bloomingdale's in the Crossways Mall, he can look out and see doves fluttering like human palms, up into the eaves of the building across from them. Often birds sail by at eye level.

Jamil loves this rush toward work. He feels as if he could live on a crust of bread, a bit of honey, and the burnt sun through the train windows, stippling the backs of heads, illuminating a hand, striking one eye, lighting it to its purest colors.

Jamil has another sort of work, which may begin on the train or as Jamil stops before the mirrored wall in the employee's men's room. Checking each detail, the bulge of his tie, his oiled hair, Jamil will realize that it is his own hand he admires, so well-molded and shirred with light. He relieves himself at the urinal and his body fills with music. Jamil writes his poetry anywhere, on the backs of receipts and dress tickets and inventory sheets:

Oh my love, is that the South-wind that I taste?
Or the burnish of your auburn hair?

He began to write poetry when he was newly immigrated and enrolled in his first English language class. He loved the sounds of "burnish" and "auburn," by the images of "wind," as well as "lips," "glass," "cry," all of which suggested things more glorious and intense than the words they became in Arabic.

He loves working because it takes him away from the boredom of his uncle's house. But Jamil is also lazy, raised not to serve but to be served. He dislikes reading price tags, having to touch men through new wool, having to march along carrying armloads of suits behind their wives. Men are brought in wearing bermuda shorts, hairy legs displayed for all the world to see, ragged nylon socks, orange golfing slacks, pant cuffs whipping around inches above the ankle. He dislikes handling the money that is given to him, often by women, turned over between buff fingernails, the women's eyes barely even registering him, or else stopping on him suddenly. Then sometimes he likes it, slipping purchases into bags as the women watch his handiwork. He makes one perfect crease in the paper, tufts of receipts floating inside.

Handing over this bit of art, he smiles, lowering his eyes; he knows that American women will sometimes look back. This enthralls him; sometimes he hears their voices:

"Thank you, young man."

Sometimes they read the name on his store tag: "Thank you, Jaimie."

He imagines them saying, "What beautiful brown eyes you have Jaimie! And *look* at those hands, those are the hands of a king or a poet, or of a *man*, a true man. You shouldn't be here, you belong in my house, among the furniture and carpets and the beautiful flowers that fill with star light. . . ."

Sometimes he is so lazy that he doesn't even enjoy writing. He would prefer to let the poetry rise in him as he lifts his stream of urine. Yet he knows he *must* write it down, that this is the only way that people will come to love him. But sometimes this recognition of others seems remote. Sometimes, downstairs in the store's basement tavern after work, he contemplates his beer, or at his uncle's house, sinking into Uncle Nezar's recliner when no one else is home, suddenly Jamil aches for fame and the longing turns to fury. Suddenly his job is unbearable and insulting. And all this, boiling in him, he turns to poetry, willing those words into steam.

> A woman, you are a poker
> You touch red coals
> You are an ember
> A piece of wood on fire.

Helwa means "beautiful" in Arabic. She can never forgive her mother for that preposterous name. Not that she was not once beautiful as all the young are, but simply that this name made her invisible. Suitors came to her father's house when she was fourteen; but there was never any Helwa there, only the perfume of *beautiful*.

She was fifteen when she was paired with her cousin Nezar, who was thirty and who had done great things in business and agriculture with his portion of the family's money. The girlchild that was married is lost. There may or may not have been a girl with pinned-up hair, the skin of figs. Her aunts and uncles, her parents, her husband, and eventually even her only sister, Jasmine, blamed her childless marriage on her selfishness.

"Who will my oldest marry if you don't give me a daughter!" Jasmine demanded, speaking of her then six-year-old son, Jamil.

Nezar brought in Father Malgreb, the priest of their Syrian Orthodox church, to speak with Helwa.

"The spirits of your unborn are filling you, my daughter. Those babies are crying out, asking for life."

They sat in the living room on the couch that Jamil had imported from America.

"They're crying for you to give birth to them. At night you won't be able to sleep because of their crying, Helwa. Believe me, I've seen this very thing before," he said, taking her hand into his. "You know your own body must eventually erode, all this beauty will eat into your skin. Only your babies can make you immortal on this earth. You must welcome your husband into your bed. It's right for you to find life in his arms. You must let the eggs go, set them free."

And every night she buried her husband in herself, in darkness bruised only by the moon. And while it was true she could not sleep, she couldn't hear children inside her either. She listened, eyes open, hearing nothing. She was afraid of death, even in her sleeping husband's arms, realizing that the risings and fallings of his breath were numbered.

She realizes now, years later, that only by leaving could she truly be *Helwa* to them. Then they could remember the girl with eyes like Turkish coffee. She never gave birth, so, she would remain a girl in people's memories. Then Nezar took them away to this other place. Despite their inability to have children, Nezar loved her more and more. He was a man with a secret pleasure, guarding it and taking it where no one else could see.

Helwa stands before a wall mirror, screwing the back on to one of her hoop earrings. Her earlobes are distended from the weight of the gold that she wears. Nezar watches her from the edge of the bed. He sees the rise of her breast as she touches her ear. She wears the jewelry for him; there is no one else to see it.

She turns her back to the mirror.

"Ah tini basra," he says to her, *kiss me.*

She goes to him. Her eyes close as they touch lips; she smells the woody smell of him, his hands and the skin of his face turned hard. He cradles her.

"I would like you to bring a wife over for Jamil now," she says to him.

Nezar stares at her a moment before releasing her. "Jamil has only been here five—or is it six—months," he says. "Do you suppose he is ready for wives already? Remember, I had to reach thirty before I could take you."

"That's because you wanted a prize—you wanted *me,* not to mention my age. Jamil is a man now and I'm afraid for him alone in this country."

Nezar looks around the room, glancing at the windows and mirrors. Then he asks, "*Is* there a wife already, my love? Someone you have selected perhaps?"

Helwa lifts her chin. "There is someone," she says.

***

Nejila touches the glass of her window. They are up where she always thought Heaven was, but above the fish-scale clouds is only more sky. Awakening, she finds she has lost all sense of time and feels that, rather than moving forward, they must have been rising straight up, where clouds press glittering against the plane.

Her eyes and throat are dry. She can't understand what is happening to her. She is losing the moisture in her body, drying up, though she is only nineteen. Perhaps she will dissolve into particles when her cousin embraces her at the airport. This is the curse that betrayed her Aunt Helwa that her mother told her about, whispering to Nejila that Helwa "was beautiful in face, but inside, here," pressing one finger below her stomach, "she was wasted, and no life could ever come from her, only through the children of her sister."

Nejila was the daughter of Helwa's first cousin. As a young girl, Nejila wished to be like this aunt whom she had only glimpsed. Draping her hair around her throat and posing in the mirrors in her parents' room, she wished she too was enchanted, living only for herself. All her aunts and her mother's friends prized babies over love and beauty! They were jealous. Why should *she* care about babies, all that shit and vomit? Nejila would turn in the mirror and look at one angle, then turn to the other side, peer at the slits of her eyes.

But now. She clasps both hands over her mouth. Why, why, why now? She can feel her womb drying inside her. When she lands on the other side she will be weightless.

In descent, the walls of her stomach begin climbing. A stewardess notices the panic in Nejila's face; she comes to her and offers water and candies.

***

The trees remind Jamil of belly dancers, blue spruce turned black in the sky around his uncle's house. His aunt and uncle would not let him go with them to the airport. The trees line the perimeter of the lawn and the long drive to the semi-circle before the front door. They shiver in the rainy wind like conjurers, creating this October evening from the points of their limbs, their spiked tops toward the sky. Rain travels the air, sparse and icy, sometimes touching Jamil's lips. He stands in the middle of the drive, letting it pass through him. Like fragments of his dreams, the bodies bent over him, a dreamed hand that parts his lips or passes over his throat.

He can't imagine what she will look like. The smell of leaves reaches him from another field, rushing to his head; he burrows into it.

The car arrives and Jamil can barely see through the watery air, watching the car mount the drive. He sees shadows in the rain-stained windows, but when the first door opens it is only Aunt Helwa, pressing her head and shoulders into the spine of an umbrella.

"Jamil!" she shrieks at him. "Mother of God, what are you doing out here! *Look* at yourself. You want to frighten your cousin to death after she's come so far?" She shouts at him under the umbrella as the rain gathers around them. "Get inside and fix yourself right now!"

Behind her the garage door opens automatically and the car disappears inside. Jamil realizes that his good suit has wilted on him and the wind has molded the wet cloth to his body, the French cuffs hanging like banners. He has embarrassed himself. The wind soaks him and pounds onto the patio.

***

Nejila looks at his hand as it rests on the table while they eat. Its honeyed color seems in place among the food her aunt has laid out. She watches the hand as it takes up a bowl of rice, the grains white against the skin, and only then does she look at him.
A husband! This man is to be held to her heart, let into her body. She can barely take it all in as he looks up from the plate of rice.
Across the table she sees Aunt Helwa nodding to her.
She is shaking ever so slightly. Desire coming in her acceptance of the thing. I will give myself, I accept, I surrender, I give myself up. I submit to what is decided.

***

Jamil finds his poetry in the mail, returned, nearly every day, his manilla envelopes, his own handwriting, his stamps. The note, if there is one, no bigger than a cash receipt, imprinted with the bitter words, "we cannot," "unfortunately," "regret," "not suitable," and, "at this time." As if the time would ever change! As if time could change words, so eventually someone would recognize the thing of beauty there. He drops the envelope on the dresser, the pages inside still fresh.
Going outside he sees that the trees have given up their leaves, fallen in the shower and forming a carpet. Down the block there are baseball players practicing in the drizzle; Jamil watches them from the chain-link fence that surrounds the field. The grass is dirty and mud smears the players' hips and arms. He hears music emerging from the field, a radio piped over the P.A. It is top-40 music, songs about love. The young men, perhaps college players, move gently, hands tilted to the ball.
It seems to Jamil that all things on this earth except for himself are allowed to create beauty. He thinks of the blond path of leaves that he had admired as he left the house—the handiwork of some egotistical God who takes all for Himself and leaves nothing for Jamil.
Again, the man on the field lifts his leg. Leaning back, his arm follows his back into a symmetry and poise, and breaking this, moves forward into the whip of the ball. Jamil is fascinated by their uniforms, outlining the thigh, the upper arm, alluring because of their mystery.
Back at home he finds his new wife in their bedroom brushing her hair. It is Sunday, after dinner, before evening, a lull. Her hair is longer, blacker than American hair, the strands spilling off the brush's sable.

Something moves him toward her, draws his hand to the hair, the repetition of the brush. She stops and turns. There is nothing about her that is not glorious, the eyes deep as a swami's, her skin and the fragrance which clings to it, which he has smelled in lying beside her. Yet he still can't bring himself to do it; he won't touch her.

Jamil greets her in Arabic, still the only language she speaks, and she lifts her hand to him. "Hello, my husband," she says.

He sits beside her on the bed, his fingers touching hers. "Do you like it here, Nejila? Tell me, are you happy in this country?"

He sees a falling movement in her eyes.

"I am happy being anywhere that you are," she says at last.

Jamil stares, moved by a desire to protect her. "Ah na bahebec," he says, stirred. *I love you, I love you.* But he can't fight these things that seem thrown between him and his feeling. He can only repeat words, "Ah na bahebec."

***

When Nejila is left alone long enough, she almost forgets that she exists. She drifts through her uncle's house, feet not feeling the floor. Thoughts pour through her.

She thinks this must be how a ghost feels, able to create noise and fear. She wonders if she has indeed dried up. At night in bed, Jamil looks at her across the pillows, but his fingers creep back into his hands. Perhaps she is a ghost and no one tells her.

Sometimes Helwa sees the fear in her niece's eyes and she remembers something about herself, from years ago. She takes Nejila shopping in the supermarkets for each night's dinner. The lights there pare everything away. Nejila hangs over the sea of produce, egg plants and onions, fruits shined into precious stones. They drift through the rows and Nejila feels blinded, her body heavy with the shining.

But often that is only half their day. Two or three times a week they drive to one of the shopping malls and look for shoes and dresses for Nejila. Helwa dresses her up, finding clothes that will barely fit around her narrow body.

"Wait until you have babies," Helwa says, patting her own belly as if speaking from experience. She runs her fingers along the materials. "Now is the time to show off what you have. After the babies there won't be much left."

Almost every time they go, Helwa buys something new for Nejila. They walk along the doorways and store fronts, the corridors stretching into a galaxy.

***

One day a group of nuns in floor-length habits comes into men's sportswear and Jamil stands behind the register, his hand barely touching the keys, watching them as if they were birds. Yards of cotton obscure their form, hair drawn into the material. He is reminded of birds he has seen rising over New York swamps, eyes flitting away, beaks opening, their call emanating from the air around them. These women finger the men's fabrics, lips moving, the words invisible, Jamil supposes, like prayer, bursts of steam understood only by God.

On his break Jamil drifts after the security guards that monitor the corridors of the mall.

He writes more poems on paper bags and hides them away, feeling that Nejila must not see them. He walks the halls, wanting the men in their guard outfits. How can he open to his young wife, show her this thing at his heart? When he sees her lying there alone on the bed, whorled into herself, how can he disturb such an arrangement?

***

Nejila turns to look up into the baseball player's face. He is asking something and the words stir around, broken and pointed as she has always found English to be. Then when he repeats himself, the words begin to attach to remembered patterns, the TV news her uncle watches at night, overheard conversations in the malls and stores, the occasional English between Jamil and Uncle Nezar, words catching into strands, some meaning: "Where do you live?"

The sound is difficult to her, she tests it in her mouth. Then, leaping over a chasm, she trusts to the beaming face and attempts a new language: "You play, yes?"

A baseball flies out, dazzling against the blue. They watch it fall, he on one side of the field's chain link fence, she on the other.

"You can't hardly speak English, can you?" he says. "Damn, you're some looker, sweetcakes."

She feels like she is going crazy; she is not even supposed to leave the house.

"Your name?" he says. "Name?" He points to himself and says, "Dell."

She nods, laughing, understanding more than he thinks she does. "Name, Nejila."

The rings of the chain-link catch the sun, the gleam running through his fingers like a bolt of lightning, and he scales it in one leap.

"They won't mind if I skip out on the rest of the game," he says.

He is big, and as he walks beside her, she is drawn to him, to his great size, the strength he seems to emanate, toward the resonance of the dozens of American westerns she's seen dubbed in Arabic. John Wayne. His eyes hold the sky's blue, urging her to fall, letting the pieces fly.

"I could teach you English," he says. "I'll show you around, Honey."

***

"'Why doesn't she write to me?'" Nezar reads to his wife from her mail. "'Is she so happy there? And her new husband? Will she be giving us a baby?'"

"God, that woman has questions," Helwa says, sighing and stretching over the bed. "All the time, questions!"

Nezar takes a handful of his wife's hair. It fills his palm with black glow. He asks, "*Is* Nejila happy? Do you know if she likes him?"

"I don't think she is pregnant," she says. "That's all I know right now. I can hardly get anything out of the child at all. She's always so quiet and withdrawn. Who knows what she might be thinking about?"

Jamil stays late at work and Nejila looks for excuses to slip out of the house during the day; she claims to need air. But when Helwa looks for her out the kitchen window, she sees the lawn chairs left empty. The air echoes with frost, etching the sky. The sidewalks are frost-stenciled.

Helwa looks out the kitchen window and a wind sweeps over the walkways and streets, and beyond to those fields where the ground is rutted and impenetrable. She can't understand this failure of theirs to conceive.

***

I look at you—
A boxful of chrysanthemums.
The thought has taken hold of me
Of you, your eyes, that follow like the wild geese.
My spirit raises and abandons itself.

Waking briefly at dawn, Jamil glimpsed Nejila before the bedroom window, turning, the sun splintering her hair, and her posture—merely the tilt of her head and model of her hands—was enough to make him suddenly feel desire before slipping back to sleep. Later, at work, when he takes up his pen the memory strikes him and he writes.

A boxful of chrysanthemums
Your hands opening themselves to me
The white stems of your wrists
Your eyes following the air
Turning to the center of this country.

He stares at his words, unsure what to do with this unruly poem. What does it lead to? It seems womanly, graceful in disarray. Then he notices his boss, Mr. Bethesda, standing in the office door, arms folded and watching.

Jamil puts down the pen and paper bag, his heart thumping. There are no customers in the sportswear department, but Jamil feels he has been caught out.

Mr. Bethesda comes forward, raising his hand and saying, "No, no—please—I don't mean to interrupt, I was just watching—"

"No, no—" Jamil is shaking his head, fumbling with the paper and pen. "This is—this is nothing."

Mr. Bethesda stops at the counter, looking at Jamil sadly and smiling. For a minute he does not speak, then he says, "You spend a lot of time alone, don't you Jaimie? Writing that poetry and stuff?"

Jamil is shaking his head, eyes lowered, stuffing the scrap of paper into his pocket.

"Why don't you let me take you to a real bar tonight. Instead of spending all your time at that chintzy joint downstairs? Come on, we'll take you some place good, show you a good, American time."

Jamil doesn't know where to look; sweat starts in his palms and slides down his fingers. "A bar? I don't know, I don't know—I've never—my uncle—"

"Your uncle—bullshit!" Mr. Bethesda shouts in a laugh, slapping Jamil on the back. "Fine! This'll be fine."

***

By five p.m. the sun is skimming the tops of the houses, a curtain just above the earth. The light makes the whole day seem as if it were always late afternoon, and the shadows trail every object.

Nejila and Helwa sit together at the kitchen table, flipping through the pages of a Bloomingdale's catalogue—one that Jamil has brought home from work. But Jamil is not home yet, and the light is beginning to dissolve. Still, Helwa resists leaning over to put on the overhead lamp; to do so would be to admit to the arrival of evening, the time that Jamil should be home, but almost never is anymore. This is also the time that, lately, Nejila will want to go out, alone in the evening.

Helwa does not speak her suspicions. The one time she insisted upon accompanying her niece, Nejila was silent and angry throughout the walk, her eyes frozen to the space ahead of her. So now Helwa merely waves her on. What would Nejila's mother, her cousin, think if she knew about these walks? Or Nezar? Or, worst, if Jamil should return early one day and find that Nejila was out and alone?

Nejila is beginning to look around, she fidgets with the page, she checks her watch.

"I think I'll go out for a short walk," she says.

Helwa grabs her wrist. "Wait." No! Not this time, she almost says, and she holds her niece a second. But Nejila's look is merely incredulous as she backs away. She removes herself. Then she is gone.

***

A light snow begins to sprinkle around her as she runs. Her breath puffs out in front of her, her insubstantial boots crunch on the sand the neighbors have spread. Already her fingertips are icy and she curls them in a ball and presses them to her sides inside the lining of the cashmere coat Helwa bought for her.

Then she sees him. He waits by the streetlight three blocks away, leaning against it. But she feels the blood intensifying between them as she runs to him, hungry, frantic for him. His arms catch her, she stands on tip toes, arching into the embrace of his mouth, his neck. She hangs on, something moving inside her, his hands playing up and down her spine, her body.

Dell is from Montana, he has told her. Nevada, Arizona, Utah, Wyoming, he names these places and the light in his eyes dwindles to pinpoints of longing. Tonight they hold hands across the table of a coffee shop and he tells her about rivers that plummet down the sides of mountains, about standing inside a basin of rocks, reading the side of the earth, taking in every spangle of light that charges over the buttes, flying like the ghosts of warriors. He plays baseball professionally. He was traded to a New York team, minor league. When he speaks of his hometown his eyes darken, when he tells her about the colors in a canyon wall, or the way mountains will float over the horizon. His favorite place is the prairies, where rivers run interlacing, the railroad coursing through corn and wheat, a bull snake half-hidden and level, as far as the eye can see.

Nejila, leaning into him as they leave, tries to imagine all this, but all she can see is the New York night around her, snow shuddering down its sides. She thinks of his prairie, land of vanishing points, and, taking his hands, falls faster.

"It's a lot quieter, but things are a lot more beautiful out there," he tells her. He turns her palms up to be kissed. They are iced by the air. In the shelter of a store-front he marvels first over the pink of her palms, at the way her fingers turn back at their tips. And her face, when he takes it in his hands, is small and pointed.

"Not everyone can appreciate the plains," he says. "Folks are stupid. They can't see the little things. Believe me, Nellie, darlin, it's the best place in the world."

And then it is time for her to run back home, bounding over the curbs and landing in puddles that splatter, catching the neon of the storefronts and the stars.

***

The beer shimmers in his mug. When Jamil's coworkers lean over their glasses their faces become more mysterious and closed. Nothing is easy to see in this place: women drift by, their skin and hair amorphous. Jamil watches them, these American women, as they lean

against the bar, trailing scent.
"You like American girls?" Mr. Bethesda asks in a voice that is warning and invitation.
Jamil half shrugs, disconcerted, looking down. The men at the table laugh. Alan from Housewares and Pete from Young Men's are also at their table. Jamil has always admired them. Beer and the taste of smoke move into his thoughts, floating up a sea of images. The words on his cocktail napkin look like Arabic and English. In Jordan he was a man, straight and well-formed. Here at this table he is conscious of his lashes, like a girl's, his lips full and soft, his eyes weak.

When he goes to the bar for another round he sees that he is being observed. Women line the bar, looking, folding over the counter, backs of the hands to their cheeks. They bend forward, their eyes seeking his. Then one of them, touching him on the back, says, "Would you get the bartender for me? He doesn't seem to pay much attention to us girls."

Her eyes are a light, American blue. Jamil feels the men back at the table watching, urging him: *Go on! Go for it! Let's see if you can.* Her fingers, turned in against a glass of beer, are painted red at the nails, the knuckles white.

***

Later, when she opens to him on the couch of her housemate asleep in the next room, her inner thighs are slippery, drained. Nejila's beauty rustles in his mind, the color of earth. This other woman is coarse, sickly in comparison, and this excites him and he seizes her legs in his hands and possesses her, moving until the couch thuds against the wall. Then, just as quickly, he is done and he slips from her. In a second of zipping up his pants and finding his coat, he moves to the door, but not before seeing the pulse in one of her eyelids as she closes her eyes. He had asked her name over and over, until she was offended, but for some reason it would not stay in his mind and now it slips from him again as he sheds her and enters the night, running from the building.

***

They enter their uncle's house at different doors, Nejila only moments before Jamil. Immediately Helwa covers the table with plates of food. The children look like animals from the woods. Beyond the picture window the sunset outlines the hills and the fir-covered mountains.

Jamil does not appear to notice that Nejila has, like himself, just returned to the house. Her moist coat is thrown over one of the extra chairs in the dining room and Jamil places his over hers. He helps his wife into her chair. Helwa notices her niece's face. She hands the serving fork to Nejila. Her niece looks at her.

"Why don't *you* serve your husband tonight, habeebi?" Helwa says to her.

Seating himself, Jamil looks at his plate. "Yes, tonight I would like to eat only the food that my wife has prepared."

The two women look at each other. Helwa has not allowed Nejila to assist in the preparation of any of the meals. Now she is ashamed of this and, glancing at Nejila, pretends to smile and says, "Tonight Nejila made the rice."

Jamil nods and Nejila silently takes the serving spoon. The rice fills the whole tureen. On top it is sprinkled with cinnamon and pignolia nuts fried in butter. She heaps it on his plate. Jamil concentrates on rice.

***

He follows her from the table, down the corridor between the rooms. She is going to take her bath as she always does this time of evening, but when she reaches the bathroom, he walks in ahead of her, squatting by the tub and twisting its knobs so plumes of steam form in the air. Nejila hesitates a moment, then undresses.

She unfastens her sweater, her fingers running down the buttons, her skirt undoing easily with a hook at the back. She slides off her shoes, bra, and panty hose. Then, naked, she steps quickly into the bath. She lets Jamil pour the water over her from his hands, sweep the lather over her neck and belly. She feels removed, careless about the shine on her shoulders, indifferent to the way her husband looks at her. His hand in the washcloth slips down her thigh as she stands; he wraps a towel around her.

They walk to their bedroom and Jamil takes her shoulders, willing himself to possess her. When he pulls her in, putting his lips on hers, she stares ahead.

"Ah Nejila," he whispers. "Ya habeebi, ah na bahebec, ah na bahebec!" Then he pulls away, looking at her. "And I am so helpless," he says in English. "I am not a husband, I know. I know what you must think. There you are, so beautiful and untouched. You must understand somehow you are—this all is—impossible for me."

He uses English to cloak his thoughts from her, which he does whenever he does not wish her to understand, unable to keep from letting her feel the weight of his voice. "Still, I *must* have you as my wife. That much is clear to me, I have claimed you in my heart as mine."

Only then, for the first time all evening, does Nejila look directly at him.

Perhaps he suspected all along that she was learning the language, perhaps that is why he chose at that moment to say such a thing. Her glance gives her away. They look at each other and there is nothing for her to do now but answer.

"And so what—what—*rights*—do you believe you have over me?" she says, and her English is slow but clear and accurate. "Do you believe that you—*own* me?"

"Ah, so you are spoiled now," Jamil says. He covers his face with his hands for a moment without speaking, then looks up. "I can hear it in your voice, already. I should have guessed this would happen. I don't know how you learned so quickly. Now you are as polluted as any American woman out there. I'd like to know now how you dare to do this in the first place, to learn this language without consulting me?"

"You are not my husband," Nejila says, her breath going high. "You don't know anything about me!"

Jamil stares at her, then a look, a kind of relief passes over his face, the look of someone passing into unconsciousness. In the next second he strikes Nejila with an open hand, all his anger going into that blow, and as she flies backward he grabs her with the other hand to strike again, her head tossing. She is limp; her body has in fact caught something of this same relief, passing beyond pain to a kind of joy. She can barely see through the blur of tears and the heat filling her mouth; he is shaking her so at last her knees and arms crumble. She is becoming dust, particles. In the midst of all this, a laughter that opens, and when he slams her against the wall, she falls into that space.

***

Poetry! How Jamil loves the language, falling as if in dance around him. As he walks into town he experiences all over the baptism of his violence. This is the force that makes language sing. Tonight the streets, iced and shorn of snow, show the moon to Jamil; he rises through them, his sense of poetry confused with the stars, floating clouds, the night spinning.

There are many restaurants and taverns open in the town and as he walks among them he can't remember which he visited earlier that day. The town is changed. He feels something like love, like being madly in love. The exhilaration is so great it feeds on itself, moving through his entrails.

"I *do* love you," he murmurs, he is looking at a green shade over a pool table, a bar mottled by light, and the half-people that wander in and out. Faces flicker, altering as they move, people lift glasses, bow their heads at the bar, under the canopy of hanging glasses.

And then someone is at his arm, asking for a light, guiding him to that bar with all its brass fixtures, the bottles glowing with their colored hearts like devils.

***

Nejila did not cry out as she was beaten, but the back of her head hitting the wall sent out a loud, low thud that ran through the house. She feels now she is in a tunnel and its length rings with voices and the sound

of her breath rushes in her like wind. She hears singing, it is he! She sees his face, the lips forming words:
 "'Hang your head over, give my heart ease.'"
 I put my hands around his neck and I am bereft, she thinks. There is nothing for me to feel, I am so empty, I have let go of everything, utterly everything in my life just to touch him, even for a second. My head fills with sentimental songs, children's games. He sings and sings and won't stop, as if he knows he is carrying me away. His eyes move so slowly, how do I begin?
 "'But remember the Red River valley—'"
 She is laughing with his hands as they move over her body. They are toughened by the leather of the glove; they move over her. Now he is touching her shoulder, now he and Nejila are in his bed. It is once more the first and only time she has slept with him and there is his surprise again, almost an anger, at the sight of the web of blood left between her thighs when they are finished.
 "My God," he is saying. "God is it me? You never told me. I'll be goddammed."
 She wants to say it in his language, to feel it in his language, the way they do in this new world. The meanings of "love" and of "*baheb*" are not the same, they cross and intersect. She speaks to him, not wholly understanding her meaning, saying, "but I love you."
 Again his fingers are moving. She is on her belly and his hands come around cupping her breasts, he presses his words into her ear, the nape of her neck. "There are mountains in the West, named for a woman's bosoms." His hands move back along her shoulders then into her hair. "This hair of yours, so damn shiny," he says. "You know, when you walk into the corn, when they're tall, at their peak, you don't know where you are. You get lost and the stalks sway in the wind and make a sound like the ocean."
 Then his hands fall to her back, tracing the wings of her muscles. "And this is the great range, this brown skin you have here, fanning out for miles. And this here," he says, touching her spine, "this is the continental divide sweeping down and cutting it all in two."
 "The what?" she is murmuring, dreaming.
 "You don't know about that? About the continental divide? It's a place that runs down the back of this continent, through Canada and America and Mexico, breaking it into two parts. It's a high place that marks where the waters separate. Everything on this side of the divide," he says, sweeping his palm over the right of her back, "flows to the East, everything on this side flows West."
 Does the divide run all around the world, she wants to ask, but he is receding from her, his face growing faint, and then gone.
 Suddenly a passage is thrown open, her head ringing with scent, something held under her nose. She falls into the light of consciousness, to her aunt's tears, and frightening pain.

***

In the center of the country now, the plains rise up and the air crackles over them. Buildings on the plains are bleached to ash and chalk, the fields like scarves flung each upon each, run in maize, brown, and amber. In the cornfields the cut stalks point. A girl walking there with her dog might try to break the spear off for fetch. She would find under its papery skin the stalk is green and fibrous, and it bends under her attempts to snap it. And running through those fields like a secret—hidden wires, barbed with an electric current that snaps at the unsuspecting hand.

There is a place in Jamil like that place; it looks open and unobstructed, where winter turns the air bitter and scours every wall and face that it touches. Here is the place he returns to secretly; it is married to his joy. The joy of unhappiness! It is his own to live, to mask from others.

***

Jamil sits in the corner of the barroom, his heart pounding. There is a hand on the bar beside him, a squarish hand, neatly clipped, a hand that suggests bread. A slim ring is wrapped around one finger. Jamil thinks of the jewelry in his aunt's drawer, bracelets and rings. Then he looks from the man's hand to his eyes. They are brown eyes, like his own, but obscured by a leather brim. The fringe of hair and tough mouth are part of a uniform—a black holster, an officer's badge. Jamil looks away and then looks back again. He can't help it.

The man, watching Jamil, raises a glass to his mouth. He sips at it, as if thinking something over, and then puts it down on the counter. Looking straight at Jamil he says, "Do I got something you want?"

Jamil stares at the man, a lump filling his throat.

"Hey, I *said*, do I got something that *you* want?"

Jamil can barely shake his head, unable to remember just what the gesture means in this country.

The officer looks away, cradling his drink and Jamil sees that he is watching a woman across the room applying lipstick in the mirror of a dinner knife. Jamil tries not to look at the man. Pressing his stomach against the bar, Jamil grips its sides. But there is this hand beside him on the bar. And the man is looking at him. "What's the matter, boy?" he asks him. "Don't you like girls? You got some kind of problem?"

Yes, Jamil says, or he thinks that he has said, yes.

"You aren't from around here, are you?" the man says, moving closer. "What's the matter? Do you like me? Do you want to go with me?"

Yes, yes.

"Do you want me to take you for a drive?"

***

When Helwa first found Nejila, a stripe of blood trailing down the wall to the back of her head, she called her husband then walked out of the room, across the hall to the door, and then outdoors. She stood in the center of the street that passed their house and looked up and down its length, as if perhaps she would see Jamil there. But there was nothing to see in the dips of the road or the pools of light shed by the streetlamps. She remembered once seeing within the light of one such lamp, a cat lying on its side. It appeared unmarred, but the body was stiff and its fur ruffled with the wind. Its head was turned into the lamplight. It seemed to Helwa as if it were asking a question.

"They're trying to make women into animals," she said in English, not really knowing who she meant by this "they." But she dug her fingers into her palms, repeating herself. "They want us to be animals." Later, she wept as the doctor, a discreet neighbor, wound bandages around the cuts that covered Nejila's head and shoulders.

Now as she watches her niece sleep, she tries to imagine who this child is. The frost paints the window in a way the windows never looked in Jordan, and Helwa can see through this glass the Catskills, dark and elegant, making her think of horses.

There were Arab stallions in her father's corral. When she was a girl they let her ride with her knees hitched high on either side of the withers and her fingers roped into their manes. She remembers the flurry of hooves and the wind tunnel of her own hair.

***

The rock music on the car stereo chases the poetry from Jamil; the heaviness that pinned him down is gone now. The radio songs call out after each truck that passes. The cars and trucks are faceless, rushing in and out of the street lanes. Inside the huge car, Jamil turns toward the driver. He sees the light on four buttons on the police uniform. He focuses on the spiral of the man's ear, barely caught in the rim of headlights.

They have been driving for what seems like hours when the man finally speaks. "Do you like to drive?" he says.

Jamil has barely noticed the streetlamps and TV lights of the suburbs giving way to tree-backed mountains, rising from the highway. They are traveling through the countryside of upstate New York.

The man's fingers tap Jamil's thigh.

There is a highway sign by the edge of the road that says "Rest Area" and the man pulls off on the ramp. "This is where we're stopping," he says. "This is where the boys go to bust hippies and troublemakers. They all hang out here."

They drive behind a grove of trees. The ramp turns into a gravel parking lot that extends along the ridge of a hill. There are no lights or other cars, only a few metal drums for garbage. Jamil can just make out

shapes along the slope that he realizes are picnic tables.
The man pulls away from the road, parking and leaving the engine run for heat. He leans back away from Jamil, tilting his head against the window and eyeing him from the shadow. "So what are you, boy? Some fancy kind of negro?"

Jamil stares into the obscured face. "No, no I—I am white. I am Jordanian."

"'Jor-dane' . . . what's—oh, A-rab—one of *them*. Worse than niggers aren't you? Kill your own babies and mothers, bomb planes with Americans on them." He laughs. He reaches out and fits his fingers around the lower portion of Jamil's face. His other hand slides up to Jamil's groin and squeezes. "Do you want to kiss me, boy? Is that just what you want?"

Jamil can hardly breathe, his breath comes in short, hard gasps into the other man's palm. Words skid along his mind in Arabic, English, and a language winding under those two. His hands rise of their own volition, grabbing the man's shoulders.

"You want it," he says to Jamil, and, without releasing him, he kisses him, their teeth scraping, his tongue forcing into Jamil's mouth then withdrawing. "Is this what you want, boy—" he is talking against Jamil's mouth, forcing him backward with his strength, pressing Jamil's head against the glass. "What you want, piece of scum—coming here—fucking up our country, piece of shit—"

His words brand Jamil's skin, electric, driving him, tears starting with the ache, his lips and teeth tasting blood in their kiss.

I love you, I love you, Jamil hears himself saying. The car door bursts open and they are outside the car now and their breaths encircle them as they move through the snow. The man is stripping Jamil's clothes off him, tearing when they won't come, pushing him down into a snow drift and the ice penetrates his spine, yet he is feeling nothing, his body is turned into a streak of energy. The man is kicking him now, his feet encased in black plastic boots, kicking to the head, to the neck, in the ribs, pushing Jamil into the pointed branches of the bushes.

"You fuck," he screams at Jamil, towering over him, in the blue and white threads of snow that converge behind him. "You think I want to touch you." His head is vibrating, a thin, black line of something starts in the corner of his mouth. "A-rab scum, suck on this."

Then he slams his boot into Jamil's head and darkness drops over Jamil's eyes.

***

There is such a sweet breath on the prairie in that time when wind turns as if on a knife-edge from winter to the merest scent of spring. Then there is that moment when the air turns its grain from bitter-cold to just scrubbing at the cheek, the nape of the neck, like a lover succumbing at last.

In a matter of days Nejila is getting up from her bed, strong again. She has gone from nineteen to twenty in this month, and although one of her eyes is still purple, the cut on her scalp tender, she opens up like young wheat, the stalk lifting its leaves. She walks easily and on her first day up she goes to visit her husband who has been hospitalized.

In the big, white bed, Jamil is tiny, discolored with bruises, like a blossom that fell upon the sheets. He is so frail she wants to take him into her hands. But his skin, when she touches him, is over-hot and tacky.

"Go to him, go to your husband," Helwa urges, seeing her niece pulling back from the bed. "He needs you now."

Nezar, who had been standing by the curtain separating the beds steps forward and takes his wife's arm angrily. "I don't blame her!" he says in Arabic. "*Look* at him, how could he do this to us? Out drinking, like every other American bum off the street and he goes and gets himself beaten. Well he deserves it, he deserves a beating! It's lucky I didn't get to him first! We're made to look like fools, no better than Indians. *He* gets beaten to make me look like a fool. After years of working in this *place*, trying to make things nice, knocking my brains out for them to accept us, and he goes and does this. We're always going to be *dirty Arabs* to them," he spits, bitterness freezing the two English words, "the ones that don't take baths, the ones that live in our own shit, still, still," he stammers. "I hope he rots in that bed, by God, I don't care if he dies!"

When Nezar leaves, it's as if he has taken all the words right out of the air with him. Helwa has never known her husband to speak like this. When she looks over the bed toward the door she is looking over an immense space. Where is she to turn? She clasps her hands on her chest. Looking at Nejila she thinks, this is a terrible country.

A breath of solitude issues from the land at the heart of the country, the acres of plains, stern, ungiving, an elegiac voice. It is no wonder that their writers are so esteemed, helping those who live there to gather some of it around them, to take the glare off a mile of planted land. To make it possible to see it again.

***

He is climbing out of it, Nejila thinks. Since Jamil has returned home the light in his face has returned. But his recuperation is suffused with grieving. What does he mourn, she wonders. The thing responsible for this beating? Depression wraps its limbs around his body and closes his mouth with its own.

There is only one activity Jamil accedes to easily. He allows Nejila to bathe him. He helps lift his weight as she rolls towels out under him in bed and he raises his arms for her to draw the sponge down, soothing his breast and face.

Nejila can barely make out Jamil's face through the damage; pain seems to wrap around him, squashing his features and pulling them out of kilter. One eye is swollen. Its lid hoods up and down slowly, a curtain of blood over the cornea, his nose tilts to one side. There is a gash from the edge of his forehead to the side of his cranium. It was stitched shut and has become partially infected. Nejila is responsible for changing the dressing on this and the other wounds scattered over his body. Every morning she peels the bandage away, wondering how much this must hurt him. She has grown used to the sight, now, of exposed muscle, the way infection and lymph slide over the surface.

Every day she dampens fresh gauze with Betadine and retapes the wounds. *He appears to have been kicked*, the doctor said, *that would be my guess*. To the head? She tries not to imagine the toe against his skull.

Jamil won't tell them what happened. Nezar took him from the hospital after only a few days, carrying him in his arms, infuriating the doctor and nurses who followed them down the hall, insisting that Jamil must stay, that it was too soon. But Nezar would not look at them, and he ignored the wheelchair that they pushed at him. His mind echoed with American words, mistakes, the humiliation of police stations, of forgetting English in his nervousness, the embarrassment over his nephew, trying to fill out a police report. The hospital had called them; a picnicker had discovered Jamil half covered by bushes, sprawled on the ground. Like a drunk. Naked, for children to see.

"If we must have disgrace, we will keep it at home, not for all America to look at," he'd said when Helwa, pointing out the infections, wanted to call a doctor. "He will live, if it is the will of God."

"The will of men!" Helwa had said in anger.

But the infections subside and Jamil does live, under Nejila's hands.

After a week or two of recovery Jamil is able to sit propped up in bed. One day, when Nejila finishes bathing him, he tells her to take his writing book and pen down from the bureau.

She has never looked at his book before. There is not much written in it; a few cocktail napkins and paper receipts are scattered among the pages. The poems written there are in English; she is still struggling with the strange alphabet and must work now to make out meanings and pronunciations, to understand the words he uses there.

She avoids looking at Jamil. His lettering is cramped, printed with the concentration of a child's hand. It feels as if he has asked her to look at something intensely secret. For months she avoided looking at him. Now, in the past few weeks she has had to look at every corner of his body, his blood and healing, and his deeper, internal pain. And now, the wings of the book parted between her hands, she sees him opening something new.

Shut the book, she tells herself, just shut it now.

But he will not let her. "Please take my pen," he says. "I would like you to be my hand."

She sits in her rocker, and as Jamil speaks his voice deepens with anger, rising through the Arabic, for he is speaking in Arabic.

This is a place of betrayals, they betray
Their dead because they do not remember
Them. They bury them and pretend there
Is no death here. There is no love here
Because it can not exist without death.

There is only unhappiness here, and fear.
I have seen things made
Unrecognizable by terror. There is
Something horrible about this fear as
it comes to possess one more body.

I will gather those that I love
Around me and return us to our home,
Or I will drown in sorrow.

***

Helwa has not told Nejila about the young man who came to their door the week after they brought Jamil home. This man had that American size that seemed bred for violence, great hands, knuckles, and neck. Nejila's name was mingled in his soft English, recurring often as he spoke. Helwa would not look at his eyes, or rather could not get beyond the voice that said *Nejila*, speaking it as a husband would.

Nejila was only a door away at the time, tending to Jamil, Nezar was still at work, and Helwa knew that she must keep this stranger's voice from reaching Nejila. She would have stopped him with her own body if necessary.

"Look here ma'am," he said to her. "Look—couldn't I just—"

"Go 'way!" she said, stringing together the only bits of English available at the moment, shaking her hand at him as she would at a dog. "You, go 'way!"

***

Nejila walks through her uncle's house, striding and swinging her arms. Her aunt and uncle look at her, surprised at her lightness. Even she can not explain it to herself, but every morning when she wakes she sees the sun has come in a bit earlier. She smells the ocean grain of wheat fields; her heart has already traveled a thousand miles west, taken her to quilts of land and sandstone, the cry of the train, and the lick of its iron tracks.

Jamil is a story to her, one of the birds in her books of fairy tales, crying out in bird language that is supposed to be poetry. His words chase each other around on the page, but it is only birdsong. She takes it all down and, at the end of each session, shows him the book so that he may read it.

***

He cannot speak properly, his tongue clatters, the words he dictates to Nejila move past her neck and she brushes them away as she would a cloud of midges. He watches her from bed and thinks of his dream: the stone woman from the church in Bethlehem flanked by angels black as wasps. She rises with lifted hands, her son's body toppling from her lap, raising columns of dust. She advances toward Jamil, disrobing. He reaches to one breast, seeing the veins. He loves her, this white woman; she haunts him, she determines the course of his thought.

He wakes with a gasp. He sees Nejila's eyes on him. She stands there, just staring, as if she controls even his dreams. The pen is in her hand.

"My book," he says. "Let me see it, I want to see what I have written."

"Certainly."

She moves to the side of the bed and holds it open. But on the page is only the same sentence in Arabic he had dictated over and over:

You will do what I say

She stares at him, then closes the book and hands it to him, turning away. Quickly he reaches out and grabs some of her skirt. "Bathe me."

Sighing, she turns and begins the task, peeling down his pajama bottoms, laying open the flannel top, exposing the frail body. She leaves the room with the pail that she will fill with suds and warm water. He hears her again sighing as she returns and the afternoon mingles with the steam, the texture of the sigh, her skirts heavy on her waist, dusty with light, arms working in the bucket and reddening to the elbows. She lifts the hand that he had once seen washed golden in a train window. She draws the sponge up his arm, across his chest. He stares into brown eyes, identical to his, burned by the light that touches her dark skin.

The sponge crosses his belly, brushes the inside of his thigh, and he is aroused.

"Nejila," he whispers, stopping her hand. "My wife. My good, dear wife." His hands slide around her shoulders, drawing her toward him. "My true, true love."

He pulls, but there is nothing there, just a moth-winged movement and she is out of his grasp, looking at him in amazement.

"I mean you no harm!" he says in English. "I won't beat you anymore, I only wish to love you. I will treat you properly—as my wife."

She is breathing hard, trying to smile, to say, I love you, but instead she is saying, "Never. Never." She rises and moves back from the bed.

"Nejila!"

"I cannot bear to have you touch me," she says in Arabic. "Your face, your ruined body, your horrible smell—I can hardly stand to be near you." She is shaking, her voice like a muscle in her throat. "I'm disgusted by you! And as for your poetry," she picks up the book from the side of the bed, "it is nothing but ashes. All of it. Ashes and ashes, words from a corpse. You force me to write down your terrible complaints and all your self-praise. It's sickening—I don't know how I had the stomach to do it for so long, but I can tell you this—I will have nothing more to do any of with it."

And she runs out, her hair rising behind her, leaving its memory in the air.

Nejila is running down the hall; there is no time for her to think clearly. Her old suitcase, stowed away in the basement, opens at her touch. All the clothes she'd arrived with were still in there, still holding the folds put in by her mother's hands. Helwa had insisted on buying all new when Nejila arrived.

She locks the suitcase back up, and then she stops for a moment, thinking of Helwa and Nezar.

Nejila walks up the basement stairs to the front door. No one comes to stop her. They are back there, in those rooms, and she feels them, but the doorknob is turning under her hand now. It is three weeks since she's gone outside on her own. She steps on to the flagstone path that leads to the street. Again she stops, looking, and down the block, standing at the corner where the chain-link starts around the baseball field, there is a man.

***

I was trembling the very first time that we kissed. You took me in your arms and, somehow, I said to you, *I'm shaking*. Why was I shaking?

Standing there she feels the out-of-bounds sunlight, everything burned down, the grass, her skin and hair burnt off, pupils burned out, stomach, liver burnt to the floor of her body, to her fingers that glaze with white heat. And then! Life springing back, wildfire in the light, grass and bushes rocking the air. Her body like a plant whipping open its leaves, froth of vine and stem, and the whole earth tilts under her so she is running toward the man who is already looking away, silent on the distant green.

***

One enters the study of another language, Jamil thinks, as into an art. It is hours later, dusk is beginning. He sits up in bed, the poetry book discarded, turning the pages of his English grammar, delicately, as he might turn the pages of a picture book. The letters turn their eyes to him, the odd, round alphabet opened like mouths, singing to him. The study

of language, such purity—
He looks up and sees on the bureau a stack of postcards that his wife left behind. With some stiffness, he slides from bed and walks to the bureau. She loved to buy postcards and spent hours sifting through them.

Jamil fans them out over the dresser top and discovers that they are not photographs of landscapes and city lights in the evening, as he had supposed. Rather, they are reproductions of artworks: paintings, photographs, and prints. They are filled with textures, resplendent with color or tones of black and white. After a moment, Jamil sees that they are all of women. There are two depictions of Venus rising, one the Botticelli riding upon her sea shell, the other a photograph of a muscular woman emerging from the froth of a dark sea. There is a painting entitled "Three Sisters," which depicts three glowering and beckoning women. There is a photo of a past screen goddess, so luminous, cheekbones and flickering lips, a flame; the face with its shadows beneath the cheekbones and eyelids as if she carried her death there.

Lining these women up, each side by side, Jamil notices a gesture repeated through the poses. The right hand falls to the breast, sometimes touching, sometimes moving toward it, the left hand touches the abdomen or rises into the air. Jamil attempts the pose himself and discovers, with the movement of his left hand, that touching his abdomen, he assumes a posture of concealment, self-protection, or, lifting his hand up, he is positioned for the making of a vow, the reverse of self-protection, for it implies that whatever is concealed by the right hand will be lifted up by the left for all to see. Is the abdomen some part of mystery, of hiding? Are these the worlds that Nejila moved between, he wonders.

The light is fainter in the bedroom windows, the glass resembles dust, it appears to be dissolving.

The shadow slides back, stitching the room with light as it falls. Jamil knows she is not returning. He puts his face in his hands.

His aunt enters the bedroom, knocking softly. "Supper is ready," she says. "Are you well enough to come to the table today?"

***

At the table dishes are passed. Jamil holds each one briefly before putting it back, taking nothing. Finally, he asks for the rice. His aunt passes him the steaming tureen, a pilaf of scent and heat. He piles the grains on his plate and stares at them. Rice, heaped before him, sticky and gleaming, the whitest of white.

Gray Marrow

Daniel James Sundahl

My mother lived in the company of two women,
One to each side of our small frame house;
Mid-way through the mornings of hot summer days
She and they would gather encountering the pace
Of one another's day—husbands held at a distance.

The heat would hang high in the elms, the air
Heavy with the season's poison. I would lie awake
At night and listen to my parents' low voices,
Imagining an interpretation: what mote-like seed
Was miasmic polio? My mother waxes the table,

Rubbing in circles, in slow movements, her figure
Loose and tired, or stands stone-faced behind
The screen door in thick humidity, praying
For a breeze, a motion, a relief from something she
Has learned to fear, the slow frost in nerves,

Believing cruelty is in the weather, is in her
Intimacy with fear, is in the jangled lives of
Two other women and ours in between, going dry,
One with a left arm withered, a stammer, the other
A right arm and wrist in a steel brace, a stammer.

On the table, a water pitcher sweats, the vacuum
Sucks dregs of dust, aspirates along the wainscot;
The phone rings, my mother goes sour in the mouth.
Father, who is sitting in a chair, says nothing,
Then rises to steady the convulsions in her hands.

This House

Larry E. Smith

is his grief, did all it could
to cover him up with plaster.
The road has disappeared
in the grass, white dust from the dry fields
drifts across the porch.

He lies on the floor
with one arm in his shirt.
Everything has tried to leave or hide—
like a son who hasn't looked back in 20 years—
except a dress on the bedroom wall.
Been there since his wife hung it up
and fell dead on the floor.

He wakes from the cloud that covered
his mind, stares at the dress and slats
the plaster left behind.
He mumbles about the chimney that walked off
the roof a brick at a time, and a son

whose face is a haze.
Outside, the day hovers dark
as neglect. Any minute
a rumbling white arm could reach down
and scrape the earth clean.

Meet the Family
David Winwood

Then there was the other granny,
who wasn't my real one,
as they all kept telling me.
Her voice a copy of my kite's
taut string shrieking at the high wind.

She was never my real granny. Only
my grandfather's housekeeper. He,
a strong man with urges, she tired.
So with marriage
an Access card to the family

she visited his grandchildren.
Flapping her arms. Never taking off.
When she'd gone to 'wash her hands',
in our lavatory without sink or tap,
my mother had to clean up after her.

"She's got a shower-head in her knickers,"
my real grandmother informed me
in a whisper. Nevertheless
she had to be asked to dinner.
Sitting stiffly she would have

"A bit of shoulder please." Toning back
her voice to a breeze of discontent as
all eyes sought to penetrate the ceiling.
An only child, only I caught that knot
in her throat

of something that couldn't be said
or swallowed.

How Was Your Day

Max Westbrook

There was a young man out in the back yard, white, mid-thirties, dying of a heart attack. He was a bachelor and lived with his parents. The neighbors said he was born with a defective heart. The prognosis was that he might live a week, a year, he could drop dead at the age of two or ten, or his heart might hold out indefinitely. So he lived with his parents for over thirty years and they took care of him, the three of them knowing all day every day that he could drop dead any second. I got the story from Bennie, who had been talking with the neighbors.

The family was having a barbeque in the backyard when it happened. The young man had just brought out some tomatoes he had sliced in the kitchen. He said, "These tomatoes sure look good," and then he dropped the platter and grabbed his chest, like he had been shot by a pistol equipped with a silencer. He bent over, took one step back, and collapsed. When I first came in, one of the neighbor ladies had the platter and was bending down from the knees, like she was in church, and picking up each slice of tomato.

The father and mother were taking it hard. They were elderly, late sixties, early seventies, and they had lost control.

The EMS supervisor had the fibrillators ready, and the two EMS techs were helping with that routine they do, clearing the body. Everything else stops—no massage, no oxygen, nothing—for what seems about five minutes. I guess it's more like five seconds, but they really are careful to make certain no one is touching the body when they pop it with the fibrillators. Rosa and a neighbor lady were trying to get the mother to go inside, but she wouldn't budge. The fibrillators made that sharp popping sound, and the man's upper torso went about three or four inches off the ground. His mother screamed. Rosa and the neighbor had to catch her and hold on to keep her from falling down.

One of the EMS guys got a blanket out of a case and started toward the young man. Both parents just about went crazy. "Don't give up," they yelled, "don't give up!" They strained against the people holding them and reached toward the medics with their arms out straight and their hands open.

I don't know what the EMS guys were thinking. They might have been thinking about a law suit. They might have been thinking they had to do something to keep the parents from having a stroke. Anyway, they stopped putting their equipment away and went back to work. They were working on a dead man.

When I had first walked into the backyard, Ernie and Bennie and Rosa were already doing everything that could be done. Ernie was trying to calm the old man. Rosa was talking to the mother, or trying to. Four or five neighbors had come in the back yard the second it happened, and Bennie was keeping them out of the way and asking questions, like who should they notify and who would be a good one to make the calls.

There wasn't anything for me to do. So I looked around.

The back yard had a high board fence starting at the garage and going all around. On the east side, where the fence was connected to the house, there was a gate. I went over and stood by the gate to make certain no curiosity-seekers came wandering in.

Standing there, I could look to my left and see the back yard, then look to my right and see the front yard.

Out back, there were no trees to speak of, just three or four saplings. The carpet grass was in good shape. West of the back yard was a two-story house set well back from the street so that it blocked the setting sun and left the yard in deep shade. The parents were still crying, still pleading. The two EMS techs, both of them real young, had a strange look. They kept working, but you could tell it made them feel weird to do it. The supervisor had kind of a grim look around the mouth. My guess is he didn't want to keep working on the heart attack victim, and he didn't want to stop.

The front yard was a completely different scene. The sun was on the horizon, and the last rays were coming in at ground level. There were three big trees that covered the entire yard, a sycamore, a Spanish oak, and one I couldn't identify. The carpet grass was even better, rich and green, and leaves had fallen from the trees and were scattered everywhere, big leaves of different colors, red and yellow and brown.

All four police cars and the EMS unit were parked close together in front of the house. Five sets of overheads were turning and turning in the sun and shadows of the late afternoon. The police units all have the new lights, strobes actually, not lights with reflectors. They are amber and red, white, and blue. They are much stronger than the old fashioned lights, and they make a high-pitched space-age sound when they're on. It's not loud, but it's loud enough you can hear it over the radio.

With four sets of strobes going, plus the EMS unit, it made a light show that had attracted children from all directions, a dozen or more, kids from about five years old up to maybe eight or ten. They saw the lights, turning and flashing their colors in the sunlight and shadows under the tall trees. Then they saw the leaves and started playing.

A little boy with a cowlick picked up a double handful and dumped them on a little red-headed girl. She squealed and clapped a few of the leaves to her head with her right hand. Then she stuck out her left arm and let the wrist flop, playing like she was an elegant lady, and pranced about and laughed.

In back, Rosa and one of the neighbors were still talking to the mother. They were trying to get her to go inside. A man wearing blue walking shorts and a Hawaiian shirt was holding the father on one side, with Ernie on the other side. The father's legs were watery. They wouldn't support his weight. The mother was turning her head at odd angles, trying to get her balance. Both of them were still crying, still telling the EMS supervisor he had to keep trying.

"Don't let him go," the father was saying now. "Don't give him up!"

The way he said it made it seem like death and the EMS technicians were in a tug of war, and the side that pulled the hardest would win.

I turned and looked again at the front yard. The children had made a game of throwing leaves in the air, bending down to gather a batch, then throwing them high in the air and bending down for more while the leaves they had just thrown were still in the air. Every single one of them was working at it non-stop. There were so many leaves in the air they seemed to be flying and dancing in the last rays of the sunset.

A call came in, a knife fight in a parking lot at a beer joint. I waved to Bennie and took off running. Bennie was already moving. Ernie was saying something to the man in the Hawaiian shirt. We keep our walkie-talkies so low people who aren't used to it can only hear what sounds like a hardly-noticeable static. Ernie was probably explaining that he had to go and saying the man should get one of the other neighbors to help with the father.

When I got to my unit and started to pull out, Bennie was running across the front yard, Ernie right behind him. The children yelled with delight and ran along with them, throwing leaves at the police officers and laughing.

We had to leave one officer at the scene. Rosa never backed down from anything, but she was heavily involved with the mother, so I guess she got stuck. If Ernie and Bennie took out running and didn't say anything to her, Rosa would be ticked off and, first chance, she would have it out with them. Rosa was a little sensitive about being a female cop and always wanted to be the first one through the door. I got a glimpse of her standing at the open gate. She was turned, ready to close it and go back, but had stopped, just for a second, to look at Bennie and Ernie running through the leaves, like they had joined in and were playing with the children.

Cops don't always agree on the best route to get to where they're going, but when I decided on speed over distance and took the freeway, both units swung in behind me. I punched it up to 90 and there they were, right behind me. Everything was going by so fast it felt like they were pushing me along in front of them, and at the same time it felt like I was pulling them along with me.

When we got to the beer joint, it was all over. A teenager was lying in the parking lot with the back of his head on the concrete, but he was not lying on his back, he was not lying on his side, and his legs were not arranged. His position was kind of twisted, unnatural. When you see a man like that, like he's been dropped from the sky and just stays the way he fell without moving an inch, you know he's dead.

There was another teenager who had been stabbed in the chest and on his arms and wouldn't lie down. A plain clothes officer was holding him and talking to him, but he kept turning around, trying to get away. So we had to take him down. With four of us to do it, we were able to lay him out like you were putting a baby in his crib. "They killed my brother," he said, but not to anyone in particular. "The son-sa-bitches killed my brother. I'll get 'em! I'll get the bastards! I'll kill 'em! I'll kill 'em!"

Four narcs were there ahead of us. One of them was a sergeant. It turned out they were hiding in cars in the parking lot, all set to make a bust, when the deal went sour and the fight broke out. They were trying to salvage something and said they would handle it. It was their case. We still had to hang around for an hour, helping to secure the crime scene, doing crowd control, and questioning witnesses the narcs figured were not involved. All the people I questioned said they were inside drinking beer when it happened, and I guess they really were.

I was getting a little tired of being a go-fer for the narcs—their sergeant acted like all uniformed officers were inferior servants—and I stopped to look at the guys the narcs had picked out to question themselves. I got to the face of one of them and stopped. It was like those computer-enhanced things in the movies when they want to make a character change right in front of your eyes. The man looked older than the teenagers he was with. He was about my age, mid-twenties, but as I began to recognize him, his face changed. The cheeks became thinner. His skin became smoother. A teenager's face emerged, like he was ageing backwards. Then, you know how it is, it happens all the time, my looking at him made him look at me. At first he was seeing another goddamn cop. There was nothing but hate in his eyes.

Then he smiled. It was a very sad smile, but he recognized me. He was probably slow because of the mustache. I haven't changed much since high school, but I started wearing a mustache in college, and it makes a difference. Anyway, he recognized me, and his expression changed. First it was the sad smile, then he looked at me straight, with no expression, and the hate settled on his face again and seemed more natural. We had had some great times together in the band, back in high school. We never buddied around together except on band trips, and I never even thought to ask why. I didn't know anything at all about his family, and I suddenly remembered that I had never seen him at a band party or a high school dance.

For just a moment there, he expected something from me, a favor, maybe a word of sympathy, I don't know. But after that brief time-jump, he came back to this minute on this parking lot, and then he probably felt the separation as strong as I felt it the second I recognized him. Being a cop can separate you from friends, neighbors, and law-abiding strangers. We get told about that even in college. No experience on the street required. You become a cop, your only friends are other cops.

As for this scum-bag one-time friend and now drug dealer, I felt nothing. His choice erased our past as easily as erasing a blackboard. I pointed him out to the sergeant and said I knew that one in high school. Sometimes you can question a suspect better if you have prior knowledge. So I told the sergeant, just in case he wanted me, now or later. Then I went on back to doing my job.

After the sergeant finally cut us loose, I drove around for half an hour, with nothing much happening. A lot of police work is like that. Sometimes Dispatch comes on as soon as you call in ten-six, meaning you're available, and sometimes nothing happens. I don't suppose there's any connection, but it reminded me of when I was about eight or nine and my mother gave me a diary. She said a record of my childhood would be interesting when I was older. I worked at it for a couple of weeks. "Played with George" took care of one day. "Watched TV with Sis" was the only comment on another day. Then most of the entries were the same words, "Nothing happened today," and after that the pages were blank.

All of a sudden I was remembering little league baseball, soccer in Zilker Park, eating popcorn with the family and watching TV, and one very special day, crazy Saturday I called it. I was about twelve, and my Dad and I, for no reason at all, played tennis all day long and got so tired we wound up giggling like a couple of idiots. The climax came when I floated one back and, just being silly, I hollered out, "Hyar she comes." Dad stood flat-footed, watching the ball drifting by, about half-a-step to his right, and pointed with his racquet and said, "Thar she goes!" We were like a couple of drunks. We laughed so hard we had to sit down.

It's weird. I used to be a six year old who thought Saturday morning cartoons were the greatest thing on earth. When I was seven, I would have traded anything I had or might ever have for one home run. And here I was in a police car with a badge, a .357 magnum in my holster, and a shotgun at my elbow. It makes you wonder.

Dispatch came on. It was the call we hate the most, domestic disturbance.

It was my call, but Smith showed up with a rookie he was training and asked if I would let the rookie take the call. He needed the practice, Smith told me. I didn't like it, but Smith has seniority on me, and I didn't want to seem like a hard-nose about procedure and be uncooperative. So I said okay. Besides, Smith is kind of crazy. He's a good cop, and I've learned a lot from him, but he's been on the street too long, and I wasn't eager to cross him. You're always afraid of what he might do next.

When we got inside, it was a scene I've walked into so many times it seemed like I've been here before and I'll be here again. The husband is drunk, the wife has been beat to a pulp, and she won't file charges. Her left eye is closed so tight she can't see through it, and blood is coming up out of her mouth. A tooth has cut her cheek on the inside. She's holding a wet wash cloth to her mouth to catch the blood and is having trouble talking and can't see out of one eye, but she's very clear when the rookie asks if she will file charges. She shakes her head No and waves him off with her free hand like what he wanted was even worse than the trouble she already had.

"He's a good husband," she was saying through her bloody mouth. "It's just his job, you know. Sometimes it gets to him and he starts, you know, drinking. But he's a good husband."

The rookie does everything right—separating them so he can question the wife while Smith talks to the husband, explaining about the shelter for battered women, finding out about a sister who would help and saying phone or let him phone her—but the wife is too whipped down inside to have any pride.

And the husband is too cocky. He knows she won't file on him. He's a stocky guy, built solid. He leans in close to the rookie's face. "Why don't you get your ass out of my house and go mind your own goddamn business."

Smith is drumming his fingers on his nightstick, looking for an excuse to use it, the rookie is arguing reason to a poor pathetic punching bag not capable of being reasonable about anything, and I'm getting so fed up I'm going to lose my temper and do something stupid if I don't do something sensible first.

So I put on my most respectful-professional manner and kind of insert my body in between Smith and the drunk.

"Sir, I think you're right. We shouldn't intrude into your home this way. But we do have a complaint, sir, and we can't just ignore it."

He started to interrupt but I raised my voice—keeping it polite and respectful—and didn't slow down.

"Now I think I have a solution, sir. If you'd just cooperate with me and step outside a minute, I believe you and me could get away from all this wrangling and talk sense to one another and get everything settled. Would you be willing to cooperate with me on that, sir?"

I tried to establish eye contact, to make it seem like I knew that we

were the only two reasonable men in Texas, and I kept my hands down to my side. I didn't even make a gesture toward touching him, and I kept talking.
"I'm sure we can be out of your home and away from here in two minutes, sir. That's a guarantee."
He fell for it.
I sweet-talked him all the way out to the sidewalk in front of his house, then turned him around and cuffed him before he knew what I was doing.
"You're under arrest," I said. "Public intoxication."
He would spend a maximum of four hours in jail, but something was better than nothing, and who knows. Maybe the wife would use the time to buck up her courage and call somebody, the shelter for battered women, her sister, somebody. Besides, there was some satisfaction in seeing him so mad he might bust a blood vessel or two.

When the shift was over and the paperwork done, it was a little after three a.m. I walked out to my pickup telling myself to go home and hit the sack. My shift was over. Other cops were on duty now.

When I turned east—I live south of the station—I couldn't believe what I was doing. It was something I have never done before in three years on the street and something I don't think I'll ever do again.

The drunk's house was completely dark. No one was stirring. The bastard was probably sleeping it off, resting up so he could get drunk again and beat up his wife again. I couldn't help wondering what it was like when he proposed and did she rush home to call her friends and tell them the good news and start planning what she would wear and who would be bridesmaids.

The parking lot in back of the beer joint was so deserted and so blank I could see my high school band marching along as easily as I could see the hate on the face of my old buddy, my now no-longer friend. There was nothing on the parking lot you could tie a rope to. The cars were gone, the people gone. The front and back of the lot were the same, the sides were the same. I could imagine myself in a band uniform, marching in formation playing my alto sax, or I could wear black and put my hands on a bleeding teenager and help lay him down gently so he wouldn't jerk around and pump his own life's blood away before the EMS unit arrived. There was nothing substantial about this deserted parking lot so late at night it would soon be morning. I could put cops and drug dealers all over that lot and march the Westlake High School Band right through it all without touching anybody.

At the house where the young man died of a heart attack, there was a faint light way back inside, probably a hallway light. I looked at the front yard. The moon was bright enough for me to see the leaves, but not their colors. I had to remember the colors. They were red, a rich dark red, and bright yellow and golden brown. Except for the little boy with the cowlick and the little red-headed girl, I couldn't remember the faces of the children, but I could almost see the whole bunch running and dancing and playing in the leaves, only it was different now. The children I saw in memory were silent, laughing and playing on the thick carpet grass, like silhouettes in slow motion, the leaves tossed and tossed until they seemed to be floating in the lonesome silence of the night.

Progress

Ron Offen

Sitting
isolated, batteries dimming
in my Walkman,
moonlighting at a mindless job
that twenty years ago
would have paid me more,
straining to hear
through a rasp of white noise
songs I once ignored,
and curiously, wordlessly
content.

This Twentieth Century

B. Z. Niditch

It's yours
to encounter:
every bloodshot day
of nervous faces
manages to make
ourselves unseen—
those four-seasoned refugees
only justifiable
by pulling out plugs
on electric velvet chairs
from totalitarian nights
and egalitarian days.

Baron's Death

Matthew J. Spireng

If you know the horror
of reaching in the dark
across a laboring
horse down on its side
and feeling its guts spilled
out on the ground, you know
a little about this
death. And if you know the
sight as the quarter moon
rises of a tall horse
standing in silhouette
trailing its intestines
twisted and glistening in
the torturing light, you
know something of what I
speak. If you somehow know
how a man must feel in
the face of certain death,
trying to put it down
and having it stand and
run at him, its glazed eyes
reflecting what little
light there is, knowing it
cannot understand or
stop until the vet slips
the needle in, you know
how this nightmare begins.

Elections

Clark Brown

When their anger had smoldered down into stony silence, she flung herself on the bed while he stomped toward the kitchen and the gin. He could get blind drunk for all she cared, though he wouldn't. Alcohol turned him bitter and gave a nasty edge to his tongue but made him more ponderously reasonable than ever. Anyway, they had worn themselves out. They had said their say.

"What do you want me to *do*?" he had thrown at her. "Tell them the rules don't apply because he wouldn't have won in any case? Tell him we only go by the book if you're 'popular'?" He had pronounced the word with elaborate distaste, as though biting into something vile. His square handsome face had been flushed and scowling under the pewter-colored hair. He stood there, fifty-three years old, still snapping to attention, with that stiffness about the shoulders, as though he swiveled from the waist but not the neck. And glaring at her, he had really wanted to know.

She hadn't replied. She had lacked an answer, but there were things she had wanted to pelt him with. *Does it really matter? Is it worth it? Is it really worth it, Harry? Think! Think of the cost! Isn't it all pretty silly?*

He wouldn't have agreed, and knowing that, she hadn't bothered, turning in upon herself, sour and stoical. *It's so like you, Harry*, she had thought. *It really is! God, is it ever like you!*

Which didn't mean he wasn't "right."

Oh, he was, she would grant. He was, as always, integrity personified—and what had it gotten them? Just once she wished he would see how irrelevant, how irresponsible his precious sense of honor was. *Look at the results, for God's sake!* she wanted to scream. *How can you think*

this is victory?
He would, of course. He would balm himself with gin and rationalization. He had gone, once again, by the "book," producing pedantic justice and general disaster, and now was there anyone in the school or the town itself (barring a few obscene exceptions) who didn't hate his guts?
And he and she had been there exactly three months.
Who could have predicted it? She possibly, but no one else. He had made a marvelous impression; he always did. He was Central Casting's idea of a high school principal—tall, elegant, silver-haired, dignified, with that mellow baritone, that wry sparkle in the searching eye, and that playfulness at the mouth corners. Distinguished in Harris tweeds (as he had formerly been in dress blues), he was firm, composed, knowledgeable, good-natured and rarely pompous. He was the answer to a school board's prayer, divine intervention, someone at last to shape up Glen Oaks Senior High!
And hadn't it needed shaping? Indeed, it had! And hadn't Harry shaped? Hadn't he tried? You couldn't deny it. And when the devilish Ray Harmon, the senior genius with the 1450 SAT score and the whizbang word processor, when *he* had ventured to strike a bargain—a fair effort by the seniors on the state achievement test in return for smoking privileges—Harry had been amused but untempted. In any case, he had told Ray calmly (eyes dancing, she imagined, and smile flickering), he wasn't cutting any deals.
The boy had turned and gone without a word, and when the results were in weeks later—scores down, mostly because of an inexplicable senior collapse—Harry had pacified the Board. ". . . These kids are pretty hip. They know this doesn't count on their records, so they don't exert themselves." There would be no increased funding—a disappointment—but no one was induced to blame Harry personally. It was just too bad.
Only—she wondered (blasphemously)—what if he *had* given in? Would it have mattered? So the kids smoked on school grounds during lunch instead of fouling and trampling the neighbors' yards. So what? The mysterious Ray Harmon might have energized his peers to put forth genuine effort, resulting in new band and football uniforms, books for the library, a first class literary magazine, plausible sets for the drama club, additional computers, and more. But, as Harry loftily said, not only did the end not justify the means, certain means called in question the end itself.
Yet again . . . she wasn't sure.
She was rarely sure of anything—her lifelong curse and fatal disadvantage in debate with Harry. She was constantly questioning people, wanting to know how they lived, what they believed, what values they held, even what brands of food and appliances they bought. Invited to their houses, she sometimes examined medicine chests and peeked into

shower stalls, not out of common snoopiness but from that insatiable curiosity that left her forever wondering—what did people choose, and shouldn't she do the same?

Harry naturally felt no such gnawing. At some distant time he had apparently considered and resolved all burning questions and put them comfortably behind him. Take religion. She was forever plowing through books about different faiths—not just the innumerable Christian sects, but Judaism, Islam, Buddhism, Taoism, Confucianism and more—alternately intrigued, confused, troubled, put off and enchanted once again. Such amateur scholarship both amused and irritated Harry. Firmly but without ostentation, he would announce— if the occasion seemed to demand it, or if there appeared to be any doubt about the matter—that he was an atheist. That settled that, he implied—courteously.

Still, she had her doubts. Would a man truly sure of himself retire so abruptly from the Navy after long years? And would he, at this age, pull up stakes and abandon a secure if not terribly profitable teaching job to go larking after an "administrative credential" and a principalship— something in which for all his impressive demeanor he had no practical experience? Was this certainty? A man at peace with himself? Or wasn't this, as she secretly believed, a man whose career had never quite achieved what he (and most people) expected?

Oh yes, "lieutenant commander" sounded splendid, if you didn't know the Navy, but when it became clear Harry would advance no further, you could bet that something had gone askew, and she knew what—that blinkered perception of right and wrong that made failure inevitable if undramatic.

In the service a senior officer wrote numerous evaluations, but if a subordinate were diligent and reliable, it wasn't enough simply to say so. Oh no! If you wished the person promoted, you described said person in admiring terms suitable for Lord Nelson or Francis Drake. It was understood, but Harry declined. He would tell you your faults—frankly and with good humor—and look you in the eye. Worse, he would tell *other* people your faults (with that same frank good humor) if asked— though he wouldn't neglect your virtues as he perceived them. This, he believed, was only doing what one should—and he was right.

But—she sometimes wanted to shriek—the result *was* that inferior people were promoted and the more deserving, if they carried Harry's restrained appraisal, were not, with consequent resentment and subtle forms of non-cooperation and revenge, something Harry never seemed to grasp. If things went badly, he became philosophical but refused to blame himself. He had done what was proper. If the world chose not to respect it, the world might go its own dismal way.

The trouble was, you had to *live* in that world. There were no others. This he didn't seem to understand, atheist or no—not as she had been made to understand it, now that *her* small but pleasant world had fallen about her like so much crumbling stucco.

She yearned for friendship, she always had, but more than ever now that the children were grown and gone their own questionable directions. After a nomadic life as an officer's spouse, she had expected to die in the last town, where Harry, now a civilian, had finally put down roots. And laboriously but relentlessly, she had *made* friends, there and now here, something that didn't come easily.

Oh, she put people off, she knew it, asking too many questions, growing abruptly personal and inquisitive, striking new acquaintances as flighty and unpredictable, as she tested ideas and opinions. ("But didn't you *want* any more children?" she might ask people she hardly knew.) At times she must have sounded almost nutty. Taking any side in an argument in order to provoke a rebuttal, she could seem dangerous, lunatic and nosey. And it wasn't exactly that she didn't mean what she said. Rather, she hoped through some sort of conversational dialectic to discover what she *did* mean, for she hardly knew herself. Somehow she expected people to know this and forgive. Not everyone did.

Some did, though: Colleen Devereux for one, and Amanda Harris, Selina Jacoby and Thelma Sorenson among others—bright, self-confident women (younger than she), who had welcomed her eagerly, unfazed by questions and probings, finding her enthusiasm and avid curiosity delightful. They had had her to lunches and taken her "antiquing" (which she adored), putting her onto a local eccentric who had miraculously corralled eighteenth-century Imari and English tin-glazed tile and would part with both for a ridiculously small sum. Women like these knew "good goods," as she called them, and appreciated *her* passion for such. Spurred in turn by her interest, they had planned and promised trips to The City—to civilization in other words, meaning first rate restaurants, theaters, fabric stores, boutiques and antique shops that featured something besides old license plates and ancient farm equipment. They had promised, in short, to take her where the spirit could breathe.

Nor was that all. Colleen Devereux was putting her up for Lamda Tau, a service organization—a little snobbish (mostly doctors and attorneys' wives) but well meaning, given to charity drives and social functions—a barn dance in the fall and once a year a formal dinner, to which she hoped to persuade Harry to wear his uniform. An artist of some talent and flair, she had already contributed ideas and sketches for decorations, notions proclaimed "smashing" and "fabulous!" Well, really, they *weren't* bad!

It was a small, tidy, silly little world no doubt, something to smile at, but it stimulated and fulfilled her. And it was a charm of sorts against the long lonely hours in this blistering valley that suggested from certain angles the backside of the moon. Laugh if you wanted. She had been grateful, even at times ecstatic.

Then had come the business with Ray Harmon, the blank-faced

inventive prankster who was said to have mailed one female teacher a pair of falsies, and made a second absurd by giving a report on a non-existent book which the teacher, showing off, claimed to have read. It was Ray too who recited soundlessly in German class, lips moving, causing Mr. Vogel to turn up his hearing aid, whereupon Ray blasted out his recitation so that the poor man quailed and fiddled frantically with his machine.

Harry had found all this funny, though not, possibly, as funny as he pretended. It was his habit—developed in the Navy—never to appear shocked or surprised by folly or impudence. If you thought you could get his goat, the pose said, think again. Such equanimity discouraged jests and rebellion, he believed, and probably he was right. When, therefore, Ray had been caught throwing a paper airplane from a third floor classroom window and was sent to the principal, Harry had smiled his measured smile, eyes almost impish (she could bet), and told the offender that he would police the quad after school.

"Police?" the boy said indignantly. "Do I get a gun and a badge?"

"What you get," Harry had said mildly—in that imperturbable baritone—"is a plastic bag into which you put whatever shouldn't be lying around."

"Police?" the culprit had said again, making it his exit line. Harry had folded his arms (so he claimed), and his smile no doubt had flickered still. "Police" was unfortunate, he admitted, a slip of the old military tongue, but what the hell?

Less amusing and less trivial was the fraternity—illegal but flourishing. "My predecessor evidently looked the other way," Harry explained. "That's what Grant tells me. To get along, go along, and all that. He seems so have accepted the smoking deal too, to get the seniors galvanized for the achievement test, or so I'm informed. I told Grant that wasn't my style." "Grant" was Grant Nichols, Dean of Boys, a round, unprepossessing little man who had been at Glen Oaks for twenty years, but a shrewd old boy, Harry maintained, very like a certain chief he remembered from Subic Bay.

"But I wonder . . . ," she had objected, in her tentative faltering way.

"You wonder what?"

"I mean . . . ," she said, "well, Harry, I mean if they're not hurting anything, the boys. . . ."

"Ah," he said, "if they're not!" And he described the lunch period congregation—the men of Delta Kappa Omega hanging out on the steps, lordly and vulgar, blighting the noon hour of fourteen hundred students, most of whom adolescent Calvinism now designated not of the elect.

She had nodded and pondered, not telling him—not then anyway—that many of her newfound friends had sons at Glen Oaks, most of whom were D.K.O.'s.

Yet it wouldn't have mattered, she felt sure, if it hadn't been for the election. Oh God, the election! How she cursed it!

Running on a "ticket" or "slate" was strictly forbidden, but when Paul Devereux, Eric Jacoby, Todd Sorenson and Jerry Harris entered the lists—D.K.O.'s all and the sons of her dearest friends and benefactors— Harry and Grant conferred and decided that as long as the affiliation wasn't mentioned, the rules were honored, technically at least. Besides, Harry wished they *would* win, he said, especially Paul, a shy charming boy who was running for President against Alan Shields, a blustering self-confident type, who in "real" life probably *would* be a politician. The students seemed to share Harry's feelings, for Paul was elected; Jerry was Vice President, Eric Secretary and Todd Treasurer. None of the races was close. Harry was pleased that a potentially difficult incident had been avoided, and she, delighted for Colleen, had spent much of the joyous evening on the phone.

Then came the dawn, as melodrama might put it, and a few hours later Alan Shields and his glowering parents waiting outside Harry's office. As Harry described it, they sat, faces stiff, eyes sharp. Their lips might have quivered; he couldn't be sure. They followed him into the office, and he shut the door, hearing a quick sucking of breath. When all were seated, Alan, tall and sullen, flanked by his dumpy wounded mother and glaring father, had wordlessly laid before Harry what had appeared at first to be a business card: LADIES AND GENTLEMEN OF SOCIETY, ENDORSE A GOOD GROUP OF CANDIDATES. There followed the names of the victors.

"I felt," Harry said—with a sigh—"pretty much like a punctured tire."

Alan claimed he had found the card in his locker the day of the election and assumed that someone shoved it through the vent. "It's against the rules!" Mr. Shields had said, pointing out the obvious. "It's running on a ticket!"

"It's not fair!" Mrs. Shields had thrown in.

They were right, Harry said, which hadn't made him like them any better. They were in fact remarkably unpleasant and unattractive people, and how they had produced their tall well-favored son was to him a mystery.

Harry had asked if they knew where the card came from. "That Harmon boy!" Mrs. Shields said with a snort. She was wearing black doubleknit slacks and a loose tunic-thing with a splashy design, Harry remembered, and her hair was a stiff beet-shaped blossom tinted a pale smoke. Her owlish glasses, framed in dark plastic, had been trained on him like gun barrels.

"Alan knows," the husband had offered, nostrils flaring, brow furrowed, a man simmering in slacks, open shirt and a windbreaker. (Except for two side patches, greased and fiercely brushed, he was bald.)

"Ray's got all this equipment," Alan had said. "He makes up cards like this all the time. He's got all these different fonts and stuff."

"Did you see this before the election?" Harry had asked.

Alan had given a pained sniff. "Not personally," he said. (Harry said he wasn't sure he believed him but supposed it didn't matter.) "All right," he had promised. "I'll look into it." "How?" they had wanted to know. "I guess," he had said, "I'll have to ask some questions."

Questions he had asked all right, without delay. That too was the Navy in him. Summoned at once, Ray Harmon skulked in, chin down, lip out, pale eyes wary. (Harry described him vividly: tall and bony, with a wan blank face, colorless eyes and dark hair cut in the stiff paintbrush fashion that made him look faintly startled. The clothes—pleated and baggy—seemed draped rather than worn, and when at Harry's command he took a chair they bagged further.)

Harry presented the card. Well? Well, what? the boy asked, sparring. *He* knew what, Harry said and wanted to know if Ray had seen it before. He was standing then, hovering over the kid, and she knew just how he must have looked, much as he had looked this evening: shoulders hunched, big hands lifted, the mouth thin and grim, dark eyes hard.

Ray had shrugged and said he didn't know. Harry had said that he did. "Did you print these things up?" he asked. "On your machine?" No answer, the eyes darting up, then away. "Goddamnit!" Harry had snapped, his voice now rough and bullying. "Did you *do* this?" Then Ray had swallowed and guessed that he had, and Harry had asked how many. Three hundred and fifty. Well, what had he done with them? A shrug. Harry had suggested he had given them out.

And so it had gone. Harry could recall every twitch, every evasion of the glass-like shifty eyes.

"Kind of," the kid said.

"*Kind* of?" Harry barked.

"Uhuh."

"When?"

Ray had claimed not to know. The hell he didn't, Harry said, voice climbing. Was it before the election? Well, Ray guessed so. No, he didn't guess so, Harry told him; he knew damn well. All right. He had given them out. Why?

"To help Paul and those guys," the boy said.

Did he really think they needed his help? Ray supposed not. Did he know it was against the rules, Harry asked, and Ray wrinkled his face in a fake-quizzical look that had made Harry want to kick him. Well, said the kid, he didn't know *exactly* if it was, but. . . . But he *thought* that it was? Harry suggested. Ray shrugged again. He thought it *might* have been, he said.

By then the depressing truth must have been clear to Harry, she realized, but he had pushed on, as she knew he would, he being himself.

"But you knew it was illegal to run on a ticket," Harry had asked. Ray conceded that he had. And, Harry pursued, Ray had been willing to jeopardize his buddies' chances. Ray claimed he hadn't looked at it like that. Oh? Then how had he looked at it?

There had come another shrug. Ray didn't know. He had just wanted to do it—that is, he guessed he *thought* the guys were going to win, and. . . .

He wanted to be a part of it?

"Yeah," Ray had said with another swallow. Then he summoned his nerve. "What are you going to do?" he asked. "You're not going to cancel the election?" (Now *his* voice had risen.) "I mean," he had plunged on, "this stuff didn't make any difference. It wasn't even close!"

"So the rules don't apply?" Harry had asked coldly.

Well, they applied, he guessed. . . .

Then Harry asked if Paul and the others had known about the cards. Probably, Ray said, though he hadn't informed them. Harry told him to go. Ray stood then, looking alarmed.

"Don't punish innocent people," he protested. "That isn't right."

"Spare me," Harry ordered. "Just *go!*"

Ray had gone.

Paul Devereux had seemed genuinely shocked and saw at once the implications. So did the others. They all had declared themselves ignorant and astounded, and, Harry had told her later, "They may well be. I am inclined to sympathize. But is that really the point?"

For him points were always clear, choices obvious, and, sensing within him some gathering and ghastly momentum, she had opposed him with stiffened spine, tightened jaw and a silence more crushing than sarcasm. He, understanding, had been moved to eloquence.

". . . He's their buddy. It's up to them to control him. It was done in their names. Maybe it didn't have much effect on the election, but people know. Alan knows. His parents know. Anybody who saw one of those cards or heard about them knows. . . ."

She had listened blankly, without a word, knowing what he would do.

He did it too, without any more conferences with Nichols or anyone else. ". . . I've cancelled the election," he informed the School Board (in closed session). The Board, like most, was a depressing combination of gravity and ignorance. Vain and touchy as judges, they were nevertheless tractable if gently handled. Porter, the contractor, had wanted to know what Harry was going to do to Ray. Nothing, Harry said. To make him the villain (though he was) was to absolve the people just disqualified. Anyway, getting your friends chucked out of office was a considerable punishment in itself—or should be. The Board had grumbled and demurred. Harry had reminded them, a little sharply, that they had asked for someone to shape things up. He hadn't made the rules, but he intended to enforce them. The Board brightened then and came around, and she was willing to bet that as they rose to go, Ruth Gordon, the hair "stylist," patted Harry's arm.

At school there had been hell to pay, though some of it was simply the teenage love of drama and the thrill of indignation. As Harry walked down the corridor a girl said, "Oh, that asshole! I can't *believe* he did this!" Meant to hear, Harry had pretended not to. The outraged had switched huffily away, slim thighs flashing beneath her scrap of skirt, painted mouth fashioning more obscenities. "Astarte in braces and Clerasil," Harry said sourly.

The assembly was another matter. The speeches had to be done again, and the auditorium rocked. Harry confessed that he jumped on stage (for once losing that insufferable Buddhistic tranquility) and told them they would all be back in their classrooms in two minutes if they didn't shut up. They shut--sort of, muttering and snarling but shying from open defiance. Alan Shields hadn't helped with his goofy grin and tactless rejoicing. *So I lucked out. Hey, you don't see me crying*! Harry said he could have cheerfully throttled him.

Then Alan won. The senior class buffoon opposed him, but the seniors boycotted the election, and the sophomores and juniors refused to back a joke candidate even in protest, and she on the phone could only blurt, "Oh, Colleen, I'm so sorry! I really am!" and to her humiliation she began to sob.

Colleen had been cool and laconic, saying in a voice that seemed to come from the stars, "I've got to go now," and the phone had clicked dead. Then it rang again, but it was only another furious caller—nameless, male and possibly drunk.

"I hope the son of a bitch is proud of himself!" the man shouted hoarsely—and hung up.

That was when she began to cry, and Harry blew up, exasperated by this misery which he took as accusation. Goddamnit! What did she *expect* him to do?

"I don't expect you to do anything!" she bawled hysterically. "I don't care what you do!" She wasn't making sense, but all at once some wall came down inside her, and she was pouring abuse on him, giving way to an astonishing grief and bitterness. When had he ever thought about her? When had he? He just went blundering along in his know-it-all way and never mind who got hurt and how! And it wasn't just her! Why had the children rebelled? Well, they had! He couldn't deny it. And she knew she was right, though she had never meant to say this, not to his face, but still, the bad marriages and destructive love affairs, the meaningless smothering jobs they had stumbled into—what was all this but a blind and fitful flight from his stern omniscience and relentless rule?

He had been wounded, had stiffened, his head coming up as though she had slapped him. Well good! *Good! Good! Good!* It served him right? But she couldn't sustain her fury or take any joy in his hurt, and sickness and despair had flowed over her, and a single thought remained like flotsam: she had ruined her life. It had all gone bad. Then she sank into a chair and gave herself up to her wretchedness, crying convulsively, letting go great hoots and honks of pain, while he stood there appalled, stricken mute by these grotesque wails. His hands lifted an inch or two, fingers apart in dumb surrender. Then the spasms had subsided. She had sniffed and blown her nose and moved quickly into the bedroom. He made for the gin.

And now she lay here, listening to him fuss with ice and glass and bottle, withdrawing like her. Let someone else bury the dead and minister to the wounded. He was quitting the field.

For a few minutes they had been naked, in a way that no marriage could withstand. Now she felt them slipping toward uneasy and dishonest truce. It couldn't be helped. The fires did burn down, and you had to look at one another, if only with sidelong glances. And eventually you had to talk. They would pretend this hadn't happened, but things would not be as before.

Was he thinking this too? She didn't know, but all at once she heard footsteps—heavy and measured—and knew he was standing in the doorway, as though waiting for permission to enter. And she knew *how* he was standing, flatfooted but straight, the weight back on heels, that pinched cast to his shoulders as though frozen in incipient shrug. His eyes would be dark and grave, his mouth solemn. The light would glint flatly off the pewter-colored hair and the glass with its clinking ice and clear bright liquid.

And so it was, and his voice, a notch lower than usual, seemed to paw and rummage words, though as always they came easily enough.

". . . Peg," he said quietly, "I know how much your friendship with Colleen means to you, but I can't let that affect what I have to do. I'm sorry. I genuinely am."

He managed, with a kind of genius, to weld humility and dignity, to be apologetic and yet paternal—and barely righteous. It was that "genuinely" that annoyed her, as though he had considered sham sorrow, as though even now he made careful distinctions and went by the rules.

"I admit," he said in his rumbling homiletical way, "that those damn cards probably didn't affect the election greatly. It may seem just a technicality, but the thing I find unendurable is Ray getting away with this, letting all these kids—and I do see them as that—believe he has some special dispensation to foul up other people's lives and not have to account for it."

She hadn't intended to reply, but now she heard herself say, "You mean you think it teaches them to defy authority?" The words carried a thin freight of bitchiness, but she tried to keep her voice neutral.

"No," he said heavily, taking his cue (he too spoke in that level reflective style). "No. Most of them don't have the nerve and never will, but I think it teaches them something worse—that authority is impotent and stupid. I think it throws them back on themselves too much. It mocks any discipline and order, and without that, as I see it, there isn't any real freedom. Well!" he said abruptly, "I'm starting to make a speech, and not a very good one. I'm sorry."

He would trick her from her anger, but she couldn't help it; it was sliding from her. She didn't forgive him or agree, but once again (how many times!) she had to admit that he had acted as he thought best, no matter the cost to himself. He could stand being hated for doing what he believed right, and this was admirable. Only, he could bear for *her* to be hated too; without a qualm he sacrificed her happiness, and maybe it *should* be sacrificed, but shouldn't it count for more? Shouldn't he struggle with his conscience a bit?

But she knew too it was just that bullheaded certainty she had craved and married for, just as he had sought in her something playful and free and enchanting to relieve his own gloomy authority. Really, what they hated in each other was the reverse side of what they loved. They had made their choices, and they were still learning the price of these elections. Nowadays people traded spouses in on different models or gave up quickly, deciding with a shrug to cut losses and move on. Not they. They accepted the consequences, because you had to if you claimed any sort of self-respect. And maybe this determination more than anything else was what they loved in one another.

Because she did love him, though she understood now that love could take many forms, was not to be confused with tenderness or desire or even intimacy, was a vocation and a discipline, the very thing she had yearned for. Its costs could be terrible and had to be paid.

So when he sat upon the creaking bed and clumsily took her hand, she didn't resist or draw away. The ice tinkled in his glass while he cleared his throat, on the point of saying something in that sepulchral chastened tone she knew so well when the doorbell sounded—not a bell at all but an inane succession of lilting chimes promising more drama and significance than the house could provide, this glum board-and-batten affair beyond decorative redemption.

"Probably the tar and feathers," Harry said. "I wonder if they brought a noose." He chuckled and rose. The bed yelped and sprang back, and he went smoothly down the hall, detouring through the kitchen to clink the glass down upon the counter, then moved with steady muffled tread to the door, which he opened with a pop and squeal of jambs.

"Hi Harry. Sorry to bother you but—"

"Not at all!" Harry said, abruptly jovial. "Come in. I was just about to open a vein or two."

There was a brief laugh, and someone stepped inside, and the door whammed shut. "Grant Nichols is here!" Harry called in a stage-husband voice, hospitable and expansive now, almost the country squire.

"I'll be right out, Grant!" she cried, appalled at her false and cheery words.

"Oh, don't bother, Peg!"

She stood, hiking her skirt into place, then she was in the bathroom, running water, dabbing at her eyes and inspecting them for redness and puffiness. With hard practiced strokes she tugged a brush through her hair, quickly reglossed her lips, and wetted a fingertip with cologne to anoint her throat. Was the skirt *too* wrinkled? Oh, it didn't matter! But of course it did. This too was a part of the discipline, this united front they would suddenly contrive, this *performance*. Places, everyone! Curtain going up!

Probably Grant wouldn't care if she appeared naked or in rags, but it mattered to her, was a sort of honor which neither he nor Harry need understand.

Entering the living room, however, she dropped her bright welcoming smile and swore. Harry had conducted their guest into what he liked to call his "study," a dreary cell of walnut, leather and brass, where he presided at an enormous desk on which rested the LT. CMDR. BREELAND nameplate, under a framed and overexposed photograph of officers (Harry among them) standing on a carrier deck, hands behind backs in a modified Parade Rest. In the dazzling light the khaki uniforms looked bathtub white, recalling the ice cream vendors of her girlhood.

"Hi Grant?"

"Oh, hi Peg!"

From ignorance or tact—impossible to tell—he didn't stand. Some men (not Harry), afraid of patronizing, had abandoned the conventions, so that these days rudeness merged with exquisite courtesy.

He was friendly as always, a round, doughy sort of man in slacks and shapeless blue cardigan, plumped down in the armchair beside the vast and immaculate prairie of Harry's desk. Near its edge rested a highball glass, and the sweetish bourbon smell mingled with hints of beeswax, saddle soap, Lemon Pledge and metal polish. Harry, she saw, had treated himself to another gin.

"Let me get you gentlemen something to nibble on."

"Oh, that's all right," Grant protested. "I just dropped in for a minute." He smiled, lifting his chubby placid face. Heaped in the chair, he suggested an amiable hedgehog or porcupine. Probably it was the bristling auburn hair.

"It'll just take a minute." She clicked off to the kitchen, scurrying expertly for board and knife, wheatcrackers, blocks of cheddar and Swiss, a half-moon of Camembert, a clutch of cold black olives and a tiny sheaf of cocktail napkins. From the study in hearty celebration Harry's voice now rolled.

". . . Well, we've taken a couple direct hits, lad, but I think we'll get 'er into port!" There came the tiny crash of ice cubes as he tilted his glass.

She stopped her flurry—amazed. He pretended triumph after all! Was all that bedroom abasement pure act? Had *that* been the charade? Or was it that Grant, fellow male and properly differential, prodded him to swagger? Yes, he was sorry if he had destroyed her life in this town, but really (so his pose and voice seemed to say), it couldn't be helped.

Casualties of war.

A slow, steady heat rose in her throat and face, and she took deep indignant breaths, lifting the tray.

". . . Well," Grant was saying, "I hope so."

"*Hope* so?"

In the pause that followed she started for the study. "You know," Grant continued, "I kind of wish you'd said something to me before you told the Board."

"Oh?"

"I understand. It was your call."

"It was," Harry said, casting an eye toward her as she entered, "and if somebody had to take the flak—and somebody did—I thought it had better be me alone."

She set the tray on the end table. "Oh," Grant said, "you *shouldn't* have, Peg! I didn't want you to go to any trouble."

"It's hardly trouble," she told him with a smile, "and it's not exactly a feast."

"Well, it looks awful good!"

He popped an olive in his mouth and with thick freckled fingers cautiously lifted a cracker bearing a wedge of cheddar. "No," he said to Harry, "I understand." And he bit into his cracker.

Did he understand? Did he suspect that Harry had slogged on alone out of fear that he was becoming too dependent on Grant? Sometimes, it seemed, he was hellbound to assert, if only for himself, who was in charge.

To her Harry said: "Why don't you join us? There's some white wine in the refrigerator."

"Well. . . ." At her entrance Grant, for all his agreeableness, had flashed a questioning glance at his superior. Now with this lord-of-the-manor invitation Harry put his lieutenant neatly in his place. *What you say to me you may say to my wife!* All the same, she was nettled.

"In a minute," she said shortly, and returned to the kitchen. In the study Harry said:

"Why? You think I blew it?"

Chewing vigorously, Grant said: "I don't know."

"You think," Harry asked, a little menacingly, "I should have looked the other way?"

She paused before the refrigerator. The voices drifted in, clear but hollow, like the voices of people calling down a rain pipe.

". . . No," Grant said, "I don't. If Ray did it you didn't have any choice."

"*If!*" Then Harry, ruffled, yanked a drawer. "You saw this?"

"No," Grant said mildly. "No, I didn't."

Absently now, she opened the refrigerator and withdrew the bottle, uncorked it and poured half a wineglass. ". . . Well," Harry was saying, "our boy Ray printed and distributed several hundred. I can tell you that."

"Did he?"

"He said he did. I bullied it out of him, but, hell, I was upset. I don't mind admitting it."

Corking the bottle, she set it on the shelf and closed the door. From the study came the sound of Grant meditatively tapping the card on the desk.

"This came from Alan?"

"You bet."

Slowly, as though masticating his words, Grant said, "*You* saw it, and Alan saw it, and Ray. And you showed it to Paul and the others?"

"That's right."

She started back, walking briskly.

"And that," Grant mused, "is probably about it."

Entering the study, she saw him flopped back in the chair, staring straight ahead in a glazed way, under Harry's frown.

". . . I can't prove it," he was saying now, "but I bet you'd be hard put to find another one of these." His eyes met Harry's and held his look. "I mean," he went on, "*I* didn't see any, and I don't think anyone else did either, no matter *what* Ray said."

She stood, glass in hand—breath suddenly shallow—looking from one to the other. Harry's face darkened.

"You're telling me," he said, "that Ray never made these up—and didn't hand them out?"

"That's my belief."

"Then why—"

"Because," Grant said, "he wanted you to think he did. And he wanted Alan to think he did."

Harry shook his head. "Even if it cost his friends the election?"

They had forgotten her. Or rather, she did not count. Wine untasted, she remained on her feet, beginning to tremble, looking down upon Grant's auburn quills and pale scalp, and on Harry's thin, wavy, pewter hair. His lips thickened now; his brow grew heavier, his dark eyes more troubled and perplexed.

". . . Ray doesn't have any friends," Grant explained. "Not really. Sometimes I think he doesn't want any. That's what you have to understand."

"But," Harry said, " he told me—"

"He'll deny it," Grant said. "He'll deny he made the damn things in the first place. If he's bastard enough, he might suggest that Alan invented the whole business. Who knows?"

"No!" she said. It was out before she knew it.

Harry ignored her, shaking his head once more in wondering denial. "But," he insisted, "he said—"

"Sure he did," Grant agreed. "And you can't prove it. And if you try, you look like you're covering your own rear, because Ray will ask,

'where *are* those damn cards? And who says I did it?'"
Wincing, she closed her eyes, then opened them. "Oh God!"
Stunned, fumbling still, Harry said: "When somebody tells you—"
She took a step, set the glass upon the table. "But," she broke in, "what about the Board?"
The round earnest face turned. "The Board probably won't know what to believe," Grant said, "but they'll wonder where all those cards *went* to, I can promise you that. Of course, they went along with it, so they're in it too."
"I see." She drew a short, painful breath, and her legs went weak. Then she nodded slowly, her throat filling once more, her pulse beating in her temples, and for a moment the pale crafty face of Ray Harmon leaped before her, the colorless eyes shining with a triumph so subtle and bright it passed for fear. Probably he *had* been frightened—and exhilarated too, living for the risk and these cheap victories. Oh, but she saw! Even as Harry was beginning to see.
Word would get out. Ray would take care of that. And as long as they lived here this would follow them. *Principal claimed there were all these cards, but I don't know. . . . Tried to blame it on the kid. . . .* Yes, Ray spied you out. The defective ear, the flat chest, the harmless intellectual vanity, the pig-headed regard for justice—these he noticed and turned to account, a desperate and lonely boy finding in others what he railed against in himself—which did not console her. When had Harry ever understood the Ray Harmons of the world? Oh when? He thought himself wise and shrewd and experienced, but in certain places his imagination failed.
Harry leaned forward. His lip came out and his big hand turned into a fist. Thumping the desk, he said fiercely, "I could kill the son of a bitch! I really could!"
She was not impressed, knowing now the full, hideous meaning of a choice made long ago. She had picked badly, and succumbed unwisely, yet it would have been all right. But now . . . They could pretend, could play their parts, but he would not recover, would not shake free of her contempt, which would grieve her more than him. Oh yes! He could storm about, but it would be mere noise and pointless strut, and if he thought he could posture himself back into her esteem—or his own either—he was wrong. But he knew that too, she saw, for his eyes, clawing at her, were great with panic and appeal.

Neighbors Near the Fence

R. Nikolas Macioci

Toward the end of a day when the sun ate
roses and fences were whiter by noon,
next door neighbors, empty as sea silence,
come to the fence, the ash of their cookout
fires stuck to their shoes like summer snow.

From the property line they extend
a simple invitation, initiate
trite words from a subtle hunger to talk,
to share the boredom of a marriage
that has betrayed them. Later, I notice
dusk has climbed our skins,
rolled a wave of night over us.

They point to constellations,
to the rattling moon,
a blistering sun in the cedar branches.
I look away, sick from their tedium.
Like chickens in a barnyard, they pick
their way through darkness to their back door,
nocturnal faces nameless now,

stones come to rest in a dead house.

A Cottage for Sale

James Cushing

All I see through an overlay of green
Plus all you hear underneath the cries of morning birds
Plus the Renaissance profile of the cacti against the furnace
Result in these twin pillows, this hundred-dollar bed,
These circles of damp wood cartoon-captioning the ceiling.

You were a reservoir a city depended on.
Let me suggest more water in your future. Look
At what we brought up by wondering out loud
About fictional characters in a psychology text,
Taking off the hesitant bits of hat and glove.

You told me your girlhood nickname was "Curfew."
I suddenly remembered the address:
One Hundred Thousand Sycamore Drive.
Chimes rang all the time then. The forest served,
You insisted. This strange hour needs an answer, even

If you mean paraphrasable content accompanied by a set
Of moral principles you get to feel guilty about
Until the unnamed thing within the work
Arises like a leopard from the veldt and stands before you
Saying "Ride me" with its shy, magnificent head.

Eurydice's Lot

Alice Friman

He packed it up—
the camel, the tasseled rugs,
the copper pots clanking off the hump—
leaving the old girl behind, veiled to the spot,
two feet jammed into one shoe.

Couldn't carry a tune
or tweedle a pipe but hero enough he'd be
to lead Eurydice out if he'd a mind to,
not giving a damn, the way he did,
if she fell or followed. One eye he had
and that forward, forward,
straight to Duluth if he knew
where that was, not that
it would have mattered in a world
where looking back with sorrow
for what never was is worse
than following a camel's rump
anywhere it goes.

And Eurydice? Mama's apple girl?
She'd have trudged behind
squinting for a sudden sign or stir,
crooning for the sly one
to come in from the high grass again
winding his surgeon's eye
the way he did that first time
when love-stiffened
he coiled
then nibbled her soft
into a sweet brown sin:

"Oh, Worm
Great Slitherer
hammer of my heel
of my heel's own heart

Subtlety of double sight
in whose salt rings
all future spins, and past,
the same as what that other
must have seen—cocoon of sorrows
prisoner of her own salt-spun eye

Here in front of me—single file—
shuffles dry duty
a different kind of cage
Sweet Vicious
Shucker of Skins
come and help me now."

God's Country

Greg Luthi

My parents' separation in the spring of 1968 stunned me, much as the Tet Offensive shocked the country a few months before. For as long as I could remember, my parents reacted to one another as if from a great distance, safely removed from affection and anger, and I saw nothing wrong or unusual about it. They were that kind of people, that was the way they did things, and I was used to it. I assumed the love they gave me was privately felt for each other, privately displayed in ways reserved for adults, which I had no business, nor the inclination, to question--until they announced their separation. Then I called everything into question, and none of my parents' explanations satisfied me. I was seventeen, and for the first time in my life I longed for the past.

My parents decided it would be best if I lived somewhere else for the summer, until they could sort things out, and my grandparents, who owned a farm in central Kansas, agreed to take me. And so, when school ended, I packed a few bags and left Kansas City. I left most of my belongings behind, grasping at the notion that if my room remained intact, so would my parents' marriage.

If I longed for the past, there seemed no better place to find it than my grandparents' farm. There was the hayloft in which I'd once led the charge against Indians, the stone tank in which I splashed after goldfish, the gabled farmhouse in whose shadow the past seemed a tangible presence. Among these things I thought I could retreat, only to discover the present followed me like an unwanted friend.

Even my grandparents, whose ordered and predictable lives seemed symbolic of the past, surprised me the day I arrived, revealing a motive for taking me in that had nothing to do with my parents' separation.

We had almost finished supper when my grandmother touched her mouth with her napkin and said, "We were thinking, Danny, you might work for a woman who lost her husband this spring. You'd work here too, of course, but anything you could do for her would help."

"What kind of work?" I asked. "What happened to her husband?"

"He was killed in the war," my grandfather said. "Didn't live to see his twenty-second birthday. He took over his folks' farm when his father died, and now Emma's all alone to run it."

"Her folks help her as much as they can," my grandmother added, "but they've got their own farm to think about. I don't know how she's going to manage all by herself. She ought to sell the place."

"Emma's a stubborn girl," my grandfather said. "Always was. She's got something to prove."

"She can't run the place by herself, Al. She works day and night, and all she gets is further behind."

"She'll clear the summer if Danny helps."

My grandparents looked at me, and there was nothing I could do but agree to help. I didn't much care one way or the other. I didn't know this woman, couldn't share my sympathy I'd reserved for myself.

I arrived on Friday, and was not to start helping our neighbor until Monday, so I had the weekend to myself. Unable to find anything else to do, I went for a drive Saturday evening, roaming the dusty gravel roads sectioning the land. The broad expanse of the fields and pastures magnified my loneliness, conjured memories I hoped to forget. Every road I took, a memory waited.

There it was: my mother holding me in her lap as she read to me. The story she read didn't matter. I was hardly aware of the bright illustrations. What mattered was her voice, her crisp, ironed blouse, her smooth, cool skin and fresh smell that made me think of the yard after a rain. What mattered were her arms around me, her breasts like pillows into which I could sink my head and feel safe, full, content, as if I would never again be hungry or afraid.

It was that way with my father as I sat in his lap and watched *The Wizard of Oz* for the first time, the television spitting shadows across the walls as malevolent as the cyclone and the wicked witch. My father was there. His broad, firm chest was a defense against evil, a rock to which I could cling and know it would hold; his arms were shields that warded off cyclones and falling houses.

I could not bear the loss. I stopped the car and got out. It was dark, the sky salted with bitter stars. I looked blindly around. The fields of ripening wheat spread like dark water over the terraces, their enormity overwhelming. I felt lost, cut adrift.

During Sunday dinner, my grandmother said, "Emma Tucker wasn't in church today."

"Art Baer saw her raking alfalfa," my grandfather replied. "She wants to start baling with Danny first thing in the morning."

"It's more than that. She hasn't been to church since Wyatt's funeral."

People are beginning to talk."

"They've been talking all spring."

"She's losing her faith," my grandmother said. "Both times Reverend Peters went to visit her, she said she was too busy to talk. The second time, she walked right off the porch and left him standing there. Louella and Vivian called her about club meetings, and she barely spoke to them. She even hung up on Louella."

"Good for her," my grandfather said, winking at me.

"Be serious, Al. Jud and Estalene are worried, say they hardly know their daughter anymore. The farm's in Emma's name, and they can't do anything but watch her go under."

"Give her a chance. Things aren't that bad. Jud's been helping her, and so have the Schmutz brothers."

"Not anymore, not with summer here. They've got too much to do."

"That's why Danny's here," my grandfather said. "He'll help her clear the summer, then she'll be okay. Right, Danny?"

I said nothing, only nodded.

The grass was bright with dew when I left for Emma Tucker's farm the next morning. She lived on a rise a quarter-mile west of us; if not for the windbreak protecting my grandparents' garden, I would have been able to see her house from my window.

Her place looked deserted as I turned into the semicircular driveway. The house had a shuttered look, closed to the morning, wind chimes hanging silently along the porch. The flowerbeds were bare except for splashes of volunteer marigolds, and the grass ran ragged over the flagstone walk. Silence filled the air, amplifying the sound of my steps on the gravel.

Emma Tucker strode around the corner of the house to meet me, her vigorous steps announcing the urgency of our mission. She was tall and lean in jeans and a plaid sleeveless shirt, her dark hair woven into a short braid. My grandmother told me she was twenty-two, but she looked deep in womanhood, self-possessed, with eyes at once penetrating and remote. The sweetness of youth still lingered in her face, but it had hardened, in danger of turning brittle.

Without any introduction, she said, "We'll do the east pasture first. The dew'll make the bales heavy, but it'll burn off by mid-morning."

We walked around the house to the farmyard, where the tractor, baler, and hayrack formed a caravan. She put on a straw hat and said, "Know anything about baling?"

"I helped my grandpa once. He showed me how to hook and stack."

"You want to do that or drive?"

"I'll stack."

"Okay. Holler if I go too fast. If you get tired, we'll trade places."

"I'll be okay," I said. Feeling my manhood was in question, I jumped on the hayrack to show my readiness.

I enjoyed baling with my grandfather, liked the slow, steady rhythm of hooking and stacking the bales, the sun on my back, muscles awakening. Baling with Emma Tucker was a different story. She drove as if possessed, at a frenetic pace that left me soaked with sweat halfway through the first load. The bales were as heavy as blocks of concrete, and my muscles screamed in outrage. A buzz clicked on in my head, and the field began to swim before my eyes, the windrows squirming like snakes across the stubbly ground.

I grew more exasperated with each bale I stacked, but I refused to ask her to slow down. My anger and frustration of the last few weeks came to a boil in the hot sun, and I needed someone to blame. So I blamed Emma. She was challenging me unfairly, testing me, seeing how far she could push a city kid; she was punishing me for my kindness, my willingness to help her when I had better ways of spending my time.

When we finished the load, she called for me to help her unhook the baler. I jumped off the hayrack and staggered toward her.

"Where's the goddamn fire?" I shouted brutally.

She looked up at me from the shadow of her straw hat, her expression unchanged. "I told you to holler."

"I didn't have time to holler, I was too busy busting my ass. You got eyes, don't you?"

"You looked like you were doing fine." She checked her watch. "We made good time. We'll go slower the next load. Give me a hand."

I helped her unhook the baler, then hook the tractor to the hayrack. Her indifference was maddening, but I felt a little better now the baling had stopped. She handed me the jug and inspected the pattern I'd used in stacking the bales.

"You did a good job," she said. "Your grandpa taught you right."

"Thanks," I said. Her compliment and the cool water had a soothing effect. "I guess I'm not used to this."

"First load's the hardest. The bales'll get lighter now the hay's dry." She jumped onto the hayrack, grunted as she lifted a bale. "You weren't kidding. Like concrete."

At the hay barn, I loaded the bales onto the elevator while she stacked them inside. When we finished, she came out into the sunlight, her face and arms streaked with alfalfa dust, shirt splotched with sweat. Her eyes looked glazed, and a faint click sounded in her throat when she swallowed. She gulped thirstily from the jug, splashed water on her face. I realized how heavy the bales must have been for her, how suffocating it must have been inside with the sun bearing down on the tin roof.

As she handed me the jug, her eyes regained their clarity and purpose. "Ready to start the next load?" she asked.

"I'm ready."

"You want to drive this time?"

"I'll stay on the hayrack," I said.

She drove slower this time, and the bales didn't seem as heavy. The humidity had burned off, and a dry breeze swept through the field, billowing alfalfa dust each time I hooked a bale and brought it thudding onto the hayrack. The heat felt good, searing away the aches and pains of the winter, my thoughts of home.

The second load stacked in the barn, we went to the house for lunch. Emma turned on a fan and we sat down to sandwiches, fruit, and cold bottles of Pepsi. Unlike my grandparents, she offered no prayer.

"How long're you staying?" she asked.

"Depends on my parents. They're separated, trying to get their act together. They'll probably get divorced." The statement startled me, for I hadn't really believed until that moment they would do such a thing. But now, suddenly, I couldn't deny the logic: people who separated got divorced. I stared at the table, my lunch forgotten, and when Emma spoke, her voice seemed to come from far away.

"Who gets you when you move back?"

I hadn't the slightest idea. I'd never considered it. I sat there in growing anger, feeling my parents had played a cruel joke on me, until I exploded, "Nobody gets me."

"What'll you do?"

"Whatever I have to," I said bitterly. "Maybe I'll join the army and get shipped to Vietnam. That'd serve 'em right."

It was out of my mouth before I remembered her husband. My anger deflated, I groped for an apology, gave in finally to the heavy silence. We finished the meal without another word. I glanced at her only once, saw nothing had changed. Her expression was impenetrable, as if she had transcended emotion. I envied her.

That evening, after we'd done the chores, she insisted I eat supper with her. While she worked in the kitchen, I got the mail. The newspaper carried a story about Bobby Kennedy, my hero that summer, who was to die in just three days.

During supper, I told Emma about Bobby Kennedy, how he would end the war and heal the country's wounds. She remained silent through it all, indifferent to everything except her fried chicken and potatoes. Impatient, I said, "What about it? Don't you think he's the best?"

"I don't think it makes any difference," she said.

"Sure it does. It makes all the difference in the world. Bobby's going to change things, make them better."

"If Bobby Kennedy wants to make things better, he's welcome to put up hay and harvest wheat."

She abruptly stood up and left the room. I thought I'd made her angry, but she returned a minute later with pie and ice cream. "Dig in," she said. "No one can say I didn't feed you."

I didn't think of Emma that night, my parents, or Bobby Kennedy, or all that was wrong with the world. I dreamed no dreams that I could remember. I was exhausted after the long day, and for the first time in weeks I fell quickly asleep.

During a break the next afternoon, Emma and I sat beneath a tree and ate a small lunch. We were baling the north field now, a plot of land surrounded by dense trees and underbrush that blocked the wind, leaving the air still and sweet with the aroma of cut alfalfa. The world where people fought, died, and separated seemed far away.

From out of the blue, Emma said, "What're they saying about me these days?"

"Who?"

"Your grandparents, the people at church. What do they say about crazy Emma living all by herself with her crazy ideas?"

"They're worried about you," I said. "Grandma thinks you're losing your faith because you don't go to church anymore. Grandpa thinks you'll be okay if you get through the summer."

"What do the others think?"

"They think you're stubborn, going to lose the farm. Grandpa says you've got something to prove."

"Do they think I'm crazy?"

"I don't know."

"What do *you* think, Danny?"

It was the first time she spoke my name; I wasn't even sure she knew it. I took a bite of my sandwich to give me time to think of an answer. I said, "I think you want to keep your farm."

"You don't think I'm crazy?"

"Do *you*?" When she didn't answer, I said, "Are you trying to prove something?"

"I'm not trying to prove anything. I don't know what else to do. This is all I've got."

"I can see why you want to keep it. It's a good place."

She smiled for the first time since I'd met her. "God's country. That's what the minister called it when he came to visit me after Wyatt died. I was working in the farmyard, and he looked around with a smile and spread his arms and said, 'God's country. This is truly God's country.' And there I was under the tractor with grease up to my elbows. I knew a sermon was coming, and I didn't have time for it, so I got up and said, 'You'll excuse me, but God's country's got to be plowed by sundown.' I walked off, and the last I saw, he was looking at me like I was off my rocker. Maybe I was."

"No wonder they think you're losing your faith," I said.

"Maybe I never had any to start with," she replied, and finished her lunch without saying another word.

Tired as I was, I was unable to sleep that night. The baling was finished, and I wasn't sure when I'd see Emma again. The uncertainty nagged me, like a half-remembered thought, though I didn't know why it should. Finally I got out of bed and stood at the window, my view of Emma's farm blocked by the windbreak. Dressing, I crept downstairs.

The night was warm, the air fragrant with the scent of soil and vegetables as I passed through the garden. I poked my way through the windbreak and stood in the shadows, where I gazed at Emma's farm. It looked dark and lonely, the house a shadow against the starry night.

I thought about people living alone, how for some it was a choice, for others a circumstance beyond their control. I wondered what it was like for Emma to turn off the lights and go to bed each night, knowing she was alone in the darkness. I wondered what it was like for my mother and father to suddenly be alone after twenty years, reviewing the past for the point at which things went wrong. Perhaps it was no different when they'd lived together. If that was the case, why couldn't they stay together? Surely it was better to be alone among family than have no one at all.

I didn't see Emma for a while, for I was busy on my grandparents' farm. I baled hay with my grandfather, tended the garden with my grandmother, shingled the garage and mowed the grass—in general, working harder than I ever had in my life. During that time, Bobby Kennedy died, and my parents grew further apart. They called every few days to see how I was doing; by design, they kept the focus on me, evaded my questions. I knew my father had leased an apartment, and that my mother had taken a weekend trip to St. Louis with her friend Joy Carter, a divorced woman who lived on our street. Beyond that, their lives were as mysterious as the pronouncement with which my mother concluded one of her calls: "Enjoy life."

Enjoy life. How was I to do that stuck on a farm in the middle of nowhere? Other than work, eat, and sleep, there was nothing to do but go to church once a week and watch the single channel my grandparents got on their TV. Besides my grandparents, I knew no one except Emma, and she hardly qualified as someone with whom I might *enjoy life*.

And yet I felt myself turn in her direction. I decided we shared a similar predicament, and the least we could do was commiserate with each other. That was why I went to see her one evening, not long before the wheat harvest.

An old, battered Chevrolet stood in the driveway, and a man with a similar beaten look sat with Emma on the porch swing. As I got out of my car, he rose and gave me a wary look, as if I'd caught him in a compromising act. He was older than my father, close to fifty, small and spare, with the air of a man who has known only hard times but believes fortune is just around the corner. I could see it in his hungry, rodent-like eyes: he could finally smell the feast he'd dreamed of for years.

Emma sat unmoving, as still as the evening air, wearing a colorful print dress that didn't soften her features. Her face was as inscrutable as ever.

"Well, I better be going," the man said, to no one in particular.

"I can come back some other time," I said uncertainly.

"Naw, I was going anyway." But he gave no indication of leaving, held by the aroma of the feast. He rocked slightly on the balls of his feet, hands thrust deep in his pockets; as he gazed across the yard, he smiled and jingled his keys, as if registering the intensity of his anticipation. I suddenly felt the urge to kick him off the porch.

Abruptly he said, "So long, Emma. I'll be in touch." As he drove away, I asked her who he was.

"Someone I know." She had set the swing in motion, back and forth in precise little arcs, as if keeping time to her thoughts.

"What's his name?"

"George Utter."

"Is he making trouble?"

"No. What do you want?"

"I came to see how you're doing, when you want me to work."

"There's always work."

"Are you doing anything now?" I asked.

"Why?"

"I thought we could do something."

"Like what?"

"I don't know. Maybe we could go for a drive."

"Where?"

"Anywhere. Just drive."

She continued to swing, as if she had no intention of going anywhere. Then she abruptly brought the swing to a halt and said, "I can't stay out too late."

I had thought we could form a friendship, but as we drove in silence along the country roads, I was ready to admit it was a mistake. We had nothing to say, like passengers on a bus. Emma took no recognition of the world beyond her farm, her gaze set firmly on the road.

My frustration grew until finally I said, "Look, that guy bothers me. What's he want with you?"

"If I tell you, will you promise not to tell?"

"I can keep a secret."

"He asked me to marry him."

I hit the brakes as if a stop sign had suddenly appeared in front of us. We came to a stop in a cloud of dust, and I stared at her and repeated, "Marry you."

"It's the only way I can keep the farm. I can't do it all by myself."

"You've got *me*," I said. "That's what I'm here for."

"It's not enough. Even if I clear the summer, I'll need someone else when you're gone. And the wheat harvest, I can't do it all by myself."

"I'll help you."

"You have to help your grandparents."

"I'll help you when we're finished."

"The wheat can't wait. When it turns, you harvest it or else. And without the wheat I'm finished."

I stared across the fields, seeing only an image of a hungry little man waiting for a feast. "Who is this guy?" I said. "What's he do?"

"He's a janitor at the high school in Chapman. He used to own a farm,

till he ran into a streak of bad luck."
 "Do you love him?"
 "No."
 "Then you're not going to marry him?"
 "I might."
 "So you'd marry a guy twice your age you don't even love, just to keep your farm."

Her mouth wrinkled into something resembling a smile. "I can't lose God's country, can I?"

On the way home, she asked me to stop by the church. It was almost dark when we arrived, the great white steeple aiming for the first stars. I parked next to the cemetery as she directed, and followed her inside to a recent grave, whose stone I couldn't read in the failing light. I didn't have to ask who was buried there.

Arms folded, Emma gazed down at the grave and said, "He wasn't there one week before he got killed. He didn't even have time to do anything. It's like they sent him over there for no reason but to die, fill the quota. Men have to die in a war, and they decided he'd be one of them, so he might as well go ahead and get it over with. Maybe it's just as well. I've heard stories how awful it is over there, how they suffer. How they change, turn into men you don't know. This way, he got it over with in a hurry."

She knelt beside the grave and ran her hand over it. "I didn't think the grass would grow so fast. Pretty soon it'll look like all the others." Rising, she looked into the darkness, in an attitude of listening. Around the cemetery the wheat whispered urgently. Heeding it, she started for the car.

At breakfast the next morning, I said, "Emma told me a guy named George Utter wants to buy some of her land."

My grandmother was surprised. "George Utter? I didn't think he had the money."

"What kind of land?" my grandfather asked. "What's he going to do with it?"

"She didn't say, just he was interested. She said he had a streak of bad luck."

"I'll say," my grandmother confirmed. "The man lost his wife to cancer and couldn't get over it. His farm went to pot, and he had to sell it to pay off his debts."

I said, "He sounds like trouble to me."

"He's a nice enough man, I suppose. The heart went out of him when Gladys died, and he's never been the same since."

It wasn't what I wanted to hear. I'd hoped for a darker secret in George Utter's life, one I could lay before Emma in all its ugliness. He wasn't meant to appear in the picture I'd framed around her and me, but I didn't know how to convince her of that.

Feeling I was in competition with George Utter, I started doing chores for her. I fed the livestock, gathered the eggs, nurtured her sickly garden back to health, whatever I could to give her more time to work in the fields, convince her George Utter was not indispensable. It was a peculiar relationship we had. We worked the same land, toiling in the heat and the dust as we strived for the same goal, yet barely acknowledging each other.

Then one afternoon during lunch, I brought up the subject of the wheat harvest. It was just a few days away, and I asked if she had help lined up.

"George is helping me," she said.

"Doesn't he have to work?"

"He's taking vacation time."

"What's he get in return? He expect you to marry him?"

"He doesn't expect anything."

"Oh really. What a generous guy."

"I'm paying him for his work."

"He doesn't want money. You know it and I know it."

Unruffled, she replied, "You know an awful lot about things that aren't your business." And she refused to say anything more.

I didn't see Emma during the wheat harvest—or rather, I saw only the headlights of her combine as she worked late into the night. Standing in the shadow of the windbreak, I watched the lights cut a pale swath as the combine passed back and forth in the darkness, like a ship that had lost its bearings. Rescue seemed at hand when another set of lights appeared in the distance, but it was only George Utter returning from the grain elevator, as lost in his own dream as Emma was in hers.

The phrase most often used at church to described Emma was "mentally unstable," and there was talk that her parents might take "drastic action," though the nature of this was never clear to me. I too received a share of attention, mostly in the form of curious looks, since I was the boy who spent so much time at her place. I didn't know what was said about me, and if my grandparents knew, they didn't say. Even they, sympathetic to Emma for so long, began to question whether I should continue to work for a woman who had cut herself loose from the community without the slightest hesitation, who was now rumored to be having an affair with George Utter. I defended her as best I could, saying an affair with George Utter was ridiculous, that, to use my grandfather's words, she was simply a stubborn girl. I wouldn't have persuaded them, however, if I hadn't told them that working for Emma made me happy at a time in my life when there was little to be happy about.

As much as I hated all the gossip, I was on the verge of believing it myself, especially when I didn't hear from Emma after the harvest. I drove over to see her one morning, expecting anything except what I found.

She was working in the garden, and when I greeted her she stiffened, keeping her back to me, and said harshly, "Go home. No work for you today." She resumed her hoeing, working slowly, painfully, as if her body were arthritic.

I went into the potato patch and blocked her way. She didn't stop, and if I hadn't grabbed the hoe she would have speared my foot. She glared at me, her battered face accentuating her anger. Her left eye was swollen purple, her lower lip split open, scabbing.

"What happened?" I exclaimed.

"I'm okay," she murmured. "Go on home."

"What happened?" I demanded, and then answered for her: "George Utter did it, didn't he?" As I stared at her, absorbing the evidence, another thought jolted me. "What else did he do?"

"Nothing. He got scared and took off." She wrenched the hoe from my grip and attacked the ground savagely, as if George Utter lay there.

As I stepped from her path, the truth crystallized. "I know why he did it. He didn't get what he wanted."

"I paid him good wages," she said stubbornly.

"You led him on. He thought if he helped you harvest you'd marry him."

"It that's what he thought, he was wrong. I told him I'd pay him."

"He was expecting more, and you know it. He wanted to marry you, you told me so yourself."

"I never said I would."

"You led him on. I don't know whether to be mad at him or you."

She stopped hoeing, her left eye squinting obscenely at me through bruised tissue. "What's it to you?" It was a question to which I had no answer. Silenced, I walked away.

I got as far as my car before she called to me. The sound of her voice pulled me back to the garden, where she stood leaning on the hoe. Her gaze passed through me, as if I were invisible. She said, "If you want to keep on with the chores, you can." I was too angry to reply. I went back to my car, followed by silence, and drove away.

I resumed my chores at Emma's because I needed a purpose, something to hold on to. My parents grew further apart, and I knew what the outcome would bring. It was evident in the way they talked, the things they talked about: they had lives of their own.

And so I returned to Emma. I tended her garden, helped her plow the stubble fields, ran errands in Chapman while her face healed. July crested, fell into August, and though the days remained long and hot, there was a feeling that time was running short.

One afternoon during the second hay baling, we stopped for a break in the north pasture. As we sat beneath a tree, lunching on sandwiches and fruit, Emma said, "We'll finish tomorrow. After you help your grandpa, we'll cultivate the milo."

"I'm going home," I said.

She gave me a rare look of surprise. "So soon? It's only the first week

of August."
"School starts in a few weeks."
"Stay till then. I'll pay you."
"I have to go."
"You told me you didn't want to go home. You said nobody gets you. You're alone, I'm alone. We won't be if we stay together."
"Would it really make a difference?" I said.
She was silent. Then, abruptly, she wrapped what was left of her sandwich and stuffed it in the sack. "Come on. We don't have all day."

The hay barn was almost full when we finished unloading that evening. Emma came outside and sat down on a bale in the shadow of the barn. She gazed across the fields, gold in the evening light. After a time she said, "I want you to stay on. You can live here, go to school in Chapman. We'll make a good team."

"I have to go home."

"I'll pay you," she said, "and cook for you. Everything. Just like we were married."

I thought of George Utter and the feast he smelled, would never taste. I thought of my parents, who accepted their failure. I asked softly, "Why is it so important to you?"

"It's Wyatt's," she said. "I can't let go of it."

Her answer was not enough. I followed her gaze across the land, trying to find her field of vision. I could not. Finally she stood up. As she started for the house, she told me to think about it, give her my answer tomorrow.

That was the night my mother and father called to tell me they were getting a divorce. They called together from the house, a final act of family unity. They talked; I listened. No explanation was needed. This was the way things happened sometimes. Some people were ready to let go; others were not.

When I think of my last day with Emma, I cannot help contrasting it to the first. On that final day, she placed me on an awkward pedestal. She insisted on doing everything: stacking every load of bales, opening gates, serving me food and water at every break, suggesting I rest if I was tired. She did it all with a cheerful smile, as if her happiness depended upon the sacrifice she made.

Finally, I could stand it no longer. As we prepared to bale another load, I told her I'd stack this time.

"I can do it," she said. She started onto the hayrack, and I pulled her off.

"Get on the tractor," I shouted. "You'll kill yourself if you keep this up. You're going to kill yourself anyway, trying to save this farm."

Anger flared in her eyes, then died. "I just wanted to make it easier for you."

"I'm not staying, so quit being nice. I liked you better the other way."

She stared at me, then staggered off to the tractor, her figure drooping

in the heat. It took all my will to keep from changing my mind.
The day came to an end, the last bale filling the barn. There was no space left, no nook or cranny into which any stray bale could be fitted. I was struck by the sum weight of the bales, the knowledge that Emma and I had pushed, pulled, and carried it piece by piece to completion. I wondered how she could want to do it again, year after year.

As if reading my thoughts, she said, "It'll be empty come next spring."

I felt her gaze, but said nothing. I tried to think of a way to say goodbye. She said, "No use standing around. I'll start supper."

"I'm going home." I meant to my grandparents' house, but it must have sounded to her as if I meant Kansas City.

"I'm fixing you supper. Go wash up."

We ate in silence, until she cleared the table and brought in a layered chocolate cake. A hole had been poked in the middle, where a candle had been inserted and removed. She stood beside me as she cut the cake. I smelled the odors of the kitchen clinging to her, the pungent odors of the farm, the sweat and grime and ache soap could not wash away. I felt her hand on my shoulder, tentative, inept. A voice said, "Please."

Through the window, the yard was growing dim in the twilight. The grass needed to be cut. It would always need to be cut. I thought of the yard at home; it had to be tended. The grass would have to be cut, the flowers watered. The leaves would have to be raked and bagged in the fall, the driveway cleared in the winter. It all would have to be tended, again and again and again.

I rose from the table, and the hand that touched me slipped away, like the napkin that fluttered from my lap. No voice called to me as I went to the door, and I did not look back. Outside, I breathed deeply the evening air, and started for my car. With each step I took, I felt I was approaching myself, until at last I stepped into the figure that awaited me all summer.

Two days later I returned home to my mother. I found my room exactly as I had left it, save for a fine layer of dust. I gave it a good dusting and went on from there, to dinners and football games with my father, to school and friends and college entrance exams.

I didn't see Emma again, but my grandparents kept me informed. They seemed to feel it was their duty to observe and record her descent, as if it were a lesson from which I could learn. Given my loyalty to her that summer, they probably thought I wanted to know.

Emma survived the fall and winter, but a hailstorm in late spring ruined her wheat crop, and she carried no insurance. To pay her debts, she was forced to sell eighty acres of prime land. My grandmother said it was God's way of taking away what no longer could be hers. Whether or not Emma arrived at the same conclusion, I don't know. But selling that land must have broken something inside her, for she gave up farming and rented the rest of her land, including the hay barn we worked so hard to fill. Perhaps she realized the futility of her struggle, grew tired of battling the odds and herself as she strived to keep something she had already lost.

And yet, in spite of this defeat, she refused to leave. She kept her house, the garden, and enough of the farm to raise chickens. Long after my grandparents retired and moved to Chapman, she stayed on alone, exiled to the past, holding on to the wish we all relinquish sooner or later.

Horror Film

Miriam McCluney

After the horror movie at the drive-in
we would play out our fears
in the dark of our attic bedroom.
In a parody of stiff arms and moron eyes,
we would move across the narrow light
of the skylight like the zombies
we had seen the night before.

We were such little girls. Such
little girls to have such monstrous
fears of dark men moving. But
it is what he did to us. Our father,
whose silhouette cut dark against
the driver's pane, laughed
at all our fears and made us
watch until the ending came.

Riding home, he chided us
for trying not to look
by saying zombies caught
only little girls whose eyes were hid.
We had no weapons but our play.
Parodies that cast dark silhouettes,
we made to disappear, then turned
to swaddle dolls and nurture them
with breasts not there.

Another Spring

Joyce K. Luzzi

Look at the way she sits
in the yard, propped up
with three big pillows,

facing dread, half dead,
torn-up body wearing brittle
as noontime grass;

and yet she dares to care
that robins trace the sounds
of slugs fed fat on buried

treasure; look at how they
cock their heads and stare,
bulged eyes ready, intent

on finding worms succulent
as sausages unchewed; and
look at Roger watching,

still as onyx, tail a crook
forced straight out stiff
behind the bush that

always smells like cats, where
she could never get the roses
going—perhaps because

the soil lacks bonemeal there.

Making Room

Kelly Sievers

Here is the entry hall where once guests,
burdened with the scent of flowers,
whispered; where my father whistled,

and built a scaffold to rip faded paper
from the walls. Up this open staircase
winding to old mortician's quarters

my grandmother led her men. And when
the voices got too loud, my father tore
upstairs to catch the flying plates,

the crashing words. Carpets of roses, worn
thin by lines of mourners and knees bent to pray
the rosary, my father ripped up, exposing

inlaid wood my mother waxed and
polished. When I helped her wax it all again,
and then again, I thought: this is what I am.

Behind these oak doors that slid along their tracks
to hide viewing room two from one, we slept
in single beds, woke to hear our parents'

litany: the kids come first . . . enough
money . . . she's your mother. . . . Those nights
I made room in bed for my mother's silence.

Here are the basement shelves lined
with the largest cans of applesauce,
catsup, and beans; cleared of formaldehyde.

In this basement my father labored each summer
on casket-sturdy benches with paint and putty
fixing windows against winter storms

to seal
the family in.

Soup and Pennies

Richard Widerkehr

I tell you I'd just love him dearly if he wasn't so crazy. I never *met* someone so into negativity. He treats everything I say as some kind of joke. It's unbelievable. The other day when I brought in my driftwood fish—the one I found that looks just like a mermaid, etcetera, you know, lying on its side—he just said, "Cheryl, it'd look better in plastic." Gross. And if there's one thing I can't stand, it's gross people. I've been living with them all my life.

He knows about you, too, Rags, sure as I'm talking to you now. He says, "Going over to Ragdale's place to rag on him?" He grins that shit-eating grin—doesn't think a woman can have a man for just a friend.

Today I go in the kitchen. I'm fixing soup, and Randy's standing by the wood stove pitching pennies in the soup. I'm thinking, Well, if he's gonna pitch pennies, I ain't gonna say a thing. But I sure wasn't eating any of that soup, and I walked out. I could take the pennies out later, don't you think? I mean, why's he got to be throwing those nasty coins?

I do care for him underneath. I really do. He's a neat little guy. He's got his music, and I know he's got to have his own space. He's got this mysterious side to him. I guess that's why he's into music, etcetera. It'd be okay if there was just some respect. He got so mad the other night when everyone was telling their stories about morgues and dead people, and I told about my mom's parakeet I drowned in the toilet and gave away one Halloween. There was this girl I couldn't stand, and I told her she better not come to *my* house on Halloween. But she came anyway—thought she'd try and sneak in with a bunch of other kids. So I give her the parakeet, right? She never came back to *my* house.

But that Randy, you know what he says right in front of everyone? He says, "Cheryl, we were talking about dead *people*. Can't you stick to the subject?" A lot he knows.

That night after everyone splits he's telling me he *likes* my mom and how come I killed that poor, pitiful bird. I say, "Randy, that girl looked like that parakeet. She deserved to get that particular bird." You know what he does? Just shakes his head, picks up his guitar, won't even talk about it with me.

Now he's got this statue set up where we sleep next to the suitcases. Or I call it a statue—he calls it Ivanhoe. It's this coat rack he's wrapped an old army coat around, and he's put a football on top of the stand for a head. Scares me to death when I come in at night. When Randy sits in the dark playing his twelve-string, staring at Ivanhoe, I swear I won't say a thing. I won't give him the satisfaction. But if I take out my art work, he starts tapping his foot at me. I don't see why some people have to be so difficult.

You know, I asked him once why he calls it Ivanhoe. Something about knights in shining armor, I think, but he wouldn't say. Just went on playing one of his twangy tunes. *Folk* music for Godsake—I mean that's history.

"You want to save the world, Randy?" I say. "Is that it?"

He goes on playing—won't even look at me.

"Me and him been together a long time," he says. "A lot of street corners and coffee houses."

"You mean you set him up right in front of people, up on a stage?"

"No, he's my audience times I haven't *had* an audience. Lots of water under the bridge. Over it, too." He grins his little grin.

Then he starts telling me about freight trains and picking apples over by Chelan, and he asks me, "You ever been broke, Cheryl?" Thinks I'm a rich man's daughter. I'm not. He ought to know that. Then he talks about this one house he lived in—the wind blew in underneath and picked the carpet right up off the floor. But why live in the past? I always say. I mean, what's his problem?

Just two months ago today, I met him on the street in Wheaton, outside the Red Dog—you know, that red-neck bar? I'd just come from the thrift shop. I'm wearing my leather vest, my deerskin boots, just trucking along. A little old man and woman come on by. They're walking this little white poodle on a silver chain. It's all trimmed and manicured the poodle is—right there in front of the Red Dog, logging trucks just slamming on by. Well, these two women come out of the Red Dog, their hair all bouffant. One of them looks at the poodle and says, "Of course, they look exactly like sheep if you don't cut their hair."

Randy's walking toward me, and we see each other. He's a short dude. Me, I'm not ashamed to say I'm 5'10", but I don't get the feeling he's looking up at me. Fact it's the other way around. He's wearing black pants and a shirt to match. He's got that twelve-string slung on his shoulder, and I think, Who *is* this guy?

Well, Randy and me, we just laugh. Later we go to the dumpster at the mall and get out some lettuce, tell the security guard we're getting it for our pigs. But it's good lettuce—those Safeways throw out all kinds of perfectly good stuff. So we get the lettuce and split and I'm feeling pretty good, you know?

Life can be beautiful. I believe that, I really do. Sometimes I just groove on how a person walks down a street. They don't have to say a word, and I think that's beautiful. All people are just *people* anyway, no matter what their lifestyle is. I used to think it was Randy's job I couldn't stand—you know, working the shake mill, etcetera. But he quit that job, so it's not that. He's more into his music now, and he talks to people, trying to find a place to do a gig. I do care for him underneath. I do. I just wonder sometimes what's the use of caring for someone for a lifetime if you can't get along with them five solid minutes.

My allergies for one thing—he just laughs at them. When I tell him how good I've felt since I came back from my folks' place in Carmel, does he care? I fasted seventeen days there—well, not entirely. I had some grape juice and some sprouts. I've felt so good. I got so many of the poisons out. Of course, you never get them all out, living in our society, etcetera. But now that I sprout all my foods, I hardly ever get hives or hysterics or more than a bit cranky.

He is right about some things, and I should listen to him more. The time I sent away to Florida for the spider monkey, and it came in the mail, dead, Randy thought I was kidding when I told him about it. "You should've been here when I opened the box," I told him. Course I sent that box right back "return to sender." He said there's a law against shipping dead animals in the mail, but I told him that's not my lookout. *They* sent it, didn't they?

I sure hope Randy can get his trip together—for his sake, you know? I am thankful for the good times, and I have learned so much from him. I think the good Lord must've had a plan in it somewhere, even if Randy does say, "You mean He saw it coming?" real sarcastic like he's wishing I'd put some soup on he could pitch pennies at. I just hope it doesn't come to fixing him cornflake and catsup sandwiches like I did to one old man I had. All I can say is if he thinks I'm full of it, at least my shit's all in one place. I mean it's *together*.

***

These two weeks since I saw you, Rags, it's gotten ridiculous. What he does now is pitch pennies when I try and talk to him, just like I'm talking to you now. And he keeps hinting there's something bad about me that he knows, except he won't tell me what it is. It's too gross to say, is what I think he means.

Today I'm fixing soup, and he's doing his old number, right? Pitching pennies. "Cheapskate," I say, "how about quarters? Silver dollars if you're so inclined." Really, I'm getting good at batting away those nasty coins. Our place looks like a goddam wishing well, etcetera, what with that croaking old linoleum with the purple flowers and the wallpaper all flowery, too, and peeling off, all those layers they papered over, though I can't complain about the rent.

Anyway, he's pitching pennies, and he's hinting he knows these *things*. I ask him what, and he says I don't have guts. Says I never face myself, just keep stewing and chewing on things. That gets me pissed 'cause I don't complain, or hardly ever. I've learned there's nothing gets him pitching pennies quicker than if I go yan-yan-yan about something.

"I can't hold things in, Randy," I tell him. "I have to get it out."

"You never do get it out," he says, and he pitches another coin.

"Randy," I say, "this isn't Campbell's Cream of Creamola I'm fixing. I cut up these carrots and celery and onions myself. Broccoli, too, you creep. And it's got lentils and potatoes, lots of sour cream—"

"No sprouts?" he says.

This time I don't say a thing. I pick up my pot of soup and—no, I don't split. I march upstairs, and that big old pot's good and heavy. When I make soup, I make enough for a week. So I'm starting up the stairs to our bedroom. I don't know what I'm gonna do with the soup yet. But at the top of the stairs, I see Ivanhoe staring at me—that stupid old football just plain staring, so I see there's no turning back.

From halfway up the stairs, Randy says, "Don't touch my music, Cheryl." Sounds like he's talking to a child.

"Some people are so difficult," I say, and I walk right up to Ivanhoe, yank his head down off the stand. I'm tired of being intimidated by a goddam football. I'm starting to feel better, but I'm not through yet. I set my soup down on the throw rug, the brown and mauve one we got from the thrift shop. I hate that old thing anyway. So I set down the soup, I take off the lid, and I dunk old Ivanhoe's head all the way in, get it good and creamy, carrots and things sticking to the leather. Pigskin is it? Whatever. Well, it's good and gloppy.

Randy's at the top of the stairs now. He sees me kneeling on the throw rug, and he's not grinning. He's real quiet, and I think, Uh-oh.

"You shouldn't've done that, Cheryl," he says real quiet. "I told you not to touch my stuff."

"Well, you shouldn't throw pennies at my soup," I say, and I get up. His eyes are looking at me this funny way, like I know I'll be seeing them staring at me after I split—kind of flat and dead his eyes are then, kind of creepy.

"Stop looking at me like that," I say. It's almost like he really does know something bad about me. I look down at poor Ivanhoe's gloppy, old head, and I look back at Mr. Deadeye. He's still trying to stare me down. Well, I don't have to take this, I think. I'm more together than this. So I walk right up to Randy. He's still watching me real close, doesn't even move. Just keeps staring. Then I'm really mad. I look him right in the eye, and I jam old Ivanhoe right in his gut—kind of hard, but not hard enough, because when he straightens up, he's still giving me that dirty look.

"Go ahead, hit me," I say. "That's what you want to do, isn't it?"

He just looks at me, like what he knows he knows, and nothing's gonna change it, and then he asks me a question I can't repeat. It's too gross.

"You don't give a shit about me," I say, and I'm crying now. I can't help looking at his stupid black shirt where I got him—it's all gloppy, and something strikes me funny, and I think, Please, dear Lord, don't let me start laughing now. Randy, he's still looking at me, and I look down at my pot of soup sitting next to Ivanhoe's stand, and I think, Goddam Ivanhoe anyway. My soup looks kind of groaty, and I say, "I think I'm gonna be sick."

I start to walk past Randy to the bathroom, and he says, "Walk away, Cheryl. Go ahead. That's what you always do."

So I split. I get done in the bathroom, and I get my stuff, and—no, I don't take my soup.

***

As I'm driving down Highway 9 toward Wheaton, I keep seeing those eyes of his, staring at me so steady and dull. So matter-of-fact, like that thing he knows about me really is true. Nothing eyes, that's what they are. Goddam him and Ivanhoe, too.

I cross the river, and it's starting to get dark. The river's brighter than the sky. I stop a minute and look at the water rolling away so smooth and nice, just one deadhead sticking up, the current making those funny ripples around it. I keep looking at the water, and then I sort of bring myself to and start the car, moving down the road past all those low, brown fields with the foothills dark around them. When I pass the billboard that says, "By Grace Ye Are Saved," I'm starting to feel better.

It's dark when I get to Wheaton, and the thrift shop's closed, but it's too early for anything to be happening in the bars. So I decide to go to the Dairy Queen. When I was a kid down in Carmel, I used to get ice cream if anything bad happened to me. Well, I know Dairy Queen isn't that good ice cream—it's got all these poisons in it, all that sugar, and it's not real ice cream, kind of more like cold cotton candy, etcetera. I mean I could taste *fibers* in it or something.

I'm still mad at Randy, but in a way I'm feeling okay or I'm wondering how come I'm not madder than I am. I'm mostly okay, I guess, but I'm expecting the bad stuff to hit me later, the way it always does. I did care about him a lot. He was a neat little guy, not little really, just mysterious, the way he could sing those songs about men in Chile dying with blood in their eyes, just like you were there.

So I'm sitting outside the Dairy Queen in my Corvair that's losing its muffler—you've noticed? I'm eating the chocolate cap off the top of the

Dairy Queen. When I start on the vanilla, I think, he didn't have to say what he did to me. I didn't hit him that hard with old Ivanhoe anyway.

And then I'm crying. I think of him pitching pennies and hinting bad things about me, and I think about the other times, like when I got back from Carmel last month, and he's holding me and telling me how he knows my parents are real important to me. And that same night he's holding me and telling me I never really broke with my parents, never grew up, and how it's never too late.

"Leave me alone," I say.

"Well, why do you keep going back to them? It's not just to fast."

"I go back 'cause it makes them feel good. They tell me, 'Why don't you move back in?'"

It's true—that's what they say. The house is practically a shrine or something, all those pictures of me petting the dog and the portraits of me done by a painter, done from photos I sent. Me with my backpack in the desert or hitching on a road somewhere. I send them those pictures, and they blow them up like that? Makes me want to cry.

My folks always make this big, flaming deal about my old room, how it's just the way I left it. Course it's a damn sight neater than I ever kept it, just like a room in *Home and Garden*. I mean the bed has this pink canopy, and there's all these stuffed animals. Oh, shit, you know?

And my mom says, "You were so beautiful." She says it kind of dreamy like I already passed away.

And my dad, he says, "You could've been anything you wanted. You could've gone to college." And he puts his arm around me, and I start feeling bad inside, and I move away. It's that frozen grin on his face when he touches me.

You know Randy met my parents when they were up here last month. We all went out for Chinese food and had about three dinners each, kept passing plates around. It's this hot Szechuan food, and my dad keeps laughing and asking for water and saying, "This is really good."

And my dad and Randy get in a fight about El Salvador, my dad being career army and Randy being a draft resister way back when, lived in Canada a while. I thought you knew that. The funny thing is my dad and Randy hit if off, even though they argue. They fight over the check, too—Randy's still working the shake mill then—and chewing on each other seems to make them both feel good. I don't understand men at all. Me, I'd just let whoever wants to pay for it. It's no big deal.

What gets me is that night in bed Randy's telling me my parents are good people, and I should give them a chance. He's holding me while he says this, and I don't like it, but he just tells me more and holds me tighter.

"You just want me to get close to them so I'll take more of their money," I say.

"No, I just want you to work things out." He keeps telling me that and telling me my parents are good people.

"But I'm 28 years old," I say.
"More reason you should work it out."
Well, I don't say much more. He keeps holding me and talking to me. And later when we make love, it's good, and I think he does care about me. But the very next day, he's back to his old number, pitching pennies. Lord knows how it starts, but sure as hell it comes down to him saying maybe I should go back and live with my parents since that's what I really want, and things just go from bad to worse until today—the soup, you know, and Ivanhoe.

Oh, why'd he ever have to look at me that way? And why'd he have to say what he did? I can still see him looking at me and holding poor Ivanhoe's crummy, old head in his arms—oh, for God sake, why do I keep calling that thing Ivanhoe? It was just a silly football. A goddam, stupid, silly.... Rags, what he said, real matter-of-fact, was: "Cheryl, your father sure gives you some funny looks."

"What do you mean?" I say.
"I mean he ever try anything funny with you?"
Well, there, that's what he said. He shouldn't've. Even to think that's bad enough. I mean, I thought Randy was different, like he did care about me, even if he did pitch those nasty coins. I mean I'd gotten used to *that*. I just never thought he'd say anything really gross to me. I can't stand people thinking things like that about me. I know he's got his music, and he's into being mysterious. But I guess I shouldn't be surprised. As I said, I've lived around gross people all my life.

Was it *true* what he said? Course not. He was just pissed about Ivanhoe. What you think I am anyway?

So that's how come I'm here, Rags. You're the only one really listens to me. My sleeping bag's in the car. I don't take up much space, and I don't eat much, just some sprouts and juice and—well, you're gonna laugh—sometimes some soup. And you, I mean you do listen to me. I do believe all people are really beautiful and like that sign says on the billboard, we're all saved by grace. I really believe that. I do. And it's just for a night or two till I can find my own place. I mean I can sleep in my car if it's a hassle or anything. Just let me—I have to have people around, and you always listen to me, so you must care some, or a little, don't you? I've got some Indian corn—here, these kernels are magic. A woman said she was a witch gave them to me. There's more in my car.

Desert

Lisa Yount

Every tenth stone
is a leaf.
Every tenth stone
breathes
in harsh olive-green gasps.

Every tenth rock
is a lizard.
Every tenth rock
reveals
scales and a tail
and a bright eye
frozen inside your own.

Every tenth bush
has a burrow,
a hole leading down
into darkness
where something lives.

Every tenth shadow
sees you;
waits.

Baglady

Louise Crago

Frail as a fried dove
or sunstruck filament spun
before an avalanche

drawn karmically to
crossroads at the second
before the earthquake hits

broken
a grannie in chains
unable to bear the thought
of kisses or arrows

dead-brained
disremembering equally
sun light and moon bane

dumb, knit tight
but catalistically knowing
the child's tale

about covering self with leaves
under the Old Wise Oak
all through night

Balance Sheet

Paul Ramsey

He knew she was untrue to him.
Both knew how much asked, and took.
But what of that? She was to him
A gold page in a grievous book.

Notes on Staff and Contributors

Alexander Blackburn, editor-in-chief, is most recently author of *A Sunrise Brighter Still: The Visionary Novels of Frank Waters* (Swallow/ Ohio University Press, 1991).

Craig Lesley, fiction editor, is currently working on his third novel. *River Song* and the prize-winning novel *Winterkill* are available in Dell Laurel paperbacks.

Bret Lott, fiction editor, has a third novel, *Jewel*, coming out from Pocket Books (hardcover), the film option bought for actress Sally Field by 20th Century Fox.

Victoria McCabe, poetry editor, has most recently published her poems in *Shenandoah, Prairie Schooner, The Hollins Critic* and *The Literary Review*. Two collections are in circulation: *The Failed Suicide & Other Poems* and *Night Company*.

WESTERN WRITERS SERIES

Ann Ronald is author of *The New West of Edward Abbey*. She is Dean of the College of Arts and Science of the University of Nevada, Reno.

FICTION

Diana Abu-Jaber is an Assistant Professor in English and Creative Writing at the University of Oregon. Some of her most recent work appears in *Seattle Review, Ploughshares*, and *Beloit Fiction Journal*. She has completed a short story collection, as well as a novel about an Arab-American family in upstate New York.

Clark Brown won a Pushcart Prize for "A Winter's Tale" in *Writers' Forum* 9, subsequently included in *The Interior Country: Stories of the Modern West*, an anthology edited by members of the *Writers' Forum* staff. He teaches at California State University, Chico.

Robert Olen Butler has published six novels since 1981, the most recent of which is *The Deuce* (Simon & Schuster, 1989). *A Good Scent from a Strange Mountain*, a forthcoming collection, includes "Love" as well as stories which have appeared in *Hudson Review, Virginia Quarterly Review, Southern Review* and others. He teaches creative writing at McNeese State University, Lake Charles, Louisiana.

Leigh Cross of Vancouver, British Columbia, earned a Pushcart nomination for his first story, in *Writers' Forum* 16. "Have no fear," he informs us, "that I'd consider abandoning the comic for. . . 'Mankind's Basic Inability to Communicate while Having an Abortion on Welfare in a Cheap Motel' school."

Peter LaSalle, who teaches at the University of Texas at Austin, is author of a novel, *Strange Sunlight*, and a story collection, *The Graves of Famous Writers*, as well as stories in numerous magazines and anthologies, including *O. Henry Awards*, *Best American Short Stories*. "The Foil Girl" is his sixth publication in *Writers' Forum*.

Greg Luthi was born and raised in Junction City, Kansas, near the farmland that serves as the setting for "God's Country." He received his M.A. from Kansas State University and his Ph.D. from Oklahoma State University, where he served as a fiction editor for *Cimarron Review*. He currently teaches English at Johnson County Community College in Overland Park, Kansas.

Clay Reynolds, novelist-in-residence at the University of North Texas, is author of three novels, *The Vigil*, *Agatite* (St. Martin's Press), and *Franklin's Crossing* (Dutton, 1991), two nonfiction books, *Stage Left* (Whitson Press) and *Taking Stock: A Larry McMurtry Casebook* (Southern Methodist University Press), as well as over a hundred essays and reviews.

Julian Silva has published six stories in *Writers' Forum*. After publication of his novel *The Gunnysack Castle* in 1981, the *San Francisco Progress* hailed Silva as "a major, if so far unsung, writer" and declared that "the excellence of this engrossing story would be apparent in any literary season."

Max Westbrook is Professor of English at the University of Texas at Austin. Of his scholarly work he is best known for his theoretical essays on Western literature, and his critical studies of Stephen Crane, Walter Van Tilburg Clark, and Ernest Hemingway. He has published three chapbooks of poetry and has recently begun to publish short fiction. "How Was Your Day," based on the experiences of his son, an Austin police officer, is his third published short story.

Richard Widerkehr's second fiction publication, "Soup and Pennies," won first prize in 1988 at the Pacific Northwest Writers Conference, Pacific Lutheran University, Tacoma; the judge was Charles Spicer, an editor at St. Martin's Press. Widerkehr won Hopgood Awards for poetry at the University of Michigan. He currently works in Bellingham, Washington, as a case manager with the chronically mentally ill.

POETRY

Louise Crago lives in Boulder, Colo.

James Cushing's collection, *You and the Night and the Music*, is available from Cahuenga Press. He lives in Morro Bay, Calif.

James Drake's long poem "Naked Manikins" was published in *Caliban #5*. He lives in San Francisco, where he works part-time as a financial consultant.

Alice Friman has been published in *Shenandoah, The Beloit Poetry Journal, Poetry*, and many others. Her collection, *Insomniac Heart*, was published by Years Press.

Joseph Hutchison is a widely published Denver poet. Recent publications include *Poetry, The Hudson Review*, and *The Chariton Review*.

P. H. Liotta has appeared this year in *Poetry, Yankee*, and *Sotheby's International Anthology*. Following a period of teaching creative writing seminars at the United States Air Force Academy, he has been assigned to the Air University in Montgomery, Ala.

Joyce Luzzi's poems have appeared in *Black Buzzard Review, The Laurel Review*, and *The Mid-West Quarterly*. She lives in Narragansett, R.I.

R. Nikolas Macioci teaches in Columbus, Ohio. His work has been published in *Negative Capability, Zone 3, Mississippi Valley Review*, and others.

Miriam McCluney teaches at Albuquerque Academy. Recent publications include *Blue Mesa Review* and *Conceptions Southwest*.

B. Z. Niditch is a widely published poet and novelist. He lives in Milton, Mass.

Ron Offen edits *Free Lunch* in Laguna Niguel, Calif. He has recent works in *Mr. Cognito* and *Poet & Critic*.

Paul Ramsey's books include *Running on the Boardwalk* (University of Georgia Press) and *The Keeper* (Irvington Press). His poems and essays have appeared in *Shenandoah, Poetry, Ploughshares, Southern Poetry Review*, and others. He edited *Contemporary Religious Poetry*, and is Poet-in-Residence at the University of Tennessee.

David Ray's books include *X-Rays, Gathering Firewood, The Touched Life*, and *Sam's Book*. He has edited numerous collections, including

Notes

India: An Anthology of Contemporary Writing and *New Asian Writing.* He teaches at the University of Missouri in Kansas City.

Gary Short is currently a fellow at the Fine Arts Center in Provincetown.

Floyd Skloot's first novel, *Pilgrim's Harbor*, is forthcoming from StoryLine Press. His poems are found everywhere, including *Prairie Schooner*, *Northwest Review*, and *The Georgia Review*. He lives in Portland.

Larry E. Smith teaches at South Park Middle School in Corpus Christi, Texas. He has previously appeared in *Descant*, *Wind*, and *Old Hickory Review*.

Matthew Spireng has poems in *The Cape Rock*, *The Hollins Critic*, *Hiram Poetry Review*, and others. A newspaper copy editor, he lives in Kingston, N.Y.

David Sumner's work has been published in *Pacific Review*, *Puerto del Sol*, *Mississippi Review*, and others. He lives in Aloha, Oregon.

Daniel James Sundahl is an Associate Professor in English at Hillsdale College, Hillsdale, Mich. His articles, book reviews, and poems have appeared in a number of journals and periodicals including *Writers' Forum*, *New Letters*, *Commonweal*, and *The Southern Poetry Review*.

Sandra Gail Teichmann's translations have appeared in *International Poetry Review*, *Aileron Literary Journal*, and *Zone 2*. She lives in Manitou Springs, Colo.

Terry Thomas teaches speech and literature in Prescott, Ariz.

Rawdon Tomlinson's publications include *The Southern Review*, *The Hollins Critic*, *Commonweal*, and many others. He lives in Denver.

Ken Waldman lives in Nome, Alaska and teaches writing at the University of Alaska. He has appeared in *Gargoyle*, *Swamp Root*, and others.

Harold Witt is a frequent contributor to *Writers' Forum*. 170 of his American Literature poems have been published in journals, including *The New York Quarterly*, *The New Letters*, and *The Chariton Review*. He lives in Orinda, Calif.

Lisa Yount lives in Richmond Annex, Calif. She has previously published in *The Minnesota Review*, *Anima*, and *Primavera*.

WRITERS' FORUM:
Index, Volumes 1-16

Writers' Forum was founded in 1974 at the University of Colorado at Colorado Springs (itself founded in 1965) by novelist, critic, and educator Alexander Blackburn (B.A., Yale, Ph.D., Cambridge) in order to encourage and publish emerging as well as recognized poets and fiction writers, especially those from the contemporary American West. The annual magazine has been ranked by *Writer's Digest* as third (first among university-sponsored) in the nation's top thirty nonpaying fiction markets. Contributors have been included in *Pushcart Prize: Best of the Small Presses* and the *Best of the West* series, and some "firsts" have gone on to win the Best Novel and Best First Novel awards of the Western Writers Association and the Iowa Short Fiction Award. In its first sixteen years the magazine has received more than 20,000 manuscript submissions from which the editors have selected works by approximately 150 fiction writers and 300 poets. In addition *Writers' Forum* has featured essays by or about or interviews with various well-known authors.

The *Writers' Forum* logo has been adapted from the ancient Hopi Indian symbol for Emergence.

Back orders are available for the following volumes:
16 (1990), ISBN 1-878359-00-2; 15 (1989), ISBN 0-9602992-9-7;
14 (1988), ISBN 0-9602992-8-9; 13 (1987), ISBN 0-9602992-7-0;
12 (1986), ISBN 0-9602992-6-2; 10 (1984), ISBN 0-9602992-4-6;
 9 (1983), ISBN 0-9602992-3-x; 8 (1982), ISBN 0-9602992-2-x; and
 7 (1981), ISBN 0-9602992-01-1. Vols. 1-6 (1974-80) and
11 (1985) are available on microfiche of archival quality.

ESSAYS, ARTICLES, AND INTERVIEWS

Adams, Charles. On 'Pike's Peak', 11: 195-208
Adler, Carol. Guided Imagery, 9: v
Anaya, Rudolfo. Interview with Rudolfo Anaya, by Ruben Martinez, 13: 14-29
Blackburn, Alexander. Introduction to 2: iii-v; Introduction to 4: v-vii; Homage to Paul Engle, 6: iii-iv; Frank Waters: Preface and Bibliography, 11: 164-70; On 'The Woman at Otowi Crossing', 11: 171-79; When You Say 'Westerns'--Read!, 12: 1-5; Experience, Imagination, and Revolt, 13: 1-7
Engle, Paul. Introduction to 6: ix-xvii
Greenberg, Joanne. Interview with Joanne Greenberg, by Patricia Brandt, 4: 1-10
Hall, James B. Introduction to 7: v-xviii
Hornsby, Bill. Tom Ferril: Finest Poet the Rocky Mountain West Has Produced, 14: 1-3
Kennedy, Thomas E. Imagination as a Way of Knowing in the Fiction of Gladys Swan, 12: 15-24
Lyon, Thomas J. On 'The Man Who Killed the Deer', 11: 180-94
McCabe, Victoria. Thomas Hornsby Ferril: Commensurate Pen, 14: 4-13
Martinez, Ruben. Rudolfo Anaya, Chicano in China, 13: 8-13
Milton, John R. Literary or Not, 10: 1-5; Thoughts on Western Writers, 15: 1-20
Pellow, C. Kenneth. John Nichols, Regionalist and Reformer, 12: 41-57
Price, Reynolds. Letter to a Young Writer, 8: i-v
Raffel, Burton. Introduction to 5: vii-xiv
Swan, Gladys. An Interview with Gladys Swan, by Thomas E. Kennedy, 12: 25-40; An Interview with Gladys Swan, by Edward J. Weyhing, 16: 1-14
Waters, Frank. A Saturday with Frank Waters, 11: 209-221

FICTION

Abbott, H. Porter. My Father's Hands, 4: 55-59
Adams, Alex. Chopin's Angel, 5: 67-96
Amberchele, J. C. So I Told Them, 14: 47-51
Anderson, Jeffrey. Sweetwater, 7: 43-60
Atthowe, Jean Fausett. You Never Mention New York Anymore, 8: 37-47; A Moon Over the Cherry Tree, 9: 114-27; The Last Frontier, 10: 82-98
Bache, Ellyn. Shell Island, 12: 206-21
Baker, Yvonne G. Rip-Tide, 1: 153-64; But How You Played the Game, 1: 165-72
Barnes, H. Lee. The Mind Is Its Own Place, 14: 14-43
Bartlett, Elizabeth. Nancy's House, 11: 149-52
Barza, Steven. Water and Stone, 14: 148-61
Baxter, Charles. The Eleventh Floor, 11: 1-17
Beeson, Thomas. The Quiet Hours, 4: 131-41
Bloom, Paul A. In the Asylum: A Rendezvous, 1: 134-38
Bograd, Michel. Blood Sacrifice, 1: 80-84
Bonner, Helen. Roadside Trinity, 7: 140-51
Boughton, Richard. Days of Black Heat, 13: 182-88
Brandmark, Wendy Rhea. Portrait, 2: 116-23
Brickebank, Peter. Prospects, 11: 125-30
Brooks, Ben. Bandana Man, 12: 149-69
Brown, Clark. A Winter's Tale, 9: 84-99; Cezanne's Fingers, 10: 6-12; Liars, 12: 96-103
Brown, Richard E. Melting with Ruth, 13: 152-71; Bootlegger's Daughter, 16: 79-93
Bukoski, Anthony. A Chance of Snow, 13: 81-95

Burski, Mark Alan. A Window for Saturday, 1: 139-45
Caple, John. The Children Grow Old, 3: 66-71, repr. 5: 29-38
Carlson, Ron. Phenomena, 12: 79-91
Carr, Pat. Buffalo Man, 5: 25-28; The Scorpion Pin, 7: 1-6
Chappell, Fred. The Furlough, 8: 1-15
Chavez, Denise. Shooting Stars, 9: 153-65
Cisneros-Pitman, Anne. Big One, 7: 130-39
Crocker, Jack. The Hunt, 8: 48-58
Cross, Leigh. A Simple and Healthy Environment, 16: 150-58
Dai, Catherine. Baksheesh for Love, 13: 221-40
Davey, William. Light and Death, 16: 32-50
Davis, Almer John. Willie Wyatt's Tale, 9: 1-26
DeFrees, Madeline. The Rye Bread in My Larder, 11: 91-96 Driscoll, Jack. from 'The Hermit Journals', 12: 92-95; Fish and Whiskey, 14: 78-90
Duncan, Julia Nunnelly. Tintype, 12: 174-85
Eis, Jacqueline. Glories, 12: 106-16
Elliott, Gayle. The Family Circle, 16: 55-73
Elrod, Rod. Salvation, 10: 44-55
Felible, Roma. Links, 1: 108-29
Ferguson, Lawrence. And You Know How Martha Is, 3: 46-52
Filer, Tom. Fiction, 14: 107-15; Rocks, 16: 114-25
Files, James L. Go-Round, 4: 81-89; Horror Story, 6: 149-56; The Long View Home, 9: 166-85
Garcia, Jenaro Mark. Julio, 1: 36-64
Geha, Joseph. Something Else, 7: 118-29
Gehling, Tom. The Leader, 4: 120-26
Gibbons, Sheila. Gobar's Map, 15: 104-12
Gilmer, Tim T. Basin's Pride, 15: 120-29
Goto, Dawn M. It Happens to Everybody, 2: 174-77
Greer, Robert O., Jr. The Can Men, 16: 130-39
Guidry, Pat. Visit, 2: 107-11
Gullard, Pamela. Immortal Buttons, 14: 55-61
Hallock, Steve. California Gold, 4: 90-96
Halperin, Irving. Uncle Beryl, 7: 97-109; Father and the Day at Riverview, 8: 16-22, repr. 9: 186-93
Harris, Mark Jonathan. Night Beat, 10: 156-72
Haugen, Mary Jane. Snow to the Right, 15: 143-48
Heibult, Sally Jean. Netchekepringel, 3: 179-86
Hendrie, Laura. Lizzy's Town, 10: 121-31
Hermann, John. Arma Virumque Cano, 5: 97-112; This Is the Way a Lady Rides, 6: 21-34; Sister Adele, 7: 61-74; Zapopan, 8: 69-81: Sarcophagus, 9: 27-64; Withold Willian, 11: 19-32; Death Valley, 12: 66-75; A Problem in Addition, 14: 119-28; Matrix, 16: 142-49
Hollister, Michael. Below the Rainbow, 11: 36-49
Humphrey, James. The Trouble Causer, 8: 182-88
Hunt, Bryan. A Wedding Book, 1: 181-90
Johnson, George. Flipside, 2: 185-92
Johnson, Jay D. Black-and-White, 15: 131-42
Johnson, William. Jenkins Pond, 2: 31-68
Johnston, Wayne. Nurse Jim & GC's Bullet, 2: 149-59
Jones, Greg. Punk: 1969, 15: 78-87

Kaczynski, David. El Cibolo, 16: 172-89
Kelsey, N. W. Vacation Crash, 1: 85-100
Kennedy, Thomas E. City of the Foxes, 13: 135-47
Knapp, Toni Graham. Sparrow, 4: 97-106; Have a Nice Day, 5: 153-90
Koster, James F. A Thinking Man's Race, 1: 176-80
Kranes, David. The Whorehouse Picnic, 11: 99-108
Landem, Jill. Wrestling Mr. Green, 9: 142-48; How Many Swallows Does It Take to Make a Summer?, 10: 61-68
Lares, Christine. For the Fish, 3: 83-86; What I Never Said, 5: 113-19
LaSalle, Peter. Roly Poly, 8: 23-36; Night Life, 10: 69-81; Shy Salvaging, 13: 124-31
Lesley, Craig. Spurs, 5: 134-41; The Catch, 6: 35-45; Hoopsnake, 7: 110-17
Light, Frank. The Great Afghan Short Story, 4: 60-70
Lochhaas, Thomas. The Empty Lot, 3: 171-78; The Woman on Tape, 4: 134-41
Lott, Bret. I Owned Vermont, 9: 149-52; The Transfer, 10: 56-60
Lowell, Susan. Los Mojados, 12: 133-48
Luna, Richard L. Terecita, 3: 127-35
McCoy, Maureen. Friends and Neighbors, 8: 105-112
MacDonald, D. R. Coal, 6: 116-29
MacGregor, Vicki. Lilacs, 2: 88-100
Malone, Paul Scott. Mother's Thimbles, 14: 137-47
Martin, Julie. Apparent Calm, 3: 107-10
Martin, Russell. Piecing, 1: 1-7; Maundy Thursday, 1: 8-14; Going Down, 1: 15-21
Melendez, Gabriel. The Scars of Old Sabers, 11: 157-62
Miller, Merritt Scott. The Sunseason Vision of Mede Mahoney, 8: 122-39
Miller, Warren C. The One Best Alternative, 6: 76-115; Return, 7: 75-96
Minton, Karen. Honest Men and Hypocrites, 15: 149-57
Moore, Dinty. White Birds, 15: 68-76
Morrison, Mark. Moving Day, 2: 69-79
Mouat, David. Kick a Rock, 16: 160-68
Nowrey, Kevin. Connections, 14: 129-34
Nye, Nancy. A Likely Story, 2: 15-18; The Edge of Night, 3: 166- 70; Notes of the Oldest Daughter, 4: 17-29; Olga and Goldofsky, 5: 11-24; Going Beyond, 6: 1-9; Black Feather, 12: 224-37
Odowan, Dakotah. The Circle of Wakanshicha, 11: 136-44
Peavy, Linda. Something Worth Saying, 12: 193-203
Peden, William. The Blue Slipper, 11: 85-88
Peterson, F. Gordon. Lila, 3: 72-75; Quarternion, 6: 130-42
Poling-Kempes, Lesley. Edith's Own, 16: 100-109
Pond, D. B., Jr. The Word, 2: 133-42; The Stalker, 3: 1-6; The Lesson, 4: 115-19
Rea, David W. The Second Coming of Errol Flynn, 4: 71-80; Gregor, 5: 48-59
Ridenour, William. The Rooster's Lady, 6: 180-203
Robins, Paul L. Bruce--In Two Parts, 4: 127-30
Robson, Deborah. Eft, 6: 10-20
Rogers, Bruce P. Wirewalkers Get No Overtime, 5: 120-33
Romjue, Nichell Roan. The Little Chief of Staff, 8: 140-55; Zarathustra, 13: 60-78; Chartres, 15: 46-64
Root, William Pitt. West of Tuba City, 10: 112-20
Roper, Peter. Song for a Summer Night, 6: 157-79
Roripaugh, Robert. Leave's End, 15: 26-42
Rubin, Michael. The Saving Graces, 10: 99-111
Safford, Dan S. Social Conditions of Unrest, 8: 166-81; Grace, 10: 140-55

Sampayo, Lupe Rendon. Torero, 10: 173-80
Scott, Ellie. Milk River, 11: 111-19
Shahan, Richard. Something About Frames, 4: 50-54, repr. 5: 60-66
Shaw, Blossom. The Day Sister Slade Saw Death, 5: 1-10
Shore, Marion. Prelude, 13: 197-220
Silva, Julian. A Sudden and Violent Death, 6: 46-75; Brave Cossacks All, 7: 7-42; Salome's Trencher, 8: 88-104; The Tortoiseshell Caddy, 10: 23-43; A Candle in the Wind, 13: 99-117
Smith, Steve. Getting Well, 2: 193-97
Soos, Frank. Jackson of All Trades, 11: 53-59
Stavrakis, Katheryn. The Room, 8: 113-21
Stubblefield, Charles. George, 4: 30-38
Sunderland, Brooke W. Aurora, 3: 136-42
Swan, Gladys. The Tiger's Eye, 8: 59-68; Backtracking, 9: 100-13; The Dancing Floor, 10: 13-22; Black Hole, 11: 76-84; Of Memory and Desire, 12: 6-14; In the Wilderness, 16: 18-28
Taylor, Robert C. Skitterbugging, 3: 111-18
Theis, Dan. Reunion, 4: 107-14
Thompson, Joyce. The Copper Mine, 11: 63-73
Toma, T. L. Harper Screamed Again, 14: 94-103
Turner, Fay Birdsong. Suburban Retreat, 3: 143-48
Uschuk, Pamela. Road Kill, 10: 132-39
Wanner, Irene. I Am Not Prince Hamlet, Nor Was Meant to Be, 5: 39-47
Welsh, Elizabeth Gilchrist. The Coming of Diana, 5: 142-52
Widner, Doug. The Helmsman, 3: 10-14
Wilson, Keith. Captain of Fires, 8: 156-65
Wilson, Miles. Fire Season, 4: 11-16
Woelfel, Monica Hall. Slow Dance, 14: 64-70
Wonn, Deborah. One Together, 3: 22-31; Quartet, 4: 39-49
Wright, Carolyne. The Blind Man, 8: 82-87
Yudkin, Marcia. Lessons, 15: 90-99
Zancanella, Don. Beneath Orion, 2: 198-208; Adobe Town, 9: 65-83
Zepeda, Rafael. Horse Medicine, 12: 117-30
ZoBell, Bonnie. Faye and the Mile of Cars, 9: 128-41

POETRY

Adler, Carol. High Loom Weaving, 10: 208; Alarm, 11: 96-97
Akers, Deborah. Sunset at Ocean Beach, 16: 16-17
Alexander, Floyce. Diptych, 13: 191-93
Anderson, Michael. The Road, the Eye, 3: 165
Antonopoulos, Nicholas. Vestige of Immanuel, 3: 104
Arvey, Michael. Grandmother of Unalakleet, 7: 185
Ashbaugh, Gwendolyn. Resolve, 1: 101-02; Night Letter, 1: 103; Receipt, 1: 103-04; If I Die Before I Wake, 2: 124; The Unspelling, 2: 124; The Jeweller's Daughter, 2: 125; Song of Pegasus, 2: 125-26; Sun Set, 2: 126; Alicanto, 2: 127; They: A Child's Projection, 3: 101-03, repr. 5: 213-15
Atkinson, Alan. Forest, 14: 116
Axinn, Donald Everett. Saturday Night on the Desert, March 1938, 7: 160-61; Where the Bad Guys Always Waited, 7: 161; Even My Memory of It Will Change, 9: 195; Daughter's Farewell, 10: 207; Old Pilots in Springtime, 11: 52; Desert, Tucson to Phoenix, 12: 169-70; The Antelope, 15: 21-22; Tiwa Pueblo, Taos, 15: 22

Bachmann, Ingeborg (trans. Aaron Kramer and Siegfried Mandel). Salt and Bread (Salz und Brot), 11: 17-18; In the Storm of the Roses (Im Gewitter der Rosen), 11: 18
Bailey, Pam. Wolf Creek Passage, 6: 275
Baker, David. Persimmon Trees, She Remembers, Not Far Away, 8: 215-16; Antioch Church and Cemetery, 1840-1972, 8: 216-17; Mad Song, 9: 203-04; Night Song, 9: 204; Small Farm Songs, 11: 75
Baker, June Frankland. Trees in a Desert Town, 6: 276
Baker, T. M. The Stormstruck Tree, 8: 237-38
Ball, Angela. The Lake in the Woods, 3: 154; The Lost Colony, 3: 154-55
Ballantyne, Lisa. No Way Out, 3: 98; Oddball, 3: 98; The Rapist, 3: 98
Barale, Michele. Why I Don't Climb, 3: 55; How to Have a Roman Picnic, 3: 55-56; Poetry Is a Matter of Oranges, 3: 56; Like a Fish on a Line, 3: 56
Barnes, Jeannette. Of a Death in the Next House, 2: 168; To a Ph.D in Education, 2: 167; Where the Grass Bends, 2: 167; The Deaf-Mute Dreams, 3: 123; Grandmother, 3: 124, Black Squirrel, 3: 125; Avis, 4: 212
Basting, Alan. First Winter in Colorado, 6: 270
Bender, Sheila. My Mother Was Here Today, 5: 218, Remembering My Father at Elliott Bay, 8: 230-231; Poem at 4 A.M., 8: 231
Bentley, Sean. The big things, 16: 128-29
Bertolino, James. Order, 10: 192; First Catch, 10: 193
Block, Ray. I Pray for the Moon Boy, 4: 167; How the World Works, 4: 168
Bomba, Bernard. Brother, 11: 135
Brewer, Kenneth W. Astronomy, 16: 141
Brody, Harry. Mark Bowden, 16: 52; The Graves in October, 16: 53
Brown, Edith H. The Marking, 3: 61
Brown, Kurt. A Woman, Separated from Her Hunting Party Near Telluride Last Monday, Is Still Missing, 8: 200-03
Bruchac, Joseph. Fort Mason Wharf, 10: 195
Bruner, Dallas. Alamosa, 3: 160
Burns, R. W. Dream of Roethke, 6: 266; Creed, 6: 267; Fantod, 10: 212; Gourds, 10: 213; Sign of the Cross, 13: 119
Busch, Trent. Uncle Ace, 16: 98-99
Byrd, Sandy. The Gun Owner, 4: 180; Anna Making Biscuits, 4: 181; The Dancer's Father, 5: 216
Cadnum, Michael. Prairie, 13: 174; Driving Through the Desert, 13: 175; Niles' Heart Attack, 15: 23
Cannady, Criss E. Drinking a Glass of Water and Thinking of Keats, 4: 203
Carpenter, Carol. Remedies, 7: 181-2
Carr, Duane. A Refusal to Make a Pilgrimage to Cristo Rey, 5: 231
Carter, Jefferson. Anger: Sonora Desert Museum, 3: 91; Milton, 3: 91-92
Carter, Judith. One Note Sung, 4: 205
Chadwick, Jerah. Attu, 1943: from the Diary of Dr. Nebu Tatsuguchi, 14: 63
Chamlee, Ken. Phases, 3: 125-26
Chavez, Denise. Birth of Me in My Room at Home, 4: 207-09
Chin, Marilyn. Counting, Recounting, 8: 212; American Rain, 8: 212-15
Clark, Patricia. Small Prayers, 6: 271; Holding On, 6: 271-2
Clarke, Steven. Weekend, 4: 194
Cleary, Victoria. The Love Stranger and the Light, 1: 146-48; After Evening News, 1: 148-49; Wood and Smoke, 1: 149; There I Was in Your Eyes, 1: 149-50
Clifton, Chas. Clackamas Breakdown, 3: 53; Family Matters, 3: 53-54; Defining Deer, 3: 54

Cooke, Robert P. A Week Off, Mathesen Bay, Canada, Fishing Trip, 15: 67
Cooperman, Robert. The Stroke Victim Exercises, 11: 120-21
Cramer, Maurice Browning. Monarch Pass, 7: 153-55
Crews, Judson. Friend of forty years, 9: 202; The conjunctions the dead converge upon, 12: 76; Ringed in a circle of singing so soundless, 12: 76-77; There were ides of change, so to speak, 13: 180-81; A collage you tossed together like, 13: 181; My saddest commentary on the human, 14: 71; A pen of wet fibers, almost a brush, 14: 71-72; The residue or fall-out flaking my, 16: 54
Crupper, Chris. In Awe of Albert, 6: 273-74
Dallman, Elaine. Three Haiku, 6: 259
Daniel, John. Dedication for a New Mirror, 13: 96; Reading, 13: 97-98; Joshua Tree, 13: 98
Dassanowsky-Harris, Robert. The Local Color (Joshua Tree, California), 15: 77
Davis, William Virgil. Pilgrimage, 13: 133; Distanced, 14: 92
Desy, Peter. The Cough, 13: 173-74
Digges, Deborah. Widow, 4: 169-70; The Museum Keeper's Birthday, 4: 170-71
Dilsaver, Paul. My German Heritage, 10: 216; Dead End, 11: 146; A Cure for Optimism, 11: 147; Memory of the Fish, 11: 148; Swine Song, 13: 176-77; Time as Terrorist, 13: 177; Fortune's Wheel, 13: 178; Divorce, 13: 179-80; Confession, 14: 116-17; Morgue Song, 14: 117-18
Dilts, Jan. It Was Sunday: The Era Was Black Passion, 3: 99-100
Ditsky, John. To Be of a Certain Age, 10: 196-97; Prismatics, 12: 204
Dobbs, Kevin. Music from Bavaria, 16: 110-11
Doyle, James. The Daily Life of the Dead Man, 11: 122-23
Drake, Albert. Red Verne, 7: 183-84
Drake, Barbara. That We Flew at All, Being So Heavy, 6: 255-56; Life in a Gothic Novel, 6: 256-57
Elkind, Sue Saniel. No Longer Afraid, 8: 224; Love Song, 8: 224-25
Etter, Dave. Community Hospital, 12: 170-71
Evans, James. The Map, the World, 5: 228-29
Evertz, David. Body Parts, 6: 267-70
Farley, Blanche. Tallying, 8: 227-28
Fasel, Ida. Dilsey, 3: 15; Genesis, 3: 15; Circling the Dark, 3: 16-17; Going Up Cottonwood Pass, 3: 17-18; Dialogue of the Dance, 3: 18; In Cologne I Remember Henry David, 4: 191-93; Old Wives' Tale, 6: 262-63
Fedo, David. Dreaming of Trotsky, 13: 172-73
Fenza, David. Afterwords, 3: 119; Catechism, 3: 119-20; Reunion, 3: 121; Vesper, 3: 121; Afternoon, 3: 122; Anthem, 4: 207
Ferril, Thomas Hornsby. Two Rivers, 14: 2-3
Fields, Kenneth. In the Place of Stories, 12: 62; Tangled, 12: 63; Imprisoned Lover Singing Freedom, 12: 63-64; Apology, 12: 64
Files, James. Pidgin Chinese, 4: 164; The Stone Fence, 4: 164; Affair, 4: 165; Separation, 5: 235; Springtime from My Window, 5: 235; Blossom, 16: 159
Finch, Roger. Portrait of a Girl with Viola, 8: 206-08; Les Demoiselles de Leytonstone, 8: 208-09; Lupines, 8: 209-210; The Strange Case of Miss E, 9: 209-10
Finefrock, Thelma. Lament for Sylvia Plath, 3: 156; Interim, 3: 157; That Summer, 3: 157-58
Fink, Robert A. The Pathfinder, 6: 250-51; The Ghostly Hitchhiker, 6: 251; To My Student Caught Cheating on the Religion 101 Final, 8: 221; The Meteorologist Explains Tornadoes, 13: 149-50

Foster, S. R. K. Uncle Benjamin, 11: 134
Fredson, Michael. Walking Back, 5: 221-24
Fried, Elliott. The Man Who Walks His Mother, 8: 228-29
Frost, Celestine. The Refusal, 15: 88
Garcia, Cherry E. Elite Cafe--Beaver, Utah, 1: 67; Love by Long Division, 1: 68; Sylvia, 1: 69-70; Yellow Crayons, 1:70
German, Norman. Trying Again, 15: 118; The Three Bears, 15: 118-19
Gonzalez, Ray. Your Mother's Mountain, 11: 163
Gordon, Robert. Kitchen Cinquain, 4: 171-72; Screwdriver Sixain, 4: 173-74
Grabill, James. In the Morning, 11: 60
Graziano, Frank, Jr. History of the Dead, 3: 87; The Hare Krishnas Came to Campus, 3: 87-88; Desemboque, 3: 88; Mary, 3: 88-89; Some Notes on Creation, 4: 197
Gregory, Michael. Cliche Pantoum, 15: 117-18
Griffin, Mary. The Lamedeer Lecture, 4: 196-97
Griffin, Walter. Fish Leaves, 12: 131-32; Aunt Ida and Lord Byron, 12: 132; Sliding Home, 16: 112
Grimm, Maury. Remembering Bear Creek, 4: 187-88
Griswold, Jay. Rio Las Animas, 15: 115-16
Gronowicz, Antoni. the emigrant's letter to the fatherland, 10: 209-11
Gvozdzius, Vidas. Fairy Tales, 15: 114-15
Hackler, Mark. A Definition: Revolution, 3: 164; Poeta, 3: 164
Hadley, Martha. The Note of Congratulations, 4: 199
Hall, Michael. My Father's Lover, 5: 217-18
Hall, Walter. Glowing in the Dark, 6: 236-37; The Last Poem, 6: 237-38; Forage, 6: 238-39; That Brings Us to the Woodstove in the Wilds, at Night, 7: 158-59; Hunting Lions with a Sixgun, 7: 159; The Hat, 7: 160
Hammer, Adam. How We Coped with the Deer, 4: 143; I Have No Taste in Anything, 4: 144; A General Comma to America, 4: 145-46, repr. 5: 203-04; Undressing Crowded Airplanes, 4: 146-47; Degrees of Polio, 4: 147-48; As an Intellectual, 6: 239-41; Quote, Said the Lips, 6: 241-42
Hammons, Jayni. La Llorna, 2: 143
Harjo, Joy. For Two Hundred Years, 1: 66; Waiting, 1: 66; Red Horse Wind Over Albuquerque, 4: 157-58; Round Dance Somewhere Around Oklahoma City/November Night, 4: 158-59
Harris, Will. The Austin Revelations, 14: 72-74
Hasan, Rabiul. A Glass Face in the Rain, 12: 222-23
Hays, Janice. On Cyprus, 10: 213-15; The Neo-Life Temple of Health Shop, 12: 223
Heineman, W. F. The Mood, 8: 234-35; The Pond, 8: 235
Hemenway, Phillip. Lesson, 4: 178; Alma, 4: 179-80
Henderson, Donna. Come One Step Closer, 16: 76
Herrman, Pamela. Images of My Brother, 2: 16-61; Daddy, It's the Wind, 2: 161-62; Brenin's Pond, 2: 163
Hill, Nellie. The Teacher, 6: 277
Hillard, Jeffrey. At the Top of the Stairs, 12: 241-42; Rain Rising, 12: 242-43
Hixon, Jane. Grandma Tells How She Got Her Glass Eye, 7: 168; The Haircut, 7: 169
Hoagland, William. Middle Finger, 8: 195-96; Dust Storm, 8: 196; Dancing with a Deaf Woman, 10: 205; December Spearing, 12: 243-44; Beaver Run, 16: 94-95; Clepsydra, 16: 96
Hoben, Sandra. Burns, 4: 200
Hogan, Linda. After Fish, 3: 105; Arrowhead, 3: 105-06; Heading for Esztergom, 3: 106

Holtby, Judy. Devils and Ghosts, 1: 105-06; To All Life, Too Harsh, 1: 106; Dandelion Wine, 1: 106-07
Holzapfel, Rudi. Those Green Fuzzy-Looking Plants, 12: 104-05; Now Is the Autumn Failing, 12: 105
Hutchison, Joseph. Ghazel, 11: 62; Robert Emmitt, 15: 24-25; The Stone Forest, 15: 25
Jahns, T. R. Jalama Road, 4: 165-66; Fugitive, 4: 166; A Myth, 4: 166-67
James, Billie Jean. A Villanelle: My Son Lets Me Have a Magical Stone, 4: 198
Johnson, David. Connection, 6: 244; Emergency Room, 6: 245; Patriarch in the Midwest, 7: 162-63; State Fair, 7: 163-67; A Time of Amateurs, 8: 193-95
Johnson, Pam. Your Child, 3: 162; Weekend in Tucson, 3: 162; Losing Ken on Galveston Beach, 4: 196
Jones, Daryl. The Impulse, 7: 175; The Passing, 7: 176; Absolute, 13: 79; Dolls, 13: 80
Jones, Richard. Nightwatches Have Glow in the Dark Hands, 16: 15-16
Jones, Richard A. Amtrak--Chicago to Martinsburg, West Virginia, 12: 237-38; Thirty-Fifth Birthday, 12: 238
Juhasz, Suzanne. but what about epiphanies?, 5: 212-13
Kane, Sid. A Warrior, 4: 200
Kawin, Bruce. Song of the Jealous Father, 3: 37; Poems for a California Divorce, 3: 38-40; Secretive, 3: 40-41; Wash Your Mouth Out with Food: Excerpts from an Apocalypse, 3: 41-43; A Piece of the Day Slides Away, 3: 43-45
Keithley, George. The River's Sister, 13: 134
Kellman, Steven G. Time Has Fun When We Are Flying, 6: 284
Kieft, Nancy Ann. Joy Ride, 2: 101; The Terrarium, 2: 101; Take Two Aspirins and Call Me in the Morning, 2: 102; The Surgeon General's Report, 2: 102-03; Leaving the Travelled Way, 2: 103; Don't Set the Alarm, 2: 103; Oral Analgesic, 2: 104; On Catching One's Death, 2: 104-05; With a Friend Like You, 2: 105; You Can't Have Your Cake, 2: 106; The Objects of Your Affection, 3: 76; Sticks and Stones, 3: 77; Suppression, 3: 77; Words, 3: 78; What's in a Word, 3: 78-80
Kime, Peter. The Letter in Response, 11: 98
Knapp, Toni. Plato and the Persian Cat, 2: 171-73
Komunyakaa, Yusef. Masks, 1: 22; Evolutionary Fantasy, 1: 22-23; Any Sunday Morning, 1: 23; Uncle Noah's Lament, 1:23; The Dog's Theology, 1: 24; Remembrance, 1: 24; East 110th St., 1: 25; Two Blues Hokku, 1: 25; Strange Star in the West, 1: 27; Untitled, 1: 28; Weldon Kees, 1: 28; Dozens, 1: 28-29; For Henry Dumas, 1: 29; The Underdog, 1: 30; Africa, 1: 30; Our Heroes, 1: 30-31; Password, 1: 31; Depression House, 1: 32; The American, 1: 32; Free Fire Zone, 1: 33; Americanization, 1: 33; Apprehension, 1: 34; Young Soldier to Wife, 1: 34; Ode to Langston Hughes, 2: 1-2; From the Back of My Mind, 2: 2; Loneliness, 2: 3-4; Oldmaid, 2: 4; Rag Woman, 2: 4; Rituals, 2: 5; Rocking-Chair-Man's Soliloquy, 2: 5-6; Man in the Country of Shadows, 2: 6; Louisiana Bayou Blues, 2: 6-7; Insinuations, 2: 7-8; The Leaving Lover, 2: 8; Eyewitness, 2: 8; A Different Story, 2: 9; Reminiscences, 2: 9-10; Improvisation, 2: 10-11; Sagittarius Approaching Thirty-Five, 2: 11; The Way the Cards Fall, 2: 11-12; Child Stealer, 2: 12-13; Mississippi John Hurt, 2: 13; Concerning the Ancient Art of Hara-Kiri, 2: 13; One Breath Song, 2: 14; Blue Burning in the Yellow Night Near Stone Mountain, 2: 14; Standing Under the Birdtree, 3: 7-8; The Tongue, 3: 8; Desperation, 3: 8-9; Punchdrunk, 3: 9; Blues Stomp Chant Hoodoo Revival, 4: 148-50; Interregnum, 4: 151; Family Tree, 4: 151-54; Urban Renewal, 4: 154; Looking a Mad Dog Dead in the Eyes, 4: 155; Passions, 5: 198-202; The Falling Down Song, 6: 247; After the Heart's Interrogation, 6: 248;

Fear's Understudy, 6: 248-49; In the Background of Silence, 7: 177; Newport Beach, 1979, 8: 203; Good-Joe, 8: 203-04; Safe Subjects, 8: 205-06; Making Out with the Dream Shredding Machine, 9: 198; Tiger Lady, 10: 197; The Dead at Quang Tri, 10: 198; Saigon Bar Girls, 1975, 10: 199-200

Kramer, Aaron. The Visits of Cousins, 8: 233-34; Fable, 8: 234; The Son, 11: 73; The Laughter of Madeline Mason, 11: 74; Charlie, 14: 118

Larson, R. A. Medicine Wind, 6: 246; Lesson on the Wind, 6: 247; Lake Kachess When Silvers Run, 7: 176-77

LaSalle, Peter. The Last of the Detroit Convertibles, 6: 273; Night Flight: In Transit, 7: 178

Lauradunn, Gayle. Chicken Every Sunday, 5: 220-21

Less, Samuel. Autumn, 2: 144; After Making Love, 2: 144; This Mountain, 3: 163; Late Night Conversation, 3: 163-64; Drawing, 4: 181-82; First Day in Georgia, 4: 182

Levendosky, Charles. Massage is a Message Spoken, 6: 280; The Scrabble Players, 8: 235-36

Locke, Duane. Speculations Upon Angelo Bronzino's 'An Allegory of Time and Love', 16: 126

Loebell, Larry. Half Gainer, 3: 93; Devotion, 3: 93-94; Love Poem, 3: 94-95; Postcards from First View, 3: 95-96; Postmarks, 3: 96-97

Lopez, Manuel Alfonso. Como un Retrato Olvidado, 6: 205; Invierno, 6: 206

Loveday, Marc. Present, 2: 182

Luna, Denise. My Father's Earth, 4: 206

Mackie, J. A Walk in an Open Field, 1: 173; Canto I and II, 1: 173-75

Madsen, Linda. Dweller of the Cliffs, 3: 149-52; The Women Weave It So, 3: 152-53; Following the Crow, 4: 189-90

Mahaffey, Phillip. Dodson, 13: 150-51

Martin, Roger D. The Shaman, 16: 140

McCabe, Victoria. Woman Song, 6: 252; Depression, 6: 252; Houses, III, 6: 253

McCarthy, Joanne. The Mourners, 6: 260-61; The Fear of Going Outside, 6: 261; The Silent Woman, 7: 162

McCleery, Nancy. The Mailman, 4: 183; Correspondences, 4: 183

McCord, Howard. Theodicy, 11: 152; The Old Beast Instructs a Callow Listener Desirous of Achieving Literary Fame, 11: 153

McCurry, Jim. Goodfellow AFB After Hours, 6: 257-58; Body Tenure, 6: 258-59; At the Moscow Circus in Denver, 7: 171; The Doves, 12: 171; Condo, 12: 172

McDaniel, Ames. Butterfly in a Strong Wind, 4: 202-03

McDaniel, Judith. It Is in the End a Private Grief, 11: 119-20

McDonald, Walter. Mirror Image, 6: 228; World War I Soldiers, 6: 229; On Father's Hands, 6: 230; Sangre de Cristo, September 6: The Holy Mountain, 7: 155-56; Waking Up Outside Missoula, 7: 156; When the Wind Dies, 11: 33; Night Skiing on Lake Buchanan, 11: 34-35; Trout Fishing in the Rockies, 11: 35; Lord Hawk, 13: 121; Riding on Hardscrabble, 13: 122; The Sting of the Visible, 13: 123; The Rainmaker, 16: 29; August of the Drinking Well, 16: 30; Colonel MacKenzie and the Ghosts of Warriors, 16: 31

McFarland, R. E. Inviting a Certain Irishman to Return from the Auld Sod, 4: 176; A Dream of Baseball, 4: 177

McNamara, Bob. 233 Walnut, Apt. #4, 3: 62; Line of Descent, 3: 62-63; Family Album, 3: 63-64; Driving, 3: 64; Letter to Bill Tremblay from Seattle, 3: 65

McNamara, Sarah J. 36 Louis Street, 5: 233; Womanhood, 6: 275-76

Meeks, Chris. On My Bed, 3: 36

Meiskey, Elinor. After the Poetry Chapbook Was Published, 16: 127-28

Melendez, Gabriel. Madrugadas y el Ritmo de Cumbias, 11: 154; Tan Lejos Estoy de Mi, 11: 155-56
Metz, Robin. December Divorce: A Theorem, 16: 169-71
Mikulec, Patrick B. Chicken Hawk, 16: 97-98
Miles, Richard. Letter from the Sangre de Cristos, 3: 32; Morning Walk, 3: 32-33; The Cellar Steps, 3: 33-34; Dawn in the Attleboro Shipyard, 3: 34-35; Friend of the Night, 3: 35
Miller, Errol. The Texas Waltz, 15: 113-14
Miller, Tom. We Have Only the Night, 11: 123-24
Moore, Wayne. Bimillenium, 3: 90
Morris, James Ryan. The Need. 4: 195
Mott, Randy. Abby, Flying Kites, 3: 103-04
Mouw, Gudrun. Rumours, 11: 121
Moya, J. Ann. What Do You Do When It's True But Sounds Sentimental?, 1: 71-72; The Infinitive 'To Boogie', 1: 73; One Up on Philip Wylie, 1: 74-75; I Want to See Too, Daddy, 1: 76; I Wear Mocassins to Walk on Dirt, 1: 77; Scorpio in 1971, 1: 78-79
Murphy, Sheila. Initiation, 7: 182-83
Nava, Michael. For an Equestrian Statue of Diocletian, 1: 65
Nelson, Harold. Dad, 5: 215-16
Nelson, Peter N. Hursh Gets Mail, 4: 212; The Bear, 4: 213; The Winter Man, 4: 213; The Wish, 4: 214
Neumeyer, Peter F. Maine Orchids, Maine Palmetto, 8: 217-18; Eng. Dept. Snapshots by a Onetime Chairman, 8: 218-20
Niditch, B. Z. The Death of a Son, 11: 109; Neon City, 11: 110; Paul Celan, 13: 195; Budapest: 1986, 13: 195-96; Daydream: It Happens, 14: 135; Liberation: For Primo Levi, 14: 136
Nightingale, Eric. Undedicated, 14: 104-05; Sex Surrogate Fragment, 14: 105; One of Them, 14: 105-06; Aftermath, 14: 106
Nolan, James. Begonias & Bus Stations, 5: 204-05; At the End of the Long White Corridor, 5: 206; Cuttings from the Jungle of Land Inside, 5: 206-08
Nye, Nancy. Between Decades, 2: 19-20; Minotaur, 2: 21; The Vegetarian and the Lady, 2: 22; Crossing the Channel, 2: 23; After 12 Years, 2: 24-26; The Lover You Might Yet Be, 2: 27-28; Lemonade Serenade, 2: 29; Uprooted, 2: 30
Offen, Ron. Going Home, 14: 74-75
Olvera, Joe. Al Frescoe, 4: 201
Orr, Denie. Reflections from a Jailhouse Window, 2: 178; Articulations of Being, 2: 179
Orr, Ed. Strawberry Patch, 13: 189
Owen, David. At a Family Plot, 2: 169; Instructions for the Burning, 2: 169-70
Padhi, Bibhu. Letters, 11: 89-90; Puri, 11: 90
Pankowski, Elsie. Migrations, 13: 133-34
Partridge, Dixie. Fish, 11: 131-32
Pasanen, Christine. Chant, 4: 155-56; Home Song, 4: 156-57; The Night Before Moving Out, 4: 157
Paugh, Bert. Widow, 4: 202
Paul, Sid. The Day Walt Whitman Died, 4: 160-63
Penny, Michael. Bear, 2: 129-32
Perchik, Simon. Untitled, 12: 173
Perdue, Lance. Corporal Jones Legacy, 3: 19; The Building and the Magpie, 3: 20; Jaswell, 3: 21

Perreault, George. Albino, 4: 175; Arthur Rubenstein, 4: 175-76; Brotherhood of the Green Wolf, 5: 191-96; These Days, 5: 196-97; The Truth As We Know It, 5: 197-98; Talking About It, 6: 222-23; Tarantula Time, 6: 223-34; Seasonal, 6: 224-25; November: The South Porch, 12: 245; December Smoke, 14: 45; Werewolf Writes an Ad, 14: 46; Listening to the Seniors, 14: 46

Peterfreund, Stuart. After a Depression of Three Years, 5: 232-33; Love Poem, 6: 225; Picking Strawberries--Age 10, 6: 226; New Heart, 6: 226; Winter Heart, 6: 227

Pigno, Antonia Quintana. Vicente, 6: 282-84; La Jornada, 13: 30-59, repr. 14: 162-90

Pitner, Erin Clayton. For a Friend Dying, 9: 211

Pound, Omar S. For Harlequin, 10: 188; The Realm of Courtly Love, 10: 188-89; An Impromptu on Juliana of Norwich, 10: 189-90

Quinn, John. Mountain Chickadee: McAllister Creek, 8: 210-11

Rael, Michael T., Jr. Raindrop, 4: 184

Rankin, Paula. The Backslider's Wife, 6: 278-80

Ransome, Richard. Corpus Christi, 1: 130-31; The Last Snow Was Old, 1: 132; Upon Learning That You Were Killed by Seven Cars on a Los Angeles Freeway, 1: 133

Rasnic, Steve. The Hydrocephalic Ward, 3: 57-58; Light and Dark in Poudre Canyon, 3: 58-59; Jonesville, 3: 60-61; Thunder and Uk'ten, 4: 193

Ray, David. Leaving Virginia, 10: 182-83; Oblomov, 10: 184;

Resurrection, 10: 185-86; The Buckeye Bush, 10: 187; The Widower, 12: 57-58; The Weddings in the Garden, 12: 59; My Children Leave for the Alps, 12: 60-61; Homage to Akbar, 12: 61-62; From Horseheads to Watkins Glen in the Old Days, 13: 132

Ray, Judy. Falling Flowers, 13: 118

Rewak, William J. Felix, 12: 205

Root, William Pitt. Looking for a Place to Live, 7: 184; Voyeur, 10: 200-01; Opening the Season, 10: 201-02

Rubenstein, Elaine. Gothic, 8: 236-37

Ruble, Shirley. Gamesmanship, 6: 277-78

Ruiz, Judy. Explain, 2: 180; Speech, 2: 180; Picnic, 2: 181; What You Are Reading Now Is the Poem, the Title Appears Below, 4: 159; I Give Me That, 4: 159-60

Runciman, Lex. Elk at Jewell Meadows, 8: 226; Journal Entry, 8: 226-27

Ruth, Bobbie. Customs of Women in Rio De Janeiro, 2: 183-84

Ryner, Julien. Non-Skid Special, 2: 145; Liza, 2: 146; Fortune, 2: 146-47; The Shadow, 2: 147-48; Threat of Winter, 2: 148; The Cleaving of the Road, 3: 81; To My Father, 3: 82

Salvati, John. The Rothko 'Black on Gray' (1969), 2: 164; Terminal, 2: 165; Priests' Retreat at Ossining, 2: 165-66; One After Her, 3: 166

Saner, Reg. Palomino Weed and One Open Secret, 8: 189; Because the Skipper Loves Color, 8: 190; Out of the Ashes of Last Summer's Green Cigar, 8: 190-91; With Anne Outside Kayenta, 8: 191-92; Language Lesson, 8: 192-93

Schiff, Jeff. Grackle at Dusk, 12: 130-31; Hoppers, 15: 102-03

Seib, Kenneth. The Chemistry of the Soul, 4: 190-91

Serin, Judith. The Lost Dog, 7: 180-81

Sha Ning Liu, Stephen. Letter Undeliverable, 4: 185

Sharat Chandra, G. S. Coming of the River, 11: 49-50

Shepard, Neil. North Platte to Chicago/November Nights, Rte #80, 2: 80-81; Woodpecker Hole, 2: 81-82; Father Poems, 2: 83-86; Greener the Earth, 2: 87

Short, Gary. Arizona, 16: 74; Rains, 16: 75

Shumaker, Peggy. Landlady, 4: 186

Simmerman, Jim. Tell Them, 16: 96-97

Skaggs, James. Decision Past, 5: 235-36

Skloot, Floyd. Leavings, 14: 52; The New and Used Bookstore, 14: 53; Holman Meadow, 14: 54; At Home, 16: 54
Slaughter, William. Alibis, 12: 185-86
Slegman, Ann. Nothing Stops Clint Eastwood, 4: 187
Sloan, Gerry. Raising Crazy Horse, 15: 44-45; Floods, 15: 45
Smith, Barbara Taylor. Sisters, 9: 205; Those Women, 9: 206; Long Fingers, 9: 207; Another Saturday Night, 9: 208
Smith, Clark. How I Learned to Cook, 14: 92-93
Smith, David James. Young Men Hitch Out of the San Joaquin Valley Towards Glory, 15: 89
Smith, James. If It Is the Spaces That Hold the World Together, 1: 65
Somoza, Joseph. China, 8: 199; Uncle Red Delivers the Cucumbers, 8: 199-200
Sorkin, Nelson. Sell Me Your Shoes, 8: 229-30
Speer, Laurel. Visits from Stallions, 7: 170; Luxury Vacations on the Colorado, 7: 170; Johnny Maquis on Speedway, 8: 232; Bomb Around in This Pickup, Clown, It Goes to the Boneyard, 9: 202-03; A Second Winter in Which Our Mother Is Dead, 10: 217; A Quaint Custom of the 30s When People Were Young, 11: 145
Spielberg, Peter. Inventory, 6: 249; Lines, 6: 250
Stafford, William. Looking Up at Night, 10: 181; Time Goes By, 10: 181
Stark, Bradford. An Advertisement for the Next Season, 6: 231; The Display Case, 6: 231-34; Picture for a Sunday Afternoon, 6: 234-35; A Sketch, 6: 235
Starkey, David. Ecce Home, 16: 113
Stein, Donna. El Santuario de Chimayo, 14: 62-63
Stene, Gregory. Earth #4, 1: 151-52
Steven, Ida. Try Touching River Fog, 15: 66
Stevenson, Kenneth E., Jr. On Discussing Revolution with a Dedicated Sister, 4: 209-11
Stryk, Dan. Swelter, 6: 281-82
Sundahl, Daniel James. In Late Autumn, the Devil's Wind Visits Mrs. Vigo Miller's Husband, 14: 91-92
Sunderland, Brooke N. Revenge, 4: 204; The Girl I Knew, 5: 219
Svoboda, Terese. Ku Klux Klan, 6: 281
Szeman, Sherri. letter to sylvia, 12: 186-88
Tagliabue, John. If Final Exams Come Can Heaven Be Far Away?, 8: 221-22; There's All Enterprise in Dancing Naked, 8: 222-23
Taksa, Mark. Trampled Courage, 15: 102
Teichmann, Sandra Gail. Note to the Model, 15: 65-66
Todd, Theodora. Pyramid, 2: 112-13; Journey, 2: 113-14; Woven, 2: 114-15; The Sun Behind a Cloud, 2: 115
Tomlinson, Rawdon. Adultery, 8: 193; The Horse Who Became a Woman, 8: 193; He Can Quote You Rimbaud, 9: 196; A. A., 9: 197-98; Ancestors, 10: 202-03; The Photograph at the County Fair, 12: 188-89; Make-Believe, Ukraine 1932-33, 14: 75-77
Tremblay, Bill. Duhamel at the Easel, 10: 193-94; The One White Horse, 10: 194-95
Trujillo, Paul. To Move Away, 7: 178-79; Minus One, 7: 179; Seven Months, 8: 223-24
Tuttle, Tory. Oh! They Say. Be Quiet, 4: 184
Uschuk, Pamela. Who Gathers Honey, 12: 189-90; Praying Mantis, 12: 191-92
VanWinckel, Nance. Letters Home, 3: 159; For Sexton, Winter, 3: 159-60
Vernon, William J. Three Days Out, 11: 88-89
Visser, Richard. I Wondered, 13: 176

Von Till, Susan A. Early Spring, 2: 209
Wanek, Connie. Lake in February, 4: 205
Ward, Candice. What There Was, 6: 272
Ward, Dorothy. The Desert Is Disappearing, 4: 189
Washburn, Walter R., III, War Memorial, 3: 36
Watkins, William J. How To Tell If You Have the Makings of a Topnotch New York Literary Agent, 16: 51-52
Watson, Carol. Poems, 3: 92
Weber, Marc. Oikos, 6: 207-18; Now We Enter, 6: 219-20; Nicht-Mehr-Da-Sein, 6: 220; Breathing In, 6: 221; Rebirth, 7: 185-93
Weir, Virginia. Expulsion, 4: 195
Wells, Will. Doing Donuts, 12: 239-40
Wessel, Peter. After Saint Valentine, 12: 239
White, Ed. Decoration, 6: 275
White, Mary Jane. His Last Mistress, 6: 253-54; A Letter, 6: 254-55; Haywood Patterson: 1948, 7: 172-75; After Reading Late, 8: 232-33
Whitsitt, Ronald G. For a Horse, 4: 203-04; About the Joneses, 5: 231-32
Whittington, Janice D. Winter in a West Texas Town, 13: 148
Wild, Peter. Pawnees, 6: 243; Cannibals, 6: 243-44; Tortillas, 7: 157; Robbers, 7: 158; The Bleeding Virgin of Marcus Hook, 11: 50-51; Stationmaster, 11: 51-52
Williams, Daniel. windchime window in Angels Camp, 16: 77; Mark Twain's cabin, 16: 78
Wilson, Keith. Songs for Dawn & Evening, 10: 206
Wilson, Miles. Vita, 5: 208-09; In Hand, 5: 209-210; Fathers, 5: 210-11
Witt, Harold. A Tarzan, 12: 77; A Vampire, 12: 77-78; Sonnets, 13: 191; American Lit: A Cask of Amontillado, 14: 44; American Lit: Susan Glaspell's 'The Verge' at Coleville, 14: 44-45; American Lit: Anais Nin, 15: 43; American Lit: Peg, 15: 44; American Lit: She'd Rather Read the Funnies, 16:127
Winwood, David. Cows, 15: 101-02
Wolk, Joel. The Horses Who Joined the Mother, 15: 100
Woodard, Deborah. In the Farmhouse, 6: 262; Hanged Man, 7: 180
Worley, Jeff. Interview, 12: 221-22; Item Buried in 'Financial Times' Section, 13: 190-91
Wright, Carolyne. Overlook Road: Late August, 5: 224-25; Boredom, Nevada, 5: 226; Spokane Reservation Schoolteacher, Welpinit, Washington, 5: 227-28; Premonitions of an Uneasy Guest, 6: 263-64; Strange Wintry Country with a Garden, 6: 264-65; Sestina After an Etching by William Blake, 8: 197-98; The Morning Mail: A Brief Irreverie, 8: 198-99; Sierra Walk, 9: 199-200; Hospital Visit, 9: 200-201; Eulene Stays the Course, 10: 204-05
Wright, Charles David. The Good Drinker, 5: 229-31
Yots, Michael. Word Hustlers, 5: 236-37; Hero's Welcome, 6: 260; In the Clock Shop, 9: 209
Zander, William. Truth, 11: 132; Autumn, 11: 133; After Goya, 13: 194; Portrait of the Poet as Pater Familias, 15: 130
Zaranka, William. Some Meaningful Statistics, 10: 190-91; An Overview of Mankind, 10: 191-92
Zydek, Fredrick. Words at Tahola, 8: 225; 15 Meditation: Clocks, 11: 61